Just Keep Swimming –

A story of hope against anorexia

Just Keep Swimming

Published by The Conrad Press Limited in the United Kingdom 2021

Tel: +44(0)1227 472 874
www.theconradpress.com
info@theconradpress.com

ISBN 978-1-914913-11-2

Typesetting and Cover Design by: Charlotte Mouncey, www.bookstyle.co.uk
The Conrad Press logo was designed by Maria Priestley.

Printed and bound in Great Britain by Clays Ltd, Elcograf S.p.A.

Just Keep Swimming –

A story of hope against anorexia

Stephanie Shott

PREFACE

After years of being silenced by my eating disorder, I finally feel able to share my story with the world.

I want to use my experience with anorexia nervosa to encourage others to carry on. Ultimately, my journey is one of hope and inspiration. It is true that mental illness may be a part of you, but it doesn't have to define who you are as a person.

One of the phrases that has stuck with me throughout my treatment is 'Just Keep Swimming,' and I briefly want to explain to you what those words mean to me and my eating disorder.

Life with an eating disorder can feel impossible. You feel like you are drowning with no way out.

Every time you find yourself trying to break the surface, your eating disorder will pull you back under again. Your head feels as though it's constantly submerged in water and each breath is a struggle.

But this doesn't have to be the end. You must ride the waves to get to the other side. All you must do is just keep swimming and eventually, you will see the light.

Never give up the fight, no matter how tiring or difficult it feels. All you must do is just keep swimming. And you will survive.

I like to personify my anorexia as a separate being to myself, and I give her the rather unoriginal name of Ana (short for anorexia.) I make it perfectly clear throughout this book that Steph and Ana are two different people, although she was the most dominant one in our relationship. She made my lie and manipulated my family and friends. She forced me to exercise to the point where I was bleeding internally. Ana nearly killed me and that is the truth of what it means to live with an eating disorder.

I couldn't have written this book without the help of those closest to me. To my mum and dad, and brother Darian, thank you for never giving up on me. Thank you for believing in me and holding that hope when I was unable to carry it myself. Thank you to my wonderful friends and April House. I wouldn't be here if it weren't for you.

In the darkest time of my life, I have bonded with so many inspiring individuals and, to those who have stuck by me, this is for you. Lastly, I want to dedicate this story in loving memory of a friend who sadly lost their life to anorexia nervosa last year. Charlie, this us for you.

I went through hell and back and I know what it feels like to have an internal battle raging on inside of you. I have received both inpatient and outpatient treatment, and I have personally fought against my anorexia. I know what it feels like to slowly kill yourself and not give a damn about the consequences.

While eating disorders are complex and deadly mental illnesses, this doesn't have to be the end. This is just the beginning of my life, and I am going to just keep swimming...

Stephanie Shott   August 2021

PART ONE:

Spiralling
Into
Despair

Anorexia Nervosa kills people! But not before it kills off relationships, family, and friends. Happiness, freedom, and joy of any kind. Recovery is hard. No, it feels impossible at times. Like an incredibly high mountain to climb, and there are moments when recovery seems completely overwhelming and unattainable. But there is a glimmer of hope at the end of the tunnel. There is a flicker of light in the enveloping darkness. I am determined to be the girl who beat anorexia. I am NOT going to be the girl who died from it. That is not happening. You hear me anorexia. YOU ARE NOT GOING TO BE THE DEATH OF ME! But I WILL be the death of you!

My name is Stephanie Shott and for most of my life I have been in an abusive relationship with my eating disorder. I like to see anorexia as a separate entity to myself. I give her a name (Ana), and I picture her as a creature of fire. Her face is just an angry ball of flames and the more power she gains, the hotter she becomes. The more the flames angrily lick the wounds of her abuse. Ana is pure evil and, whilst she lives, I am trapped in a burning cage with only her coercive behaviour for company. When someone comes too close, she pounces and burns off all human contact, so it is just you and her. She is a killer. This is my story of how I am fighting tooth and nail to survive. Ana is trying to hold me down, but I am gradually breaking free. I need to keep on swimming and, eventually, I will come up for air. I will be free. I will expose her for the killer she is.

***

'Mirror, mirror, on the wall, who's the fairest of them all.' A saying I'm sure many of us are familiar with. If you are anything like me, Disney was a huge part of my childhood, and I often dreamt that one day I would meet my own Prince Charming. A silly fantasy, but a happy one. Whenever I glimpsed my reflection in the mirror I would be confronted by my 'fat face' and 'protruding stomach.' I was no 'Fair Princess,' and I was to have no 'Prince Charming.' I was filled by an overwhelming sense of disgust and self-hatred. Have you ever felt as though you want to tear apart your very skin? To rip apart your body and simultaneously combust? Have you ever just wanted to saw your head off and stick it on another persons' body? Like you want to crawl up into a ball, all alone, and never show your face in public ever again? I have. And I know I am not alone. These are the constant thoughts that never stray far from the forefront of my mind. The avoidance of food and preoccupation with my body completely consumed me to the point where I was no longer able to function within the community.

For a while, there had been a battle raging inside my head. Well, it had now escalated to a full-on war. My head was a violent battlefield, and I was losing the fight. I was failing at my job, at being a good friend. I was failing at being a sister, a daughter... I was miserably failing everything in life. Everyone would be better off if I went to bed one night and didn't wake up the next day. The world would be a better place if I wasn't in it, taking up so much space. That's what I thought. It's what my head was screaming at me and I fell for the lies. I fell hook, line, and sinker. The only way I can think of explaining it to you would be that it felt like I was stuck at the bottom of a pit with nowhere to turn. No light and no way out. An empty darkness which was closing in on me in every waking moment. Every time I felt like I had hit rock bottom, it turned out that

I had even further to fall. Every single time I attempted to free myself from this hellhole, the rungs of the ladder were ripped from under my feet. I fell deeper and deeper into a growing pit of despair. Trapped, lost, and feeling completely and utterly alone. Like no one else in the world understood the self-inflicted pain that I endured. I had only my destructive thoughts to keep me company.

I was trapped in my own head, and it was suffocating. I was in freefall and I did not care for the consequences. I had scant regard for my own safety, and I put my health at risk multiple times. There was only one question I could continue to ask myself: How did things get so bad? What was it that tipped me over the edge of the cliff? What went wrong? That's all I wanted to know. Surely, that's not asking too much, right? Eating disorders affect many people. It doesn't matter if you're male or female, tall or short, gay or straight. This condition does NOT discriminate. Anybody of any age and of any social standing can develop an eating disorder, and it won't necessarily be anorexia. It could be bulimia nervosa or OFSED (unspecified eating disorder) but that doesn't mean that your demons aren't real. Whatever it is that you're struggling in life with is irrelevant. A struggle is a struggle. It is still a serious mental health condition of which weight is only a possible symptom. Eating disorders manifest themselves in several different ways. There is no 'one size fits all.' Everyone's battle is real, and you deserve to have a voice and be heard. Listen to me when I say that you are ill. Your illness is valid, and you are fully deserving of help. Having a good upbringing, a close group of friends, stable job, or whatever else you have, does not make you immune from mental health.

Do NOT question why you are struggling. Do NOT put yourself down by saying that you shouldn't have any problems because you've had a good life. Depression, anxiety, eating disorders... none of it works like that.

Depression: 'You're not worthy of a life. No one likes you. Hell, nobody even loves you. They won't miss you if you die. In fact, it'll be doing them a favour.'

Steph: 'Hey, why are you hounding me so much? I've had a good life. My family and friends are amazing. I've had a great education. I have no right to be feeling this way.'

Depression: 'Oh, Okay. Sorry, I'll just leave you then...'

Yep, it sure doesn't work like that. Mental illnesses won't leave you alone just because you can't understand why you're struggling. That's what makes it so difficult to understand and diagnose. Quite often, it is those who seem okay that are struggling with the most inner torment. People put on a façade. They wear a mask so, on the outside, it appears as if everything is just hunky-dory and that they are coping fine. A smile can hide a million fears. Just because people laugh and smile, that does not mean they are happy. Remember that. Happiness comes from within, and it is so easy to hide what people cannot see. Speak out to seek help. Believe me when I say you are NOT wasting anyone's time, nor are you taking up a bed. You NEED that support; you NEED that bed or medication. So, don't be a doormat for your mental health to trample all over. My eating disorder told me I was an imposter and that I was wasting all the doctor's and therapist's time. My depression told me I was an attention seeker. My inner critic told me I was a waste of fucking space. It. Is. A. Bully. It lies to you and tricks you, lulling you into a false sense of security. It

11

manipulates the truth and turns friends into foes. My struggles are not representative of everyone. It is simply one person's fight with a terrible, vicious, and debilitating illness. This is MY life, this is MY fight, this is MY war.

***

My struggles began when I was just thirteen years old. I was hitting the teenage years… and puberty. I've always seen myself as a bit of a Peter Pan; I valued the innocence of childhood and was in no hurry to grow up. You're a child for such a short amount of time. The naivety and carefree nature of youth is precious. I wasn't into make-up or dresses, instead opting to wear my brother's baggy tops and leggings. A proper tomboy. However, I attended an all-girls Catholic school. Inevitably, that meant I was surrounded by girls who were all going through puberty and their bodies were changing. Mine was not. Body dysmorphia is when you see a morphed or distorted picture of yourself. It is true that I never had a big bust, but instead of accepting my body for what it was, I became fixated on what I didn't like. For me, that was my bust and 'fat stomach.' I thought if I had a larger bust, then my stomach wouldn't stick out so noticeably. Body dysmorphia is something that I have grappled with for most of my life. There's not a single part of my body that I love, but I know that my reality isn't other people's reality. I can't change my body. I just must learn to accept it for what it is and appreciate it for all that it does for me. I have abused my body a lot recently and, frankly, I'm amazed that I haven't caused permanent damage. Our bodies are amazing things, and we might not be in love with ourselves, but that doesn't mean we can't learn to be at peace with our bodies.

I am going to be slightly contradictory here. Although I was desperate to prolong my childhood, I also envied people's changing bodies. I felt claustrophobic, trapped in the body of a toddler. Let me just clarify some things here. I didn't want the responsibility that came with adulthood. I wanted to feel like a 'normal woman,' whatever that means. Yet, I craved the carefree nature and magic that being a child allows you to have in abundance. Being surrounded by people experiencing physical changes, but not really changing myself, led to feelings of increased inadequacy and shame. I have clear memories of me stuffing rolled up socks into my bra to try and make myself feel 'more normal.' I'd buy padded and push up bras, grabbing the first one I could find in the shops, to try and create the illusion of womanhood. I still am unaware of my bra size. I have never been measured nor have I ever bought myself a fitted bra. I was too embarrassed and afraid that people would laugh at me.

Steph: 'Maybe I should get measured.'

Inner Critic: 'Oh yeah, and what exactly are you going to get measured? There's literally nothing there. I mean, you're so flat chested it's a joke. Are you sure you're not a boy?'

My inner critic was a vicious taskmaster. I would often joke about things to try to hide my disgust at my body, but this only fed my eating disorder. It started off as a seed, a tiny thought. But gradually that seed grew and took over my body. Like a weed, it infected my brain and destroyed all the good things I had in my life. At times, I tried to talk myself out of feeling this way. I tried to reason with my demons and find some self-love, but it didn't matter what I did, I was hugely dissatisfied in being me. I could, and did, examine my body

13

from every possible angle, and I hated what I saw. Wanting so desperately to be anyone but me. Wanting to escape my own body. Wanting to be free from the prison of my thoughts. I was a slave to the illness, and it was only going to be more powerful. The seed was being watered, and that would lead to its growth. Instead of nurturing the positives in my life, I was nurturing the negatives.

Looking back at my childhood, I realise just how strong the pull of 'thinness' and perceived attractiveness was. It reeled me into its little web of lies. I found myself constantly wondering what it would be like to be anorexic. A girl that I went to school with was diagnosed with anorexia and I remember wishing I could be that skinny. I know how fucked up that sounds, and I can't believe I'm writing this, but I wished I could not eat. Comparison is a huge problem with eating disorders, and I would find myself unconsciously comparing my 'messed up' body to that of my peers. I felt like the elephant in the room. I was appalled to be me. Baggy clothes were my go-to to try and disguise my 'deformed' body. I thought I was the ugliest person alive. There would be no point in trying to look nice, and no amount of make-up or pretty clothes would make me in any way desirable. Alone in my room, I would constantly berate myself. The inner critic in my head was overwhelmingly strong and I would repeatedly say to myself: 'You're a big, fat, ugly pig who deserves to die.' It was a complete pro at selling falsehoods to me, and you could have shouted out all the logical facts to me, but I would not have listened. I was blindsided by my inner critic and Ana. The more self-hatred I expressed, the more my eating disorder grew.

Getting changed for PE was something that filled me with

unprecedented levels of dread. While all my friends were wearing bras, I was still donning a babyish vest. Staring down morosely at my own body, I would wish my breasts to grow, cupping them together in my hands to create the illusion of a bust. Why was everyone else going through puberty yet I was not? My brain willed for a body I would not get. My thoughts went straight to restricting food, but my understanding of eating disorders back then was limited, and it wasn't until my struggles bubbled over, that the reality of the condition sunk in. They are not born out of vanity. Eating disorders prey on the sensitive, and it becomes a way of controlling something when you feel like everything in life is drowning you out. The illness plays games with your mind. She cruelly tricks you into believing that you are in control, when really Ana is the one in the driving seat. I would make fun of myself and this would lead to friends also making fun of me. This only reinforced my anorexic thoughts of self-condemnation. And so, the cycle repeats. On and on it goes until it breaks you before you can break it. My eating disorder and self-criticism became a way for me to numb my feelings of repulsion. I couldn't magic myself a bigger bust, or straighter teeth, but I could limit what foods I consumed. That was her way in. That was how Ana wormed her way into my life. And she has long outstayed her welcome.

***

Technology and I have not always been compatible with each other. I never really got into technology. I never had a PlayStation or games console. I never had a Nintendo Wii and didn't follow any YouTubers or bloggers. It wasn't until my teenage years that I got my own laptop. We had previously shared a house computer but most of my time was spent being immersed in reading. I loved books. I loved being transported to a different world by my favourite characters. It was a chance to escape my own head and live another life. I was a bookworm and could happily sit down with a good book for hours on end. It's a sad thing to admit, but I felt like an outsider and thought I was boring. I felt that I had nothing interesting to talk about. I wasn't into fashion or makeup. I wasn't watching any cult TV shows, and because of this, I felt a bit like a fish out of water. Maybe I did self-isolate from friends, but that was because I genuinely believed I was uninteresting and had nothing of note to talk about. Throughout a large part of secondary school, I was put in a lower tier from most of my friends. Whilst they were all in the higher group together, making new friends to add to our friendship circle, I began to feel left behind. So much time was spent in our separate classes and, outside of lessons, I felt myself very much teetering on the edge of the group.

It's strange because, in a way, you become a prophesier. You end up telling yourself that you have nothing to talk about and you go mute for fear of other people thinking you're dull, drab, and an idiot. You push your own thoughts onto others and that leads to you clamming up. If you don't speak much, then the likelihood is that others sense your discomfort and won't talk to you as much. Hence, you fulfil your own prophecy. I'm sure a lot of it was blown out of proportion by my inner critic and no one, in any way, is to blame for my eating disorder. I know I made some mountains out of molehills and I'll openly admit that. But I cannot change the past. I can only work on myself in the present in order to improve the future. I tend to very quickly retreat into my shell, and I can find it difficult to be vocal in large groups, even if I know all of them and have a good relationship with them. Makes no sense, right? Even I don't understand it properly. But because of my lack of self-belief, I then tend to think other people share the same harsh views I do. In my head, these are so much more than simple thoughts. This is my reality. I hate myself so therefore, everyone else must also hate me. It's taken me a long time to realise that this is not the case. It's something I still must work hard on, but I *am* working on it. I am at least trying to change how I, and others, perceive me. Ana makes her presence felt and takes advantage of any little thing she can get her grubby mitts on. I'm still not on the other side but I am making slow and steady progress. Meal by meal, day by day. Even as I'm typing this up, I'm fighting my own demons. The fight doesn't stop, it just becomes a little bit easier and a little less tiring. I am nowhere near recovered. I am, however, on the road to recovery and that's a place I never thought I'd reach.

***

One thing I have noticed whilst being in an inpatient setting, is that this illness is merciless in her attack against you. You become your own worst enemy. Eating disorders show you absolutely no mercy. Whilst some sufferers have a noticeable trauma that triggered the illness, many do not. It is a culmination of lots of different things, which separately don't amount to much, but collectively, they can destroy a life. That's exactly what happened to me, and it catapulted me right off the edge of that cliff. Whilst I had never restricted food during my teenage years, the intense self-loathing was burning inside of

17

me. I felt ugly, fat, repulsive, and freakish. I felt inadequate, stupid, and foolish. No one verbally put me down. I was the one doing the damage, but when you already have shaky foundations, it is easy to knock the entire thing down. It was me whose self-deprecating nature led to little or no self-esteem. My parents would always praise me, and never pressured me into doing anything I didn't want to do. They would constantly tell me how proud I made them, and how intelligent I was. My inner critic, however, had different views.

Parents: 'Steph, we're so proud of you.'

Inner Critic: 'No, they're not!'

Parents: 'You're smart, kind, and funny. Wise beyond your years.'

Inner Critic: 'Fuck that! They're lying to you. They're not saying this stuff to you because they mean it. They're telling you all this bullshit because you're their daughter and that's what parents are supposed to say.'

Parents: 'We love you so much Steph.'

Inner Critic: 'THEY'RE JUST BIASED! They don't mean any of it. It's all false. You hear me. None of it is true…'

Reading this out loud to myself, I am suddenly hit with the realisation of how immensely powerful my inner critic has always been. I feared having a big ego and getting above myself, so I went in the complete opposite direction. Instead of finding the right balance, I went to the other extreme, and that can be just as damaging. It all too easily became second nature for me to become the group's fool. By some miracle, I managed to keep a lid on my feelings throughout my adolescent years. Yes, the thoughts were constantly there, but they were just thoughts. I hadn't turned these thoughts into actions yet. At college, my self-effacing nature reared its ugly head to a whole new level. I was faced with boys... boys I fancied too. At this time, I was in the middle of growing out my short pixie cut and, because a lot of my clothes were baggy, I felt stupid. Dreading the decision of what outfit to wear each day. Telling myself I couldn't wear the same outfit twice in one week. That would be completely unacceptable. Undesirable, unattractive, and vile. Those three words sum up how I felt about myself. I told myself that no one would ever love me. Hell, I don't even remotely like myself, so how can I expect someone else to show me love? I told myself I would never get married and that I would die alone, with no family, no friends, no children... no nothing. It didn't matter if people said they liked me or that I was intelligent, I just convinced myself that they were all lying to me so as not to hurt my feelings.

The only person I felt I could trust was the voice inside my head... but little did I know that it was the toughest foe I would ever have to face. Somehow, I made it through college, achieving five A Levels. For most people, this would have been a huge achievement. But not for me. I was disappointed in myself. I could have, should have, done better. Once again, I had failed the high standard my inner critic had imposed upon me. I told myself so many times that I only got the grades I did because they felt sorry for me, and they weren't going to fail me because that would reflect badly on the college. The more I told myself this was the case, the more I believed it. I could never satisfy my inner critic because it demanded perfection. And someone who strives for perfection knows that it does not exist. When I received my results, my parents praised me, repeatedly telling me how proud I made them. My brother hugged me and said, 'well done, I knew you could do it, sis.' Was I happy? No. Did I feel like I'd achieved something even remotely special? Hell no. I told myself that I did 'average', and anybody could have done it. I did nothing special. I was nothing special.

Deciding to go to university and stay in education was an easy choice for me. I craved freedom and independence. Most importantly, however, I didn't know what I wanted to do in life, so I reasoned the best chance I had would be to get a 'good' degree from a reputable university. Next stop: Religious Studies and Theology. Destination: Cardiff. Luckily, I got the grades required to get into my top choice university. Instead of seeing this for the achievement that it was, and feeling proud of myself, I downplayed it. I convinced myself that they felt sorry for me, and I got in purely based on luck. My reasoning behind my acceptance was simple. If not, simply flawed. I thought they must be desperate to have people on the course to try and make up the numbers. In my head, I got in purely out of pity. I doggedly pursued this line of argument, refusing to listen to reason. The next chapter of my life was about to begin and, boy, was it a page turner.

***

I recall entering university halls for the first time. The memory of it is so vivid, it's as though it only happened last week. The name of my accommodation was Roy Jenkins. If first impressions are anything to go by, it did not fill me with any excitement. It was a small, drab building with just three floors and six flats. It housed only thirty-six students and, to me at least, it looked a bit like a prison from the outside. I'd never really been apart from my parents before. The longest I had gone without them was during a trip to Fairthorne Manor when I was in primary school. Fast forward eight years, and I was preparing to settle into university life. As I waved goodbye to my parents, I was filled with a mixture of excitement and fear. Excitement at being away from home for the first time and meeting new people, and fear of the unknown.

University was, for me, a rocky road, full of ups and downs. They say university is supposed to be one of the best times of your life yet, for me, it was one of the hardest. I met some wonderful people and gained a lot of independence, but I struggled with being me and accepting who I was.

Shortly into my first semester at university, I decided to colour my hair. I hated myself so much that I wanted desperately to change just one small part of me. I thought it might help ease my self-loathing. Did it work? Perhaps, but only for a little while. I soon reverted to my endless cycle of hatred. I changed my hair colour so many times. I've been red, purple, black, blonde, not to mention various shades of brown. Nothing I did was ever good enough. I could spend hundreds on new outfits and makeup, but nothing worked. In fact, I felt vain for trying so hard with my appearance. I thought if I could change myself on the outside then I could change how I felt about myself on the inside. Ana, however, had me in a vice-like grip. Everything I tried so hard to amend, or change for the better, stemmed from my body dysmorphia and crippling lack of self-belief.

***

Of course, being at university is not just about the social side of things, or about my self-discovery journey. Primarily, I went to study in Cardiff with the intention of getting a degree in Religion and Theology. But instead of loving my course, I loathed it. People joked that I hadn't taken a 'proper' degree and I did nothing to contradict them. I only fuelled the comments and kept them coming. Encouraging the jibes, I laughed at my own expense and frequently complained about how much I hated it. I provided my friends with plenty of ammunition to use against me, that's for sure. I was setting myself up for failure and disappointment, and it wasn't about to stop there. I soon stopped trying with my course. I immensely disliked it, yet I stubbornly refused to change, instead opting to ride it out. Maybe I was foolish in persisting but, come hell or high water, I was going to complete my course. The grade I got at the end was of no importance to me anymore. For me, it was just a matter of getting through it. As my drive to do well at university dwindled, my inner struggles only got more and more out of control. I remember sitting curled up on my bedroom floor, crying inconsolably to Ed Sheeran's *Kiss Me*. I had a razor in my hand. Rolling up my sleeves, I dug the blade into my flesh and felt small droplets of blood on my skin.

I didn't care what I was doing. All I wanted to do was cause myself pain. I thought I deserved to suffer. That I was not worthy of any happiness, it was a punishment for being the awful person I thought I was. I then picked up one of my photo frames, balled up my hand into a fist, and repeatedly punched the jagged edges. I just wanted to bruise my knuckles, inflict some level of pain on myself. I pushed my own thoughts onto others and if I believed that I was a good-for nothing worthless idiot, then everybody else would also share that same view. That probably sounds stupid, but I just couldn't understand how anyone would like me when I hated just about every part of my body. Feeling unworthy of happiness, friends, and life, I wanted to hurt myself, but it didn't really work. I grew frustrated. Yet again I had failed. I couldn't even self-harm properly, being the complete and utter twat that I was. Pathetic - that was me. Pathetic, useless, hopeless, unlovable, stupid, weak-minded... the list of insults is endless. There were a few occasions during my first year at university where I self-harmed, usually with a razor. I have not self-harmed to the religious and extreme extent that others have, and I don't want to sit here and say I know what it feels like to self-harm because I feel that would be an injustice. Yes, I have attempted self-harm in the past. Yes, I have purposefully cut myself, but this was only something I did occasionally, and I have not done it for the past four or so years. The wounds have long since healed, but there is still the temptation to hurt myself, particularly when things seem overwhelming and stressful. On reflection, maybe it was a cry for help. Maybe I did want people to sit up and take notice of me. Notice that I wasn't at all okay. I was fed up with playing the role of the happy one. I wasn't happy. I wasn't mentally well. I was a mess, but no one could see it. War was breaking out inside of me, but people could only see the wall I'd built up around myself. They couldn't see the crumbling mess behind it.

There is a huge stigma surrounding eating disorders and I want to dismantle people's preconceived ideas that sufferers are stick thin or on the brink of death. This is a lie. People suffering with any kind of eating disorder (this does not just apply to anorexia nervosa but extends to all other eating problems such as bulimia and OFSED,) come in many different shapes and sizes. You can be a so-called healthy weight and still have the internal battle of your eating disorder. I feel like restoring the weight is the easiest part of treatment. The hardest part is putting up with the constant battle in your head. The hardest part is standing up to your eating disorder and telling it to fuck off and leave you alone. The hardest part is maintaining that weight and trying not to relapse. The hardest part is trying to live without your eating disorder, which has become such a huge focal point of your life. Whilst I am blessed to have had the support I've had, and everyone in my treatment team is truly incredible, the system is inherently flawed.

Eating disorders are NOT determined by the number on the scales, or your BMI. A saying I have frequently heard whilst being in recovery is 'scales are for fish' and I don't think I could find anything more accurate. Humans do not need scales. They are not a necessity. Your mood and happiness should not be dependent on a stupid, little number. I was only considered bad enough for inpatient when my weight dropped to a certain amount. My discharge from hospital was because I was mostly weight restored. First and foremost, eating disorders are MENTAL HEALTH illnesses. The physical problems, such as bowel incontinence, low weight or lanugo (fine hair which grows over the body to try and preserve heat,) are symptoms of the condition. You may get all of them or you may get a few. But they do not define the condition. I told myself I was not anorexic or 'ill enough' for such a long time because that number on the scales wasn't where it was supposed to be. I refused to accept that I had a problem and, according to the medical professionals, I was within my healthy BMI range. I would spend hours trawling through Instagram, staring at food blogs and diet posts. I would dream about all the 'off-limit' foods I would have. A deep, big bowl of pasta with cheese on top and garlic bread on the side. A stuffed crust Texas BBQ domino's pizza. A takeaway burger and chips with onions inside and a big dollop of ketchup. Chocolate ice cream. A bacon sandwich on thick, white bread with all the crusts, slathered in tomato ketchup. A rare, sirloin steak with peppercorn sauce, chunky chips and fried onions. A steak and ale pie with creamy mash potato and baked beans with all the sauce. A proper cooked breakfast with pork sausages, egg, bacon, white toast, beans, and mushrooms. Chicken Tikka Masala complete with naan bread and prawn crackers. A ham, cucumber and cole-slaw bagel with a packet of cheese and onion crisps and a hot chocolate with marshmallows to wash it all down.

I could fill pages and pages with all the meals I dreamt about eating. I just couldn't permit myself to have them. There's a common misconception that people with eating disorders do not like food, or that they don't think about food at all. Let me tell you one thing. It's all lies! Many sufferers, just like myself, really enjoy food but they deny themselves that pleasure out of a crippling fear of what consuming these foods will do to them. You have an all-consuming fear of 'fatness' and taking up more space than you are worth. You can't concentrate. You can't function. You can't live a life worth living because that would mean you'd be happy and doing normal things, which you're not allowed to do according to your eating disorder.

Doing normal, everyday things means you're not ill enough, nor are you a 'proper anorexic' (whatever the hell that means.) Often, eating disorders are not actually about being skinny or pretty. Instead, it is about having some sense of control when you feel like things are getting too much for you to handle and are hurting due to traumatic events.

Steph: 'I really want to have pasta covered in cheddar cheese. I really want a massive pizza all to myself. If I want it, I should have it, right?'

Anorexia: 'Wrong! You silly cow. If you start eating these foods now you won't be able to stop. Everyone will think you're greedy and taking up too much room. You'll gain a ton of weight and you're already the size of a great whale.'

Steph: 'But surely the more I deny myself, the more I'll crave it? Everything in moderation, right?

Anorexia: 'Wrong! Wrong! And wrong again! Gosh, you really are thick, aren't you? Those foods are BAD for you. If you cave in now, you won't be able to stop yourself and you'll lose all control. Plus, I won't allow it.'

Steph: 'Wait, what? What do you mean?'

Anorexia: 'If you eat pizza and pasta and all this FAT then you simply can't have an eating disorder. I mean, it's obvious right? C'mon Steph, a blindfolded ape could figure it out quicker than you.'

The inner dialogue continues. The battle rages on. There is no respite. The saddest thing about this illness is that NOTHING will ever be good enough. You will NEVER be thin enough. You will NEVER exercise enough. You will NEVER eat few enough calories. You will NEVER be dead enough. You will only succeed in wasting away before your family and friend's horrified eyes. But before this happens, you have osteoporosis, or you can't even sit down properly without your bones hurting because they're unprotected. You have lanugo growing all over your body, your skin is as thin as paper and so pallid you appear almost grey. Your heart will struggle to keep pumping blood around your body. Your organs will shut down. The cold, hard truth is that your eating disorder desires nothing more than your death. And she is militant in her demands. I was weighing myself five or six times every day, and the number on the scales never satisfied Ana. In fact, the more it went down, the more it encouraged Ana to keep going, keeping her alive and burning. I have come to only one conclusion. Screw the scales. They screw with your head and make you feel like a 'failed anorexic,' so I'm going to tell you what I want you to do. You are going to go up to your bathroom, or wherever your scales are kept. You will pick them up. You won't stand on them, regardless of how strong the anorexia is pulling at you. Stay strong for just a little while. Close your eyes if it helps but pick the scales up in your arms. You will now go outside. You will raise it above your head and say the words 'fuck you, scales!' You will then smash it on the ground and shatter it to pieces, just as it has shattered the real you. Shattered all your thoughts and dreams and hope. Destroy it, bin it, banish it. You are stronger without it.

***

Ana makes you lie and manipulate the people who care about you the most. The people you love and the people who love you. She tricks you into thinking she's your best friend and anyone who questions her is an enemy. She tells you most convincingly that she is your one and only friend. Ana is the only person who ever speaks the truth. Everyone around me is just too afraid to tell me the harsh reality because they don't want to hurt me. I believed Ana's taunts and jibes. I have openly lied to my friends and family. I never wanted it. I never intended to hurt them. Ana did though. I hate the fact I've hurt those closest to me. It breaks my heart living with the knowledge that I put my parents through so much pain and heartache. My heart might have been breaking, but so was theirs. They were literally watching their daughter deteriorate in front of them. I was angry, miserable, rude, and on edge all the bloody time. I can't take away this illness. I wish I could. I wish, with all my heart, that I could just reach into my chaotic, disordered brain and take out all the nasty thoughts, but I cannot do that. As nice as that would be, this is something I've got to learn to live with. I don't know if I will ever kill off Ana, but I can banish her and send her into a deep coma. My past is my past and it's a part of me. I am now trying to work with my family and fight against the anorexic thoughts. The lies would all too easily tumble from my mouth as I clung helplessly onto my eating disorder. She was turning me into someone I didn't want to be, and I was powerless to stop it.

***

Somehow, I managed to muddle through university. I came extremely close to dropping out of my course in my final year. In fact, I would have dropped out had it not be for one thing: my family. They saved me in more ways than one. I was in the middle of writing my dissertation, struggling with an exercise addiction and anorexic thoughts around food. I was one track minded. I had to lose weight. That was it. When people complimented me on my weight loss or said things like 'I wish I had your discipline, you've got so much self-control,' or 'wow, you've lost so much weight,' I was only spurred on to do more. I was unable to see the weight loss. In my head, I was still fat, and I couldn't understand how I hadn't lost more weight given everything I was doing. All the exercise I was doing, the twenty thousand steps I was walking every day, the food I had banned. Deciding I needed some time out and feeling like my head was about to explode with everything going on, I booked a train home for the week.

I felt like I could finally breathe when I came home. My parents listened to my concerns, they let me cry as I admitted to them my fears of failure. They spoke sense. And I listened to the voice of reason for once. They reminded me that I'd already made it through two and a half years, I was touching distance away from the finish line. It would be a massive shame to pack it all in now and throw away all my hard work. They were right, of course. I'm only sorry I couldn't be the daughter I wished I could be. I'm sorry for hurting you. Forgive me. But don't let me forget how ill I became. Don't let me forget that I could have died from this illness.

After I completed my course and received my results from university, my next hurdle was graduation. Normally a day of celebration and giddy exuberance, it instead became a day I wish I could forget. I was so focused on how disgusting and huge I felt in a fitted dress, that I was unable to fully appreciate the special occasion. I remember bits of the ceremony and going out for a meal at my favourite restaurant, Miller and Carter, but it was marred with my continuous preoccupation with food and my body. All throughout the meal, they only thing I could think about was the number of calories in my food and how long I'd have to run for the next day in order to burn everything off. Ana told me that all the guests in the restaurant were watching my every move, scrutinising me, judging what I was eating, and thinking how much of a repulsive oaf I was. If I were to listen to logic, I would have realised that most people there were having the same food as me, if not more. They weren't judging my food and I certainly wasn't judging them. The thought of them being fat or disgusting did not even cross my mind. Yet this reasoning completely flew over my head and out of the window. It was okay for everyone else to enjoy themselves and indulge in the occasional treat, but I could not apply the same kindness to myself. I'm not sure why this is. The thought of anyone else suffering is not something I wish to think about, and I wouldn't wish this illness on my best friend, or worst enemy. No one deserves to punish themselves so harshly. No one deserves to be so self-critical and demanding that they wear themselves into the ground and have no real quality of life. Life is too short to spend every day of it being miserable.

Eating disorders suck! Full of false promises, they will always let you down. She tells you that you will achieve happiness if you reach a certain weight, but as soon as you reach it, the goal posts are suddenly changed. Just because I wasn't dying, Ana convinced me I wasn't ill. People struggle with eating and the physical consequences of starvation for years. What I had been through was insignificant in comparison. I had no right to complain when I was still eating, working, and meeting friends. If you have any sort of life, you can't have an eating disorder.

That's what she constantly tells you. Throughout my graduation all I was focused on was looking thin in my fitted dress. It was a beautiful salmon pink dress, with sequins and a low cut back, but I felt unworthy to be wearing something so pretty. I felt I couldn't do the outfit justice and thought the dress would look better on anyone other than me. I am not deserving of wearing nice things. I am not deserving of happiness or achievements. I am not deserving of family or friends. I may have got a 2:1 in my degree, but I believed that I only got that grade out of pity. I merely did 'okay,' but that was only because it was a super easy course, and anyone could have done it. I just blagged my way through, without any talent or ability. It was potluck and I had nothing to be proud of. Nothing at all.

***

In the absolute depths of my illness, I thought eating any kind of nice or indulgent food was greedy. I could survive without nice foods; it was just a matter of will power. If I caved in, I would be giving into temptation and, would therefore, be weak minded and a failure. I just wanted to live on the absolute bare minimum. To eat for pleasure was completely out of the question. I could not understand, for the life of me, how I was still so 'fat.' I had done everything I could think of, but nothing worked. A few of my friends were also undergoing weight loss journeys of themselves. Whenever I looked at them, their hard work was instantly apparent, but I couldn't see any noticeable changes in myself. This only served to anger Ana even more. People commented on my weight loss and how well I was doing, how disciplined I was, but I just couldn't see any results. In my head, all I could see were my rolls and rolls of fat and my disgusting stomach. My wonky teeth, my protruding stomach, my thunder thighs… I hated what I saw, what I could feel, what I could touch. I hated who I was. In the blinkered view of Ana, I was still massive, and I grew increasingly upset and frustrated over my lack of results. How was everyone else in control and losing more weight than I was? How were they succeeding where I was always failing? I was doing all the necessary things – dieting, exercising, restriction, the weight should have been falling off me. But it wasn't. Ana once more made me feel like a failure and a waste of space. I couldn't fathom why this was happening to me. What was I doing wrong? How were they still eating food for enjoyment, and having foods I deemed to be 'bad?' Feeling so disheartened, Ana bullied me into thinking I hadn't done well enough.

It needs to be acknowledged that this was not the case. I had lost a significant amount of weight since college, Was I satisfied? You got it in one – of course I wasn't. What I should be saying, is that it was Ana who was unhappy. In fact, she was mightily pissed off. I wanted to drop down to seven stone. When I reached that milestone, I wanted to drop down to six and a half. Then six. Then five stone. Then four… and so on… I didn't want to weigh anything at all. I wanted to be as light as a feather. I didn't want to exist. Whatever I weighed was too much, but it wasn't because I wanted to be prettier. I was under no illusion. Losing weight would not bring me happiness, nor would it make me more attractive. I hated the way I looked. Absolutely detested it, and it didn't matter what the number on the scales read. I still hated, hated, hated, my body. My overriding concern was that I felt I took up too much space, and I was unworthy of a life. I could have had a healthy complexion and been a decent weight, or I could have been all skin and bones. It would not have made a difference with how I felt about myself. I didn't want to be me anymore. I was useless. I was greedy for taking up more space than I deserved. I was a waste of fucking space.

When I walked on stage during my graduation, I vividly remember sticking in my stomach to appear thinner and minimise the amount of space I greedily took up. Too much of the lift was taken up by me… too much of the car… too much of the sofa. I was not worthy of space, or time, or love. I might not have been in control of my thoughts or other people's view of me, but I was in control of what I was eating. I was in control of how many steps I did each day. I was in control over how many calories I was burning off from running. Reflecting on this, I now realise that I had no control whatsoever. Ana was controlling the reins and I was merely a slave to her bidding. I was drowning in a sea of self-criticism. Whenever I looked at my reflection, I would instantly hear the anorexic voice start up in my head. I would be drawn straight to my stomach, scrutinising it from every possible angle. I would suck it in. I would try and push my rolls of fat down, my hands like a rolling pin trying to flatten out all my imperfections. The more I dwelled on the parts of my body I hated, the more intense the hatred became. The more prevalent those feeling of self-hatred and unworthiness became. It's a vicious cycle. You see what you consider to be a flaw. You spend hours and hours, days and days, years and years, examining it in the mirror. You try your very hardest to disguise your 'fatness,' sucking in so hard that you can barely breathe at times. But despite your best efforts, it does not go away. Instead, rather cruelly, it becomes more prominent. It consumes your thoughts and, eventually becomes you, controlling all your thoughts and actions. Until you can't take any more and your vicious thoughts break you into a million little pieces. Until you reach crisis because you just can't cope any more. And this cycle of hatred and disgust does not go away, it just repeats itself. You find other ways of hating yourself and punishing yourself.

***

Upon graduating, I decided to stay on in Cardiff for a year, getting some money from working a part-time job. Those were my intentions at least. I didn't spend too much time applying for jobs when I got a position as a door host at a restaurant in Cardiff city centre. Although all the staff there were friendly enough, Ana was a sergeant, and I was firmly in her line of fire. At the end of every single shift, without fail, I would convince myself that I would be fired. That I would lose my job for being such a clumsy oaf. Every time I dropped a glass, or seated people at the wrong table, I would get increasingly frustrated with myself. No person is perfect. Everyone makes mistakes from time to time. Whilst I could easily accept other people making mistakes and not always getting things right, I was unable to show the same compassion to myself. I refused to listen to reason. I was in a constant state of nervousness, always on edge and fearing those two little words: 'You're fired!' I was convinced my days there were numbered. I thought I was crap at my job, so therefore everyone else must also think I'm rubbish. I think I am incapable of doing anything, therefore I am. Therefore nothing. These are just thoughts. Just Ana's thoughts. They are not real. Although I might have a hard time believing this, I'm just going to have to fake it till I make it. And I will make it. Someday. Someday, somehow, I'll get there.

Each section of the restaurant was given a name and, it just so happened, that one of those sections was called 'anorexic.' Now, I am in no doubt that this was just a silly name to help organise the restaurant and waitresses, but it highlights the utter lack of understanding there is of eating disorders. Nine times out of ten they are not about starving your body. You don't suddenly wake up one morning and say to yourself 'hey, do you know what I'm going to do today? I'm going to become anorexic and starve myself.' It just doesn't work like that, okay. Do you think it's easy to go against every single survival instinct in your body? To the point where you no longer experience hunger pangs? Do you think I'm not eating out of vanity? That I want to starve myself and feel cold all the time? To experience internal bleeding because I couldn't stop myself from running six hours, each day, every day. I didn't want any of it. But Ana compelled me to do it because I felt unworthy. I took up too much space. I took up too many people's time. I took up a place in this world that I was not worthy of. Ana made me believe it was as simple as that. I couldn't control how isolated I felt and how out of touch with the modern world I felt, but I could control food and exercise. When I felt everything in life was getting too much and was out of control, at least I could do this. I could numb myself to all my feelings and just fade away into nothing…

I imagine that the 'anorexic' section of the restaurant was called as such, because all the tables were close to each other. Whenever I walked through, the anorexic voice inside my head would play a little game with me. Ana likes to play games and mess with your head. Whenever I passed them, I had to see if I could do it without holding in my stomach. If I was unable to do this, my head took it as evidence of me being too fat. I would then have to compensate by skipping out a meal or going to the gym, on top of my daily runs. It was a ritual for me. I was willing to run myself into the ground, to hurt myself, to cut myself off from friends and family. I was willing to die for Ana. Whatever it took. Nothing was too much, or too demanding, for my eating disorder. Whatever Ana ordered, I did. Whatever cruel task she set, I followed. I realise how silly this sounds, but back then I was too caught up with my illness to see past her façade.

My anorexia and inner critic joined forces with each other, making an even more powerful foe.

Inner Critic: 'You're rubbish. A baby could do a better job than you. And it would certainly be prettier. Everybody loves babies. But nobody loves Steph.'

Anorexia: 'You take up too much space, fatty!'

Inner Critic: 'You are so NOT going to last here, literally everyone hates you. You see how they're all looking at you, talking about you behind your back, laughing about how stupid you are.

Anorexia: 'You can't call yourself anorexic. You still must suck your stomach to fit between the tables. You're a joke.'

Inner Critic: 'You have no idea what you're doing, do you? Bloody hell it's an embarrassment. You're an embarrassment.'

As well as battling my inner demons, I also had to contend with my worsening eating habits and exercise addiction. Orthorexia was something that greatly plagued me, in the sense that I struggled justifying foods that were 'nice,' 'indulgent,' or considered by the media and public health messages as being 'bad' and 'naughty.' I became so caught up with these food labels that I lost sight of what is important. I didn't know what balance meant anymore. Eating these foods was something that I couldn't justify. I didn't need them, I just wanted them. I would be a greedy, fat, pig if I gave in. I only placed those strict rules on myself, nobody else. They were all deserving of enjoyment and a life.

What I decided to do with my day or how I felt about myself, was totally dependent on the number on the scales. Despite my obsessive weighing habits and negative thoughts around food, I fiercely denied that I had an eating disorder. So, I might have a slight problem with food but that was it. It was nothing more. Nothing serious and, certainly, nothing for anyone to be concerned about. I thought if I ate these foods in front of people who were beginning to get suspicious, then I would trick them into believing everything was fine. And, for a while at least, this seemed to work.

***

One weekend, I was on the phone to my parents when my dad mentioned to me that my old primary school was offering a teacher training course. I had briefly considered becoming a primary school teacher and was looking at potentially doing a PGCE the following year. I loved children and wanted to do some good in the world. This seemed too good an opportunity to miss, so I looked it up online and made a few phone calls to try and find out more about what the course entailed. Maybe this is what I needed to give me the extra boost in life that I craved?

Maybe I did have a purpose to get out of bed each day. Maybe I was going to become a teacher and set up my own pastoral care unit. It did not take long for these dreams to be shattered.

When I first heard about the course, I was filled with a sense of excitement. I wasted no time in completing my application but, the more I investigated the course, the more the self-doubt started to creep in. I was 21 years of age and had only just left university. I was still a child at heart. I am now 23, and although I have grown up a lot this past year, facing many adversaries, I still have much more growing to do. I do not think you ever stop growing and learning. When I'm old and grey, I will still be learning new things. I might be an adult but that does not mean I know everything. There's a lot I don't know, and a lot that I will never know. And I'm okay with that. You don't stop being anorexic when you reach a healthy weight. You don't stop growing when you reach a certain age. I had little experience working with children and, as I got further into my application, I realised this was a hurdle I had to overcome. In order to do the course, I needed to have recent experience with children and have a DBS check. I had none of that. The most experience I had was when I went to the school for a year ten work placement years back. Turns out, rather shockingly I know, that that wasn't enough.

I have no chance. There's a greater chance of hell freezing over. I'm too young and inexperienced, they wouldn't want me teaching kids. I don't deserve such a responsibility. I was entirely the wrong person for the job. I was going to fail before I'd even started. I didn't have it in me to be a teacher. No one would want me teaching their child. What the bloody hell was I thinking? I think you get the idea. I was beating myself up, second guessing everyone's reactions based on my own self-deprecating views. I didn't give people enough credit to assume they could make up their own decision about me. How I viewed myself was the only way anyone could see me. There was no good, only bad, and if people truly got to know me, then they wouldn't want to know me better. I wouldn't be worth their time of day.

I pictured them laughing their heads off reading my pathetic personal statement. I was just a stupid little kid who was way out of her depth. I didn't have to wait long till I was put out of my misery. About a week after I sent everything off, I got a call. My application had been accepted and they asked if I could come down that week for an interview. I said yes. I didn't think about, I didn't hesitate. I thought they must have made a mistake, so I made sure I replied quickly so that they couldn't change their mind.

I was shocked. My initial feeling of happiness was marred by my inner critic, harshly telling me that they only accepted my application because they felt sorry for me. You may notice a trend appearing here. Whenever something good happened to me, or I achieved something, I always told myself that it was out of guilt and was no true reflection of my actual ability. Everyone just felt sorry for me and gave me praise, or good grades, because I was embarrassing myself. It was done out of sympathy and not out of merit. I was, and still am to a certain extent, incapable of giving myself any credit for fear of having a big ego. Despite my inner critic rearing its goddamn ugly head and trying its best to thwart me, I tried hard to fight it. The problem was, I was tired of fighting for so long. Tired of people thinking I was okay because I was laughing or smiling.

39

Or because I had amazing friends and such a supportive family. But. I. Am. Not. A. Fraud. I am not an imposter and, although I don't believe it yet, I will continue this mantra until, one day, I will believe. And I won't have to try so flipping hard.

I caught a train home for the week to take some much need time off work, but most importantly, to attend the interview. I had a mere two days to prepare a presentation for part of the interview, so I hastily cobbled something together the day before I was due to be interviewed. Saving it to my emails, my mind was going ten to the dozen, trying to come up with excuses as to why I couldn't attend the interview. This was stupid. I was going to make such a fool out of myself. This was a disaster. What was I thinking? Oh god no, help me please, I'm so out of depth here it's ridiculous.

GET OUT OF MY HEAD!!!!

Yeah, you heard me, get out and leave me alone. I don't want you ruining my life anymore. Go screw yourself Ana. Go screw yourself inner critic. Go screw yourself anxiety and depression. Guess what? I don't need you anymore. I'm done with you. And *you* reading this can be done with your demons too. Mental health is a part of you, but that does not mean it has to define you.

I remember distinctively how anxious I was the day of the interview. I could barely sleep the night before I was so restless. I was sorely tempted to pack it all in and not turn up at all. Did I turn up? Do you know what? I did turn up. I made it. I could have not gone, that would have been the easy way out, but I faced my fears.

Having just had my hair freshly highlighted, I did my make-up and put on the most formal outfit I could find. I'm going to make a little confession here. The clothes I wore for the interview weren't mine. They belonged to my mum. I felt I had nothing suitable for an interview. I didn't like any of my clothes and thought I looked like a baby in all of them. I wasn't allowed to wear blue jeans or leggings and I practically lived in them and hoodies. Again, I found myself getting angry. I was an adult, yet all my clothes looked like they were made for young children. I wasn't mature enough. I had the body of a little girl; they were never going to accept me in my wildest dreams. Even highlighted hair and make-up failed to make me look even vaguely presentable. I hated myself more and more. Feeling woefully inadequate, I tried to push the fears to the back of my mind, but that did little good. They were still there, raging away, and I couldn't extinguish the burning flames. The interview itself lasted six hours and I underwent several tests, a presentation, and a brief interview with three head teachers. There were six of us, including me, but I was by far the youngest. All the other aspiring candidates were already working in schools as a classroom assistant whilst I virtually had no experience at all. My inner critic was firing from all cylinders.

Steph: 'Well, that was okay. Hopefully, they might recognise my passion and give me a chance.'

Inner Critic: 'You don't stand a chance you stupid little girl. You're never going to become a teacher... EVER.'

Steph: 'They MIGHT pick me. I mean I have youth on my side, so...'

Inner Critic: 'They are NOT going to pick you, stop kidding yourself. You're rubbish at everything. You have NO experience. You have NO chance. If they do accept you, it's out of sympathy and nothing else. They'll just pity you. You're not worthy of anything!'

Steph: 'Hold on a minute...'

Inner Critic: 'You're a waste of space.'

I left the interview feeling distinctly deflated. I should have prepared a better presentation. Why didn't I do more? I should have done more. I tried in vain to push it to the back of my mind. A few days later I received a phone call. With bated breath I answered my phone, mentally preparing myself for failure. I was left speechless when they told me I had been successful. I had finally proved my inner critic wrong. I had been accepted and was due to start working as a classroom assistant the following school term. Because I didn't have any recent work experience with children, they offered me the role of classroom assistant and, at the start of the next school year, I would begin my official training. For a split second, I felt genuine joy. A sense of achieving something for once. But this did not last long.

Steph: 'Oh my God, I actually did it. They accepted me. I must have done well. Finally, something I actually succeeded in.'

Inner Critic: 'Umm, nope. They're only taking you on out of pity.'

I pushed these thoughts to the back of my mind, trying to get my feelings of self-doubt under control. When I told my parents, they were so proud of me. They said they always knew I could do it and they never doubted me for a second. But I did not believe them. They were just empty words to me. As my parents it was their job to praise me. They were obliged to make me feel better, but I was bound to let them down sooner or later.

***

In the following months, I rapidly declined. On Christmas Eve, 2018, I woke up at seven o'clock in the morning to go for a twenty-six-mile run. I'd been training for a year and was determined to complete the mileage. It was a solo run and I purposefully decided to do it at this time, to try and compensate for the extra food and drink I might have. I was tired and cold. I felt weak from running every single day. After reaching the twenty-mile mark, I hit a bit of a wall. My legs were on fire, aching all over, but I could not stop and let myself off the hook. That was simply not an option. I had to keep running. There was no choice in the matter. It was a matter of life and death according to Ana. If I didn't run, I didn't deserve to eat, and I would have to find more ways of restricting and punishing myself. I had to keep running. Every time I felt my persistence waning, I would chant to myself 'just keep swimming.' Whenever I wanted to give up, I would say 'fat, stupid, ugly, cunt' on repeat. After four and a half hours of pounding the pavement, I made it home. I'd only started running In January 2018. In under a year, I had gone from not running at all to running marathon distances. When I had finished, I should have properly refuelled my body, but instead I decided to listen to Ana.

Grabbing two rice cakes from the cupboard, I spread a thin layer of honey on top and munched down on my rather pitiful snack. My stomach was making loud noises, rumbling away, and I wanted, I NEEDED, more food. My body needed something more substantial and carb heavy. That wasn't me being a pig. That was me being sensible and treating my body with a bit of love and kindness for once. Ana twisted this and used it against me, accusing me of eating unnecessary calories

43

too close to lunch. I'd come back from my gruelling run just before noon. This meant I had missed Ana's allocated breakfast time, and she forced me to wait it out till lunch. My parents demanded that I have something to eat, saying that I need to replenish my energy stores so I had the smallest thing I could possibly get away with. Wait. That's all I had to do. Just wait and ride out the feelings of hunger. Eventually, they would pass if I could learn to be more patient. For me, it was very much about mind over matter.

My mind was stronger than my body. If I ever dared to show weakness and listen to my actual body, I would become annoyed for being so pathetic and feeble. Listening to my body was a sign of weakness and something I could not do. My mind was strong. Stronger than everything else, and I was in control. Christmas is typically a time for indulgence and joviality. This year, however, Christmas was neither of those things for me. I was increasingly miserable and constantly thinking about how I could compensate for eating too many 'bad foods.' No food is bad. That's one thing I want to make perfectly clear. Food cannot be, is emphatically not, good or bad. Everything is good for you in moderation. Chocolate and carbs have got a bad press over the years. But food cannot harm you unless you eat it excessively. Some of these sugary, processed foods that are demonised by the media can have a benefit to your mental health. Imagine you and your friend meeting up for coffee. They might have a doughnut or slice of cake and a latte with full fat milk and cream on top. But you have a bottle of water and a cucumber stick. Where's the enjoyment? You'll just end up being miserable that you can't participate and join in with everybody else. You'll just be constantly reminded of a life that is out of your grasp. It's hanging over you, but you can never reach it. You will never be normal, successful, or happy if you listen to your eating disorder. But sooner or later, you will be dead. The only thing you are depriving yourself of is a life. The only thing you are starving yourself of is friendships and family. The only person you are killing is yourself.

Begrudgingly, under instructions from my parents, I had two days of rest. But, as soon as I was able to, I was out running ludicrous miles again. My parents and I had arranged to meet with my Uncle and Aunt for lunch shortly after Christmas. I quickly checked, double checked, and triple checked the menu of the pub we were going to for lunch. Counting all the calories and working out how much I would need to run in order to burn off the food was all I could think about. I knew if I refused to go out or had some salad or something, it would arouse too much suspicion. They already thought I wasn't eating enough so I didn't want to give them more ammunition. Ana was hanging on by a weakening thread, and she was determined to keep me in silent pain. It was time to slip my mask back on and put on a happy front. It was a militant operation.

Let me just give you some insight as to the type of thoughts that circulate my mind daily, and which led to my exercise addiction. Every day I would set myself a running target. Anything from six to twenty miles, but no less than six. That was the absolute minimum I permitted myself to do. Being sick, ill, tired, in pain, or just not feeling it, I would still have to go. I had to exercise because if I didn't that would make me instantly unhealthy. If I gave in and accepted that I couldn't run, it would ruin all my diligent efforts to lose weight. All I had to do was keep on putting one foot in front of the other. It could take me the whole day for all I cared. As long as I finished what I started. As long as I kept Ana's flames under control.

After spending an unthinkable amount of time looking at menus and comparing dishes, I made the difficult decision to have a steak meal. I did this for several reasons. The first was that I needed to prove to myself, and to everyone else, that I was okay. The second was because I wanted people to get off my back and stop worrying about me. I was fine. I wasn't fine, I wasn't even remotely okay, but Ana was having none of it. Using MyFitnessPal, I did some calorie counting, and amended all my other meals to make up for me being a 'greedy, fat, repulsive, pig.' I think, for a while at least, it did help put my parent's mind at rest. They knew something was amiss as they had begun to comment on my eating behaviours. I was treading a dangerous path. I wish, with every fibre of my being, that I could say I had a healthy relationship with exercise. But that is far removed from the truth. I don't know if I will ever be able to build up a healthy relationship with exercise, without it turning toxic. I have never been able to get the right balance before and my future around running is unknown.

Instead of exercising out of love, I was doing it out of fear. Fear of what might happen if I just sat with my feelings. I hated my body. I hated everything about me, but I didn't do anything about it. What was the point? I was never going to like myself. I was never going to succeed in anything. My thoughts weren't my own. They belonged to Ana. Days were spent counting calories, running miles for hours on end, scrolling through weight loss pages on Instagram, day after day. I never laughed, I never smiled, I never joked. I just ate the bare minimum and ran. That's what my world revolved around. The only thing in existence that was important to me. Sadly, I lost sight of who I was as a person. My family, jobs, relationships, nothing at all, mattered to me. With all these thoughts swarming around my mind, it really was no surprise that I didn't enjoy being a teaching assistant. It was the beginning of February when I had my first day working at my old primary school. Memories come flooding back to me. Good memories. Memories of me reading in the library, taking part in the school play, playing dodge ball in the school playground. Times of true happiness. It's something I wish I could hold on to forever. After going through all the tedious paperwork, I found myself standing in front of a year two classroom, with pupils addressing me as Miss Shott. This filled me with pride. It felt good to be back in a place that brought me so much safety and joy growing up. In my head, I already had a preconceived idea of what teaching would be like. I thought I would be making a difference, doing something good in a world where there is so much wrong. That I would get some sense of satisfaction from doing something good. How wrong was I?

***

I threw everything I had into this job, but I felt so very lost. I spent so long believing that teaching was my vocation in life, it was the perfect path to take. But suddenly, I felt as though the curtains had been pulled shut on my parade. My dreams came crashing down a lot faster than they had built up. My hopes fell apart. This was nothing like I had imagined.

Steph: 'I thought I would be helping people, making a difference.'

Inner Critic: 'Fucking hell Steph, you can't do anything right, can you?'

Steph: 'I thought this was my dream, my perfect job come true. But I'm rubbish at it.'

Inner Critic: 'Damn right you are! Oh, c'mon stop moping you twat, it shouldn't even come as a surprise to you. You're shit at everything you do. And now, you're going to fail at being a teacher too.'

Steph: 'But…'

Inner Critic: 'There are no buts. Just fact. And the fact of the matter is you're a massive let down. You're a failure. A failure. A FAILURE!'

Steph: 'Now hold on a minute… this is just new to me right now. It's going to take time for me to get a handle on things, but I will get there. It's just not going to be instantaneous, that's all.'

Inner Critic: 'No, you won't. You will NEVER achieve ANYTHING! No one here likes you. No one respects you. You don't belong here.'

It was like a game of table tennis. Back and forth, back and forth. It went on and on and on. My inner critic firmly had the upper hand, and I believed every lie it was feeding me.

**

In 2018, the school was appointed by the department of education as a hub centre. As a result of this, other schools would send representatives to see how this was achieved. Every two weeks, inspections would take place in which people from other schools would come in and visit, seeing how their 'excellence' was implemented. On occasion, I would be teaching in a corridor when the inspection took place and this, not only made me feel extremely uncomfortable, but also a bit unreliable. Like they didn't trust me to do a good job and they were just waiting for the right time to throw the book at me and tell me to leave. I understood that, as part of the hub, the school was obliged to have these frequent inspections and it was a testament to how well they were doing. This did not, however, stop me from feeling incredibly nervous and on edge whenever they came around. I felt like I was supposed to know what to do without having been given proper instructions. It's like throwing a baby into the deep end of the pool to see if they sink or swim. Sinking is what happened to me. Or at least that's what it felt like. I want to make it perfectly clear that the school did nothing wrong. Logic tells me that I was respected and valued, but that didn't change how I felt. It is no criticism of the staff; everyone I was involved with was wonderful. They had belief in me. I didn't have belief in myself and that was the underlying problem. People can praise me and support me, but I was struggling to believe their words because of how much I hate myself. It's difficult to build yourself up when the foundations are already shaky.

Every morning, I was filled with a building sense of dread. My only reason for getting up in the mornings was to run. I did not want to do anything else. Work made me feel constantly anxious and uncomfortable with myself. I felt a let-down and a disappointment to all the teachers. I felt as though students didn't respect or appreciate me. I was half expecting at the end of each day to be fired for being so bloody useless. I was unsure on whether to be strict and discipline the pupils or leave everything to my teacher. Marking class books led to an increased level of anxiety. Confused and lost, I found myself at a bit of a crossroads in life. I hated teaching. I thought I would love it, but I didn't. So, what the hell was I supposed to do? Teaching was not the dream job I envisioned it to be. I had absolutely no idea what I was going to do next.

***

Not only was my professional life falling to pieces, so too was my personal health and hygiene. I didn't change my bedding for months; I didn't hoover or tidy my room. I wasn't even able to put all my dirty clothes in the washing basket. I didn't even have to put them in the washing machine. My mum was doing it for me, but I just couldn't bring myself to do anything other than restrict and exercise. I did shower but that was the extent of my cleanliness. I would turn my pants inside and out and wear them for days on end instead of washing them. I know that's disgusting and I'm horrified with myself for doing it, but I just didn't care. The world could be on fire and I wouldn't give a damn. I could be so exhausted and dizzy, I thought I was going to collapse, but I wouldn't give a damn. I could be dying, and I wouldn't give a damn. I didn't have a sodding care in the world and that's not like me. That's not who Steph is as a person. Steph loves people. Steph wants to live a life where she is helping people and fighting for what she believes in. Steph cares. Ana does not. But that's the difference between me and her. Ana may have corrupted me and made me into a person I was ashamed to be, but I am not that person. Not on the inside. Not where it counts. That's why I'm not going to let this beat me. Steph is strong and independent and stubborn as hell. And she is sick to the back teeth of having fucking anorexia.

Anorexia is a sneaky illness. A little bastard that thrives off death and destruction. She somehow tricks you into thinking you're indestructible. You hear of other people collapsing, dying even, from eating disorders. But you end up believing that nothing will ever happen to you. Ignore it. Before it is too late. Ana desires only one thing – your death – she won't stop hating you, belittling you, and starving you, until your heart stops beating, and you die. If you don't stick your finger up to the illness and turn your back on her toxicity and evilness, you will forever be a slave to this master. And the unrelenting harshness of it is that it will eventually lead to your organs packing up. To ridiculously low blood pressures, to freezing cold body temperatures that you cannot regulate properly. To your death.

This book is not written to scare you, but to help you. To increase understanding of eating disorders and to try and help you to reach out and seek treatment before it is too late. The cold hard truth is that eating disorders are killers. They take away your life and could, just as it did for me, lead to long hospital admissions. It is not fun. It is not joyful. It is not a life. The more you isolate yourself from those who care, the happier Ana becomes, and the stronger and more relentless those lies become. Ana hates those who question her, who challenge her beliefs, and she doesn't want you to start listening to sense and logic. But the more you accept logic, the less of a grip Ana has on you. If even a tiny part of you wonders what life would be like without an eating disorder, then you can begin to stand up to the bully. No one deserves to suffer. No one deserves a death so harsh and miserable and soul-destroying. No one deserves their family to be torn to pieces. NO ONE DESERVES TO

HAVE AN EATING DISORDER!

Ana made me believe that I could only eat bland foods. My body was in desperate need of carbs. It was shouting out for fuel, but did I listen to it? No. Should I have? Yes. My body doesn't hate me contrary to what I may sometimes think. Ana hates my body, but my body doesn't reject me for putting it through so much crap. My body is still here for me, still fighting back, still working normally, and for that I am truly blessed. I do not hate my body. How can I possibly hate something that helps me to survive?

***

Whilst it's true that I may have been consuming little food, thoughts about food were consuming ninety-five percent of my life. The mind and body work together, they should not be vying with each other over who can come up on top. The mind is not more important than the body, and vice versa. They work in harmony and it's time we respected our bodies. If it wants a day off, give yourself some time to relax and repair. If your body wants the extra slice of pizza, or bowl of pasta, then you give it exactly what it needs. Our bodies don't crave things for no reason at all. Listen to it. What's the worst that can happen? You piss off Ana, but you don't die. You'll still wake up the next morning. You'll survive it, but not everyone survives having an eating disorder.

During my downward spiral, my family and I adopted a dog in November from a rescue centre. A Pomeranian cross named Simba. Normally, I love animals, but I found myself unable to connect with our new, furry, friend. It's a difficult thing to describe, but I felt detached from everything that was going on around me. I couldn't connect with anyone or anything, and I just didn't feel any sort of love towards Simba. I didn't feel anything at all towards him, and that scared me. Normally, I'm a person who is in touch with their feelings and can easily display emotions, but here I was, struggling to feel anything other than numbness. Months rolled by, and it was the beginning of April when things took another turn.

***

I had been working at the school for about three months and, instead of my feelings of inadequacy diminishing, they only intensified. It was the Easter Holidays and I had been hit with a bad bout of gastroenteritis. It took everything out of me. For about three or four days, I had bad diarrhoea and was barely able to eat anything. I just about managed one plain slice of toast. Not the best thing to happen when you have an eating disorder I must admit. It only served to set me further back into the illness. I was just reaching the tail end of a persistent cough that had lasted for about a month, and this knocked me for six. On reflection, I think part of the reason I was consistently under the weather is because I had a weakened immune system. My food and drink consumption had largely diminished, and I was denying my body of essential nutrients.

During the holidays, I accompanied my parents on a trip to stay in my Uncle's cottage opposite a beach up in Bamburgh. It's such an idyllic part of the world, tranquil and stunning. A Place of joy and calm. But nothing could put my mind at ease. Nothing could seem beautiful to me. Everything just seemed despairing and desolate, and I was unable to appreciate the beauty of this world. Unable to appreciate the beauty of living. Bamburgh is honestly one of my favourite places in the world. Throughout my childhood, we would often go on holiday there, visiting Edinburgh, the Holy Island, and Grace Darlings' lighthouse. We would go on boat rides, seeing all the puffins and wonderful sea creatures. We would go to quaint pubs opposite the sea and have good wine and food. But not this time.

Gastroenteritis proved to be a huge factor in my ailing health, and eventual hospitalisation. When we first reached Bamburgh, we made a quick pitstop at the walk-in centre. My stomach was persistently rumbling, making strange noises. I could barely walk because my stomach hurt so much, and I constantly felt nauseous and weak. I had never felt so physically weak and drained before. As a rule, I'm quite good at getting on with things when I feel ill, and I don't like to make a fuss because I feel like I am wasting everyone's valuable time. And that's not fair because I don't matter. But this was different. I willingly went to see the doctor. I just wanted to feel a little less shit, both mentally and physically. I was tired of all of this. After doing a stool sample and waiting for several minutes, I got prescribed some anti-sickness and inflammatory tablets which eased some of the pain. I basically had to ride it out and wait for my digestive system to get back on track. Ana's face lit up at this new prospect. A proper excuse to not eat anything, which wouldn't arouse suspicion in the slightest. Perfect! In all honesty, this was the worst thing that could have happened to me. It's bad enough to go through when you don't have a nagging eating disorder wearing you down but having them both together was a recipe for disaster. It made me more determined than ever before to lose weight. It also gave birth to my laxative abuse. I was constantly opening my bowels and I became addicted to that feeling of emptiness. I knew taking laxatives wasn't a tool to aid weight loss, but I found the feelings of fullness intolerable, and I wanted to rid myself of all this disgusting food I was poisoning my body with.

Don't make the same mistake I did. Don't rely on laxatives and/or diuretics to make you feel less greedy. It won't work. In the short term, it may alleviate some of those feelings of guilt and shame but, in the long run, it could cause serious health problems. If used continually it could cause the bowel to become lazy and stop working properly. You could lose control of your bowel and suffer from incontinence. You could, in severe cases, lose a part of your bowel altogether. The few moments of relief it may give you is NOT worth the lifetime of pain and misery it may cause. Believe me, it is NOT worth risking your future for. It does not help you to lose weight. It is not good for you. It is an addiction. I became addicted to the feelings I got through taking them, and once you get dragged down into that pit, it becomes incredibly difficult to climb your way back up. Don't risk the fall. You won't lose the weight, but you may lose your life.

Over a short period, my stomach pain began to die down, and my appetite returned, although I was still suffering from quite a bit of diarrhoea. My parents, particularly my mum, were paying close attention to what I was eating, and she recently disclosed to me that she thought I was purging whenever I went into the bathroom. She would stand outside to try and hear sounds of me throwing up. That's a hard pill to swallow. A difficult thing to hear and it brings a lump to my throat whenever I think about it. I was not purging. I wanted to, and

I did try several times to make myself sick. I looked up how to purge online and tried to stick two fingers down the back of my throat. I tried sticking my toothbrush down, tickling the back of my mouth to get my gag reflex going. All futile attempts that served the sole purpose of making the anorexic voice even more loud and violent. I never intended for things to get so bad. They just spiralled and I lost all control. I lost who I was as a person and, to a certain extent, I am still trying to rediscover myself. I am still trying to find out who Steph really is, and the prospect of that is terrifying. What if I don't like her? What if Steph is a boring twat? I don't know, but I might as well try and see who I am without an eating disorder. What's the worst that can happen? I don't like myself. But then, I can easily revert to the eating disorder. You see, I have nothing to lose from dipping my toes into unknown territory. It might even be better. The real Steph might be amazing, but I'm not going to know unless I try. The same goes to you too. I am confident that the real you -whoever you are, whoever you want to be – is a terrific person. Amazing inside and out. Everyone I've met along my journey has been an incredible human being. Just remember that when you lie or hurt others around you, that's not who you really are. You are not your eating disorder. Burn her, destroy her, nourish the real you, and you will flourish.

After most of the gastroenteritis had cleared up, I began to feel a bit more human. My parents were pushing me to eat more, and I knew I had to do something. I could use this as an excuse to eat some of my 'forbidden foods.' I had not eaten much for quite some time, and I knew I had lost a fair amount of weight, so I decided to have one of my favourite meals – burger and chips – to throw my parents off the scent. Naturally, this caused Ana to have a massive fit.

Steph: 'I haven't eaten for several days now, so I have a few calories to play around with. Plus, I want a flipping burger. They taste good.'

Anorexia: 'You don't deserve a burger. You don't even need to tie your trousers up to stop them from falling. Therefore, you're still too big. Do you get it now? Your clothes aren't baggy enough. You're not ill enough. You're still huge, fatso.'

Steph: 'I am not fat. The clothes I wear are kid's sizes. That's not normal. Anyway, my body craves a burger so I should listen to it for once and honour those cravings. I always listen to you but maybe I should start listening to my own self. Plus, my parents are getting super suspicious, so I need to put that mask back up.'

Anorexia: 'That's my point dimwit. If you eat the burger, you cannot be a proper anorexic. You have no right to call yourself an eating disorder sufferer. You're not dead yet…'

Steph won this battle I am pleased to say. I had the burger and chips, despite the mental torment it caused me. Ana may have loathed it, but Steph bloody loved it. Throughout this holiday, I was able to eat a few of the foods Ana forbade me to have. Every time I went into the bathroom, or anywhere with a mirror, I would roll up my top to examine my stomach and how bloated I was. Overcome with disgust, I would often lock myself in the bathroom after a big meal, fighting hard to hold back the tears that threatened to spill. Staring at my hideous reflection in the mirror I would punch the sink, overwhelmed with self-loathing. 'Why are you such a disgusting piece of trash?' Ana taunted me. I grabbed my toothbrush in turmoil and tried, once more, to stick it down the back of my throat to try and purge the food from my body. That failed so I resorted to sticking my fingers down, tickling the back of my throat. That too failed. I couldn't be a good teacher. I couldn't be a 'good anorexic.' I couldn't even purge properly. Giving up, and still in tears, I made my way into my bedroom and sobbed my heart out. I spent the next hour looking at recipes and cooking posts on Instagram. I could almost taste the food I was eating. I wanted nothing more than to be able to eat the foods I enjoyed, without constantly thinking about how fat and greedy I was, and how I would compensate to burn off all these calories.

Although I was on holiday, I still made myself go for a run along the beach every single day. There was one night where Ana came perilously close to losing her much sought-after secrecy. I remember it so clearly. It was late in the evening and my dad sat me down on the sofa next to him. He grabbed my bony hand in both of his and hugged me tightly. I felt safe in his arms, I didn't want him to let me go. He was hugging Steph and quashing Ana. As soon as he let me go and relinquished his hold over me, Ana surged back up again and stopped me from being honest. He expressed his worry for me and stroked my hand with his thumb and forefinger. 'What's wrong Steph?' he asked me, his voice a little more than a whisper. 'It's… nothing' I lied, my heart hammering loudly against my chest. I wanted, so badly, to tell the truth but I couldn't bring myself to say those three little words: 'I need help!' Try as I might, they just wouldn't come. I was worried that I was overreacting, or that people would think I was just doing this all for attention. That's been a massive fear of mine since my struggles began. The fear of people thinking I'm not 'sick enough' or that I was a disgrace to people who have been struggling with severe mental health problems and anorexia for years. What pain and torment had I gone through? Nothing in comparison. Was I being fraudulent in saying I have an eating disorder? Did I have all this wrong, and was I trying to be healthier by exercising more and losing a bit of weight? What was the answer? What was I supposed to do? DEAR GOD, TELL ME WHAT WAS I SUPPOSED TO DO???

I didn't know what normal was anymore. I didn't know what it meant to have a balanced relationship with food and exercise. I didn't understand how I could balance everything without it dictating my every waking moment. Instead of being kind to myself and taking it easy after my holiday, Ana welcomed me back into her cold embrace.

The first thing I did was go upstairs and weigh myself. I had lost some weight but not enough to satisfy her. So, what did I do next? Did I stand up to Ana or did I succumb to her? Yeah, you got it in one, I succumbed to her. I let her rule me once again. I carried on restricting, setting myself even harsher boundaries and more punishing long-distance runs. I would not cut myself some slack.

***

After my previous failed attempts at purging, I made the drastic decision to turn to oral laxatives. A tiny part of me felt guilt and shame at resorting to such extremes, and potentially damaging, methods but Ana threw her weight around and said I was taking them for my own good. That they would make me feel less full and help me to lose weight. I knew what I was doing was wrong and that I shouldn't be hiding such things from my parents, but it still wasn't enough to stop me. It was the first packet of many that I would buy and stash in my room. For me, laxatives became a safety blanket, and I was addicted to feeling like I had nothing in me. Please don't make the same mistake I did. If you feel like you might be at risk of developing addiction, or already have one, then ask for help. You might think you don't have a problem but that's the thing with Ana. She makes you think you are fine; you are indestructible. But no one will survive everything. You can survive a lot, but your body has a limit, regardless of what lies she feeds you. You wouldn't begrudge someone with a physical health condition asking for help, so why do you think you're anorexic for attention? Mental health is just as important as physical health, if not more so. You can see when someone is physically ill, but you can't always see when someone is burning with pain from the inside.

Due to my limited intake of food, I was suffering from constipation. But taking these laxatives alleviated some of this discomfort and enabled me to go. The more pills I swallowed... the less noise Ana made. But here's the thing: the more noise Ana is making, the more progress YOU are making. What happens when you try and get rid of a bully? They fight back. They grow stronger and louder to try and gain back some of the control that is slipping away from them. That is precisely what Ana is doing. She is running scared shitless. She is making such a racket because she is growing fearful. Fearful of you moving on and having a life. Fearful of her life ending, of her flames being put out, because you are slowly beginning to destroy the bitch. Keep on attacking her, and there will come a time when you are sitting in the driver's seat instead of your eating disorder. It just takes time, effort, and a whole lot of patience. But what's a few years in comparison to a whole life? Exactly, it's nothing at all.

Abusing laxatives had very nasty side effects. I would often lose control and soil my underwear. It would suddenly come on and there nothing I could do to stop it from happening. There was no warning. I was a young girl, and I didn't even have proper control of my bowels. I was devastated. Completely and utterly distraught, I was disgusted with myself. How the fuck did this happen? I was young, fit and healthy, wasn't I? I shouldn't be punishing myself like this, should I? It's not normal, is it? Tell me I've got this all messed up? Tell me I'm not okay and I need help? I need people to know that my life is going to shit, and I'm scared I might die? Who do I turn do? Who do I tell? What the actual fuck am I supposed to do? Please tell me, what am I supposed to do?

Now what I was supposed to do and what I did are two different things. There was one time when I was back in Cardiff for a house party and when I was walking in town, trying to get meet my increasing step count, I remember losing control. I tried to hold it in, but I just wasn't strong enough. I couldn't stop it and I felt my underwear go wet. Fighting back a waterfall of tears, my breath came out in short, erratic gasps. 'Oh shit, oh shit, oh shit.' I was like a baby. I was an adult for god's sake. What had I done to myself? What had I turned myself into? I was so stupid. Stupid, stupid, stupid. 'Dumb cunt' my inner critic said to me. I ran to the nearest Superdrug and bought a pack of sanitary pads. From that day onwards, I took to always wearing them over my pants for when it happened again. And it did... happen again.

Even when I was sedentary, I would still sometimes end up soiling my underwear. I thought I was just releasing some trapped wind, but more came out than I bargained for. I was making more frequent, mad, toilet dashes. My eyes had lost their glint. I was giving people empty smiles, empty words. I didn't have a spark in me anymore.

I began wondering what I was capable of.

Inner Critic: 'Being a complete and utter FAILURE! That's what you're good at. About the only thing you manage to succeed in. LOSER!!!!'

Overpowered by Ana, I was being backed into a corner, her little puppet. On top of my mental health declining, I also had to contend with being back at work after the Easter break. I was always second guessing myself and I felt abnormal. My desire to be a teacher was also dwindling fast, and I was seriously considering whether I had made the right choice. Before I could officially start my teacher training, I had to book a professional skills test. I am not exaggerating when I say I must have booked and re-booked the test about eight or ten times. There were several papers I was supposed to do online for practice, but I couldn't bring myself to do any of them. I think the closest I came to doing some work for it was typing in professional skills test on google. The real me knew I needed to revise. The real me knew that in order to pass and do the best I possibly could, I would need to put time and effort into this and do the practice papers. I wasn't even vaguely motivated. I didn't give a toss about anything. Anything apart from running and losing weight. It would get so bad that it would literally be the night before the exam, and I had not done a single minute of revision. I had nothing. Zilch, zero, nada.

***

2019 was a tough year for me. I spent the first half trying to keep my head above the parapet, and the second half was spent in hospital. There is no way I can sugar coat what happened. Ana was using me like a puppet, and I would unquestioningly follow her. My brain wasn't functioning, and Ana overruled everyone and everything. She became the only thing in my world, so I didn't have room to think or study.

Someone else I was working with was also applying to do a teacher training course. She bought thick revision books for her professional skills test and would often ask me what I'd studied or how much revision I had done. I was too ashamed to admit that I hadn't done any work for it whatsoever. To try and mask my embarrassment, I stupidly lied and said I'd done a fair bit of revision and was in the process of doing the practice papers online. Pride firmly put its foot in it, and I wasn't even able to be honest with myself, let alone others.

My existence was nothing short of miserable. Each day I would just focus on counting down the hours until I could go back to bed and switch my brain off for a few precious hours. Although, even night provided no real respite as I was often struggling to get to sleep, and I kept waking up during the night. I couldn't get comfortable either. I had to sleep curled up in a ball, but when I put my legs together all I could feel was bone. It was too uncomfortable, and I resorted to putting either the duvet or a cushion between my legs to try and protect my bones. Things came to head on the 28th of April. I was already perilously close to breaking point. My parents had arranged for us all to meet up with my Godparents to go somewhere to eat. I had not seen them for years and I was incredibly nervous. My head freaked out. What if they saw me and asked why I was still so fat? What if they questioned what I was eating and thought I was a pig? How was I supposed to calculate all my calories now?

Ana immediately grabbed hold of the reins and steered me once more towards the internet. Frantically, I started googling the restaurants in town, downloading all the menus I could pick a restaurant where I could order something under 600 calories. Ana made me go for the lowest calorie option, the blandest-looking food. The 'healthiest' and 'purest' meal I could get away with having. There were meals I craved, red meats I could almost taste, and carbs that made me want to salivate. But it was nothing more than a want. I had to put out the fire and extinguish the desires for such disgusting indulgences. I resigned myself, much to Ana's delight, to having a skinless chicken breast with a small side salad. That was the least amount I could get away with eating. Ana also ensured I skipped breakfast that morning – too much food – and went for an extra-long run. She was a rigid taskmaster, sending out all the orders for me to dutifully obey. My memory of the meal itself is a little vague. What I do remember, however, is exactly how I felt in that moment. How empty and alone I felt. How isolated I was. How unrelenting and cruel I was to my own body and mind. How much I hurt all over from acting like I was okay when, really, I was dead inside.

Whilst everyone else tucked into their delicious-looking meals, I just sat there, miserable as sin, with my pitiful salad. They didn't have a care in the world. They weren't bothered by having a few extra calories. They didn't feel like they needed to punish themselves just for having a good time. They didn't care what the number on the scales might read the next day. So why did I care so much? Why could I not be more like them? Why was I my stupid self? Get a grip, pull yourself together Steph. A huge part of me wanted to join in with them, and enjoy myself, but I couldn't bring myself to do it. Giving in would be a sign of weakness and it wasn't worth the mental torment my eating disorder would put me through. Just a few moments of enjoyment wouldn't make up for the number of hours, days, weeks, and months I spent hating myself.

If I had let myself eat these foods when my body craved it, I wouldn't have mentally fixated on them so much. I would have had my fill and then been able to stop because my body would know it would be fed again soon. Right now, my body did not know when the next meal would be. It had no idea if I would eat again that day or not. It was trying to keep me alive. If I craved food, it was because my body needed it and was in deep need of fuel. You can't run a car on no fuel in the same way your body can't function without food. I spent so long thinking my body hated me and I just had to look at food for me to gain the weight. The reality couldn't have been more different. My body, my amazing, wonderful, body was trying to protect me. It was trying to conserve what little energy it had so that I could make it through each day without passing out. It wasn't going to suddenly balloon after one meal, it just wanted what it needed to live. What it needs to thrive. And I denied it that basic right. I am so angry at Ana. Angry towards her for always making me feel like a complete pile of shit. Like I am not worth the time of day. Anger at missing out on living. That all got stripped away from me, replaced instead with an intense burning of hatred and disgust. She ruined me, inside and out, and I am done with her bullshit.

FUCK YOU, ANA! FUCK YOU, INNER CRITIC! YOU DON'T DEFINE WHO I AM AS A PERSON. JUST BECAUSE YOU SAY THESE THINGS, IT DOESN'T MAKE ANY OF IT TRUE. YOU ARE INCAPABLE OF SPEAKING THE TRUTH BECAUSE, YOU KNOW WHAT, THE TRUTH KILLS YOU. YOU THRIVE OFF LIES AND ISOLATION BUT I AM PUTTING MY FOOT DOWN AFTER YEARS AND YEARS OF HELL. YOU'RE NOT BEATING ME BACK TO THE GROUND THIS TIME. I'M GOING TO SPEAK THE TRUTH. I'M GOING TO SPEAK OUT AND I WILL END YOU. YOU TRIED TO DESTOY ME AND FAILED. SO NOW, I'M GOING TO DESTROY YOU. AND TRUST ME, I'M NOT GOING TO FAIL. I WILL KILL YOU, JUST AS YOU TRIED TO KILL ME. BUT WHERE YOU FAILED, I SHALL SUCCEED. I CAN. I SHALL. I WILL. SO, PISS OFF AND DON'T YOU DARE COME BACK!

**

Recovering from eating disorders are not as easy as just restoring weight. Throughout my treatment, I have had a handful of professionals make off-hand comments such as 'oh, why don't you just eat more?' 'You're here to gain weight' and my favourite one, 'Come on, it's just food.' No shit, really? I'd never thought of that. I know it's just food, but thanks for the advice. Do you want a round of an applause? Or a medal for figuring it all out? Bollocks! That's what it is. Eating disorders are incredibly misunderstood and even more complicated. Even

I don't fully understand the condition and I've suffered with it for many years. It is not possible to fathom the impossible. And Ana is just that – impossible. She makes no sense. It is often about control, about trying to cope with life. For me, I think a part of my illness was down to me being afraid of life. I had hated university, I had hated teaching, I didn't know what to do with my life. I felt pressured into getting a job, but I was convinced I'd fail at everything and get nowhere. I felt out of place in the world, and different from a lot of people my age. Instead of embracing that, I interpreted me being different as me being wrong. I submerged myself in my anorexia because it seemed safe, and she was always there for me. No matter how bad I was feeling, Ana was there, always there, waiting for me.

She was my one constant in an unpredictable world. As I struggled with my perfectionist ideals and self-loathing, it didn't take long for me to snap. It was the 4th of May 2019: the day my truth came out. The day I took down my walls and revealed the broken mess I was. The day Ana lost her prized secrecy. This had been bubbling away for nearly a decade, and there was about to be a massive fallout. I had never been able to articulate my struggles to my parents in person. I did try, but I always stopped myself before I said too much. I was too scared of the consequences. Ana feared losing her control, and Steph feared people thinking she was an imposter. I had to do something. Things had gone on long enough and I didn't know how much fight I had left in me. I plucked up the courage to write my parents a letter detailing my mental health battle. It was one of the toughest decisions I've ever had to make. To be so raw and open and honest for the first time in forever. To name and shame my demons. I was petrified. What if they thought I was just doing it for attention? I was just being selfish and stupid. I hadn't suffered. I hadn't tortured myself enough physically or mentally. I fucked everything up again. I couldn't even diet properly. I couldn't even exercise without messing it all up.

Inner Critic: 'Stupid, stupid, dumb, cunt!'

That's all I could hear. It drowned out any logic or sense. It was relentless. But it was the only thing I was listening to. I refused to acknowledge the truth. I refused to listen to people who said 'are you okay? What's wrong? Something's not right.' I blocked out their concern and dismissed their questions. My anorexia and inner critic were taking up all the space inside my head so there was no room for anything else. They had been poisoning my thoughts for so long, infecting me with their venom, it was time to say no. I was so close to chickening out. This letter explained why I hadn't been myself. It explained why I wasn't eating properly and had stopped drinking alcohol. Why I no longer smiled or laughed. Why I was unrecognisable. I had poured my heart out and I was pleading for someone to listen to my cry. I was pleading for help and acceptance. I couldn't accept a single part of me, I just wanted others to accept me for who I was. I needed to know that it was okay to be me. That I wasn't the freakish, fat lump I thought I was. I believed Ana's lies. I was convinced I was boring, ugly, stupid, dumb, irritating, childish, fat, quiet... I hated myself so goddamn much, but I wanted others to like me. I convinced myself everyone hated me and were only talking to me, or being friends with me, to keep up pretences and to not hurt my feelings. They were with me out of sympathy and nothing more. People could not possibly hang out with me because they enjoyed my company. No chance of that happening, my inner critic scolded me.

I kept the letter with me for about a week. I kept waiting for the right time to show them. I kept waiting for exactly the right moment. But I very quickly realised there was never going to be a good time. Unless I bit the bullet and did it now, I would constantly find excuses to get out of it. I was delaying the inevitable and the only person that was hurting was me. I had to just do it. Grit my teeth and do it. I didn't need to say anything, the letter said it all. The only thing I needed to do was hand it over to them. The rest would be out of my hands, but at least I could finally let that mask slip all the way down. It was now or never. Do or die. 'Just fucking do it Steph. Don't be a coward' I told myself, trying to build up the courage to release the emotions I'd spent so long trying to contain. It was the evening and, as I sat in the lounge with my dad, time was running out. Fast. My mum had just recently gone off to bed. It was a Sunday night and I had work the following day. The prospect of going into work was something I really couldn't bear to think about. I just couldn't do it. I couldn't focus on anything, and I was afraid I might snap at the children and lose my tether. There was no energy left in me to work. No energy left in me to live every day. My mouth kept opening and closing as I tried, and failed, to find the right words. Time was ticking. Panic began to rise within me. All I had to do was say, 'can you read this dad?' Just those five little words. Just spit them out Steph, come on, you can do it.

With trembling hands, I picked up the letter. I cleared my throat to try and get my dad's attention and said 'dad, I've got something important I need you to read.' That was it. I'd done it. Now, all I needed to do was hand the letter over and wait for the missing pieces of the puzzle to fit into place. The pieces of paper left my grip as they found themselves in my father's hands. I had ended the letter by saying 'please don't blame yourselves. It is NOT your fault… please help me. Please don't hate me!' I only hoped these words would strike a chord and I wouldn't be alone anymore. I couldn't be alone with my own thoughts for a second longer. It was torturous. Grabbing a cushion from behind me, I clutched it over my face, digging into the fabric until the tips of my fingers turned white. There was no going back now. His reaction was something I couldn't bear to see. What if he was crying? What if he was angry? I had done that to him. It was all my fault. I didn't have the strength to put my head up. Silent tears rolled down my cheeks as I hunched forwards, curling into myself. The wait was agonising. It was the most painful ten minutes I've ever had to sit through. I was waiting for my dad to read it and digest the enormity of what I was saying.

Doubts were already bombarding into my mind, and I felt compelled to rip the letter from his hands and tear it to shreds. I just wanted to bury my head in the sand and not face the reality of the situation. The reality of what was happening to me was scary. I was scared. I thought I would die soon. Maybe I wanted to die, so I didn't have to suffer anymore. So I could end the raging flames of Ana. She had scarred me, and those wounds will never truly heal. The marks she left are forever imprinted in my brain. It was much easier to ignore the gravity of the situation, and how much my illness was impacting my loved ones. But if I kept it hidden, kept it a secret, it wouldn't be so real. I could still pretend. But not anymore. What had I done? Anorexia was not going to like this one bit. Damn was I right, Ana hated me more than ever and she ramped up her burning engine.

Anorexia: 'Why did you tell them?'

Steph: 'Because I had to. I can't do this alone. I can't do any of this anymore. I'm so, so, tired, I'm not strong enough to keep standing.'

Anorexia: 'You don't even have a serious enough problem. You haven't been dealing with your struggles for long enough yet. You're an insult to people with genuine eating disorders. You may think you have a problem, but it's nothing in comparison to what other people have gone through. You know what your problem is? You're weak! Too weak and feeble to do anything.'

Steph: 'No! You're wrong! I am not okay, and I need help. My struggles are real. My brain is torturing me all the bloody time. Even when I go to bed, I can't switch my brain off. It's not normal to want to weigh nothing at all.'

Anorexia: 'Look, we all have body issues okay, but let's be real here – you're fine! Get a fucking grip and stop being a drama queen and blowing everything out of proportion.'

Steph: 'It's more than that. Weighing myself countless times a day isn't normal. Abusing laxatives isn't normal. Running when you're in pain or sick isn't normal.'

Anorexia: 'Yeah, well, you're not normal. But you still aren't ill enough. You've ruined everything.'

The comforting arms of my father wrapped themselves around my slim frame, holding me in a tight embrace. He had tears in his eyes. We both did.

'I'm so sorry you've been going through this alone, Steph.'

'It's okay' I said.

It wasn't okay. Nothing about this was okay. We just cried and held each other for some time. His protective hug of me made me feel safe and comforted. I didn't have to fight this monster all by myself anymore. I had another soldier fighting the war with me. I was getting stronger. Not a single world was uttered as we sat in poignant silence. Eventually we broke apart. I felt a mixture of feelings. Both fear and shame, but also a sense of relief. No longer did I have to carry this terrible burden alone. It felt as though a great weight had been lifted off my shoulders as I told my dad the full extent of my problems. I explained how gastroenteritis had been the catalyst to my laxative addiction, how I couldn't allow myself a day off running. How Ana wouldn't stop bullying me. I revealed the terror of where I was heading. How worried I was that I was going to cause irreversible damage to my body. Even though I knew what I was doing was wrong, I couldn't stop. I was under Ana's spell.

With my dad's support and kind words of encouragement, I retrieved the pills I had accumulated over the past few months. Picking up all the packets, I made for the stairs to hand the tablets over and surrender 'my' control. I stared down at the laxatives. In that moment, I'm sorry to say, I caved into my eating disorder. I hurriedly retreated into my bedroom and put two of the packets in my underwear drawer, haphazardly covering them so that if my parents did go into my room and open the drawer, they wouldn't find anything. When my dad asked me if that was all of them, I looked into his eyes and lied straight to his face. I said I had given him all the pills. I promised, I swore to him that was everything. Dad, I don't even know what to say to you. I hate lying. Steph hates manipulation and dishonesty. Yet I wasn't honest with you. I never wanted you, and mum, and Darian, to get hurt. I never wanted to reduce you to tears. I never wanted any of this. My eating disorder was thrilled to leave behind such a wave of destruction, but Steph was not. I am not my eating disorder. I am not the anorexic. I'm Steph, who happens to struggle with anorexia, but I have other qualities who define who I am as a person. I want to distance myself from Ana because I hate what she does to me. I hate that I become a liar and manipulator. That I become a military man and berate myself so much. I hate that I push my body to the point where I am physically in pain. I hate that I pretend I'm alright, and I try to be someone I'm not because I'm too scared that, if people got to know the real me, they wouldn't like me. I hate all of that. Steph is not like that. Steph likes to laugh with her friends. She likes to run and raise money for charity, but she also wants the freedom to stop. Steph wants to be healthy and in control. Steph wants to be happy and smile from ear to ear. Steph wants to live. I choose life. I choose life over Ana, and you can kiss my ass goodbye.

After handing over some of the laxatives, and hugging my dad for a while longer, I traipsed up to my room to go to bed. I felt completely wiped out, and just wanted to close my eyes and forget about everything that had happened. After taking a few deep breaths to try and calm my nerves, I retrieved the laxatives from the drawer. I popped out ten tablets and quickly necked them down with a sip of water. My stomach was making some very disconcerting noises, but I ignored it, instead sucking on chewing gum to try and distract myself from the emptiness and hunger I felt. I don't quite know how I managed to fall asleep that night. Maybe it was because I was so exhausted from crying. Maybe it was because of the sense of relief I felt at no longer having to suffer in silence. I have no idea. But I did fall asleep. The tears had all dried up and I felt I had nothing more left to cry. That I had nothing more left to give. Exhaustion overtook me, and I was dead to the world.

***

In the morning, I opened my eyes and then closed them again, hoping I had imagined what had happened last night with the letter. No such luck. I had done the unthinkable and outed Ana. What was going to happen now, I wondered? What were we to do next? I didn't have long to dwell on these uncertainties because, shortly afterwards, my mum came into my bedroom. Her eyes betrayed her sadness, and I knew instantly that she had also read the letter. We sat down on my bed together and just talked. Naming and shaming all my demons.

It was a tough conversation to have. It is heart-breaking to see how much this illness affects not just the sufferers, but also all the carers and everyone around them. Part of the reason this talk was tough is because my mum, I think, blamed herself. To be honest, I think both my mum and dad felt a certain extent of guilt. I think they blamed themselves for not saying anything earlier and not noticing something was so very wrong. But mum, dad, when you read this, I want you to know something. I need you to believe me when I say this because I mean it with every fibre of my body. You are in no way to blame for this. In no way to blame for any of it at all. This has got nothing to do with you, okay? It is not your fault, and I won't hear a bad word said against either of you. Life throws at you many curveballs and it isn't possible to dodge all of them. Some will hit you, but that doesn't mean you're damaged. That doesn't mean you're out of the game forever. It just means you need to take a step back and look after yourself. Sometimes, bad things happen, and there's nothing you can do to stop it. It does not matter what cards you are dealt, but rather how you play them. We held each other close and just sat in each other's company for a while. No words were needed. Just the love and safety of my family. Neither of us wanted to let go. But we couldn't stay like this forever, no matter how much I wanted us to.

I would have to face the music, and the prospect of dealing with everything petrified me. No longer could I bury my head in the sand. It's strange, because burying my head almost made me feel safe. I didn't think about the reality of the situation and I could live in denial, in my own little bubble. The sense of security it gave me was false. It is not safe to run away from your problems. It will not bring you closure. It will not go away, and it certainly won't get better. Everything will just overflow and overwhelm you. The most difficult thing to do would be to face up to the harsh realities, and accept you have a problem. The bravest thing you can do is stand up to it and fight back. Face your fears. Face them until they no longer become so fearful. Things are only new once. The more you do something the more 'normal' it becomes. Don't let your fears destroy you. Use them to make you stronger.

After so long of being secretive of the weight I had lost, I finally told them exactly what I weighed. They hid the bathroom scales from me, and we agreed that I would weigh myself once a week and this would be recorded and written down on my weight chart. I wanted to have my usual, 'safe' breakfast of apple, but my parents encouraged me to have something else. It was only a piece of dry toast with a poached egg, but I cried the whole way through it. Just having a simple breakfast like this reduced me to a blithering mess. I could barely swallow the food properly because I was sobbing so much. My hands were shaking, and I felt lost. I wasn't supposed to be eating this. Why was I ingesting such filth? Why was I so weak? I have a slight memory from a few weeks previously, where my mum had made me a pitta with some salad in it. I had just been for a seven-mile run and was due to work a twelve-hour shift. My mum had decided to make me an early lunch.

It was only some dry wholemeal pitta with salad. That was it. No sauces or meat. Nothing particularly calorie dense. I should have been able to eat it without giving it a moment's thought. I should have been able to eat and then move on with the rest of the day. Sadly, this was not the case. Although I managed to force it down, I was in floods of tears at having to eat so close to breakfast. In my head, this was all unnecessary. Had I been a 'true anorexic' I would have thrown a massive hissy fit and chucked it in the bin. I didn't have to eat. No one was forcing me to, but I had made the choice to finish it. How messed up was that? That I felt greedy for having a necessity such as food and water. Defying all logic, anorexia is an impossible illness to understand because she literally makes no sense. You can't reason with the unreasonable. You can't reason with eating disorders because you won't win. You won't stand a chance of defying them because they twist everything and turn you against yourself. You are made to feel unworthy of anything and you deny yourself basic human rights. That's how much of a bastard this illness is. She made me believe that I could only eat during specific time frames. There was no exception. I had to stick to these timings, I couldn't deviate from them by even a minute. It really was that intense.

Breakfast could only be consumed between 8 a.m. and 10 a.m. Lunch could only be between noon and 2 p.m. Dinner was only to be had between 5 p.m. and 7 p.m. If it were even one-minute past I wouldn't allow myself to eat that meal. Cruelly, I made myself wait until the next one. Even if my stomach rumbled, or I felt weak from hunger, I could not give in. I thought it was too close to my next meal and if I ate outside of these times, it would ruin everything, and I would lose control and just binge eat. Hunger signals, which are completely and utterly normal by the way – were interpreted by Ana as me being greedy. I saw these pangs of hunger or feelings of numbness as an achievement in an odd way. It gave me a twisted sense of satisfaction that I was able to deny my body food. That I was able to stay strong and ignore these signals until, eventually, I no longer experienced real hunger. Not many people could starve themselves, but I could. I could refuse to eat and that made me feel special. I am aware how ridiculous this sounds, but when you're caught up in your eating disorder, they could tell you to jump out of a plane and you would. Ana told me that I deserved to be run over with a bus, and I believed her.

***

The day after my letter had been read, my parents took me straight to my GP. During my appointment, I managed to hold things together. I didn't break down at least. The doctor I spoke to was lovely, and I didn't feel ashamed for talking about my mental health. I felt listened to, and that's a feeling I haven't often experienced. I was signed off work with immediate effect and was also prescribed anti-depressants. Along with this, my doctor also referred me to April House which is one of the only eating disorder units throughout the whole of Hampshire. I owe my life to this place. I genuinely do not think I would still be alive today had they not seen me so promptly. Anorexia would have claimed another life, my life. Of that I am certain. Originally, I was put on the waiting list, and when I rang them up, I was told I could be waiting up to six months to receive any proper treatment. Hearing that broke me. The waiting list was, and still is, huge and there simply aren't enough eating disorder units out there. They don't have the capacity or staff, and eating disorders affect so many individuals. You could be a young child; you could be a teenager. You could be a young adult; you could be middle-aged or elderly. Your age does not mean you are safe from suffering. It does not mean you are immune, and you don't need to feel like a fraud. I don't care if you've had anorexia for ten months or ten years, you don't have to live in silent torture. You wouldn't say to someone suffering with cancer that they only have 'true cancer' if they've been ill for x number of years. Physical illnesses don't have the same stigma that mental illness does. But your illness and worthiness of help is in no way dependant on how long you've been suffering for.

When I got told of how long the waiting list was, I remember dissolving into yet more tears. 'I need help' I remember saying to my parents. 'I can't do this. I can't wait six months to get help. I'm already crumbling, I can't do it anymore. They clearly don't think I'm ill enough so I'm just going to have to make myself worse in order to be seen. I don't have a choice; this is what I have to do.' None of this had an ounce of truth to it. I was ill. I didn't have to make myself worse. But I thought I wasn't anorexic enough, and that I had to prove my allegiance to the illness. After several reflective chats with my family, I think we realised that we did not hammer home the seriousness of the situation at first. I had mastered the art of appearing to cope, having practiced it for many years, and I gave the distinct impression to the doctor that I was still able, by and large, to get through life with no real disruptions. This couldn't have been further from the truth, but I couldn't expect him to read my mind. Doctors are amazing in what they do, but they can't read minds. They can't predict how you feel or what will happen unless you are honest and open with them. That was a mistake I had made, and I was about to pay dearly for it.

I had been on this course of anti-depressants for about a week when I got hit with a severe allergic reaction. One morning, I woke up with my arms and the top of my legs on fire. There was a burning sensation going all the way down my arms, and I absentmindedly scratched them to try and calm the itching. I was scratching so vigorously that I caused my skin to bleed. I was in so much discomfort, I'd never experienced anything like it before. When I went to the bathroom I was horrified when I caught sight of my inflamed skin. The whole length of both my arms were covered in ugly, angry-looking red spots. On top of this there were scratch marks and flaky skin from where they had been so itchy. I went to the toilet and noticed that the tops of my legs and neck were also covered. Instead of doing the sensible thing and going straight to my GP, I got dressed to go for a run. I could always go to the doctor's later, but running was my priority. If I didn't do it now, I would never get around to doing it later and I was not about to let that happen. Dutiful, as always to Ana, I changed into my running gear, which I don't think I had washed in about three months. I rubbed deep heat down the back of my burning legs and tried to blot out the discomfort of the rash. I looked ill. Gaunt, and grey, like you could snap me in half just as easily as a small twig. Tying my hair, which had gone dry and brittle, into a ponytail, I went to wake my dad up to go for a run with me.

I would have gone for a run by myself if I could, but my dad was adamant that he would come with me whilst he could. I think to say he was shocked by my appearance would be an understatement. He took one look at my arms, and immediately said I needed to go to the GP. Refusing to miss my run, I put my foot down and demanded that we go for a run. The rash could wait. I told a blatant lie. With my priorities completely skewered, (thanks for that Ana), I told my parents it wasn't that bad and looked a lot worse than it was. I was fine, so let's stop wasting time. My dad persisted and I eventually relented, agreeing to stop into the surgery on the way back from our run. As our feet pounded the pavement, my rash got more and more unbearable. I wouldn't stop running, but I had to constantly scratch my arms, legs, and neck. If I stopped and gave up that would be a sign of weakness. Just keep going. That's all I had to do. I really was one track minded. Just start the run and finish it.

We were doing a three-mile run that day, and the route my dad had chosen passed our doctor's surgery. We ground to a halt and went straight into the pharmacy. Thankfully, there was hardly anybody else in there so my dad went with me up to the counter and explained the situation. I got taken into a little side room where a pharmacist checked me over. She examined my arms and neck, and I also told her about my legs.

She asked me if I was taking any medication. I told her that I was, and that I had started a new anti-depressant. She took my dad and I out of the pharmacy and into the main surgery waiting room, quickly speaking to the receptionist behind the desk. She was honestly amazing, and they acted so promptly. She said I needed an immediate appointment to see the doctor so I could be prescribed with antihistamines. My appointment was made for 11 a.m. that day. Feeling thankful that I would soon have some relief from the constant itching and scratching, we walked out of the surgery and ran the rest of the way home.

I had just enough time for a shower before we had to go back to the surgery. I couldn't be bothered to brush my hair or wear matching clothes, so I just threw anything warm on. It might have been around April time, and the weather was heating up, but I was constantly freezing. My mum had taken the car to go to work that day, so we had no choice but to walk back up to the surgery. Ana was jumping for joy at this. More steps to fit in. More exercise to burn off all my fat. This was bloody brilliant. We made the short walk to the surgery and I got seen to promptly. I was told it was an extreme allergic reaction to my medication, so I was given some antihistamines and a new antidepressant was prescribed.

It didn't take long for the rash to clear up after this. It was still itchy but with the tablets and cream, the redness started to fade, and the itchiness ceased. I was relieved when it started to get better. My mood was still low, and I was still obsessed with food and running, but at least I wasn't constantly itching myself to the point where I had scratch marks covering my body and was bleeding. I had just about recovered from this when I was struck down by an ear infection. It was like a dominoes effect; I was hit by one thing and then another. There was no respite. My immune system was too weak to properly stave off infections which meant things as little as a common cold really affected me. Not long before I had the allergic reaction, I was also plagued with a nasty cough. I had lost my voice, and my appetite, and I was feeling hot and cold all the time. This lasted for about a month when I was hit by yet more ailments. It would take me a long time to recover from something and, as soon as one problem vanished, another eagerly took its place.

***

Ear infections hurt. Never, in all my life, have I experienced pain like it. The agony was constant. I couldn't sleep and there was a constant ringing in my ear. Whenever I rested it up against something like a pillow for instance, brown gunk would seep from my ear and it was almost glued to the material, so I had to literally prise my ear off. It was horrible. I also ended up throwing up a few times due to vertigo. My balance was affected in my ear, which led to dizziness and several bouts of nausea. I was bed bound for the most part of a week. My ear was pulsating all the time, and shut eye was impossible. I resorted to taking blankets and cushions down to the sofa so I could rest my eyes with my head propped up. I was unable to lie flat due to the pain that hit me whenever I lay straight. Every night, I would have a warm, damp, cloth to try and ease the incessant ringing and pain that emanated from my ear drum. The medication I was taking was insane. But despite all of this, the pain stubbornly refused to budge. My hearing was muffled and, whenever I spoke, my voice seemed distorted. Almost like there was an echo in the room or my head was

82

submerged under water. My strength to walk had vanished and I spent my days and nights confined to the sofa with a banging headache and painful ear. Turns out I had more than just your average ear infection. When my ear was getting worse and I started throwing up, I made yet another trip down to the doctors. It was fast becoming my second home, that place. How I managed to get myself down there I will never know. I was exhausted and I felt rotten. Utterly drained and in constant torture physically and mentally. They were dark times for me, and I wanted nothing more than to just succumb to darkness and not have to put up with so much shit.

I felt like death, and death seemed like a sweet release from everything. I was in the waiting room, about to be called in, when I suddenly felt nauseous and raced to the toilet to throw up. Thankfully, not much came out, it was mainly me dry heaving, but I sat down with my head against the cold toilet bowl and closed my eyes. How long was this going to last for? Would it ever stop? I wiped my mouth with some toilet paper, flushed the toilet, and made my way back to the waiting room. I was diagnosed with a perforated ear drum. In laymen's terms, I had a hole in my ear, but I was given a course of antibiotics and, with these, I gradually began to improve.

My cognitive ability was also non-existent. Days were spent looking at food, dreaming about food, and thinking about food. I stopped having contact with family and friends as I became a mere shell of my former self. In short, I stopped living. After I had completed my course of antibiotics and my ear was eighty percent back to normal, I started running again. It's strange because although I had little energy to do anything else, I was still able to run. I should not have been able to manage it, but I somehow did. I would weigh myself before and after every run. My parents had hidden the scales since they had read the letter, but that didn't stop me. When my dad was out and my mum was downstairs on the phone, I went into their bedroom and hunted for the scales. I looked in drawers, under the bed, behind the wardrobe. Any hiding place you could think of, I looked. It wasn't long before I found it pushed down the side of my mum's dressing table. Quickly, and as quietly as I could, I took them to the bathroom and weighed myself. I then returned them to their hiding place so my mum and dad would never be any the wiser. After weighing myself for the first time, I would then go to the toilet and weigh myself again. After running, I would also weigh myself, and at several points throughout the rest of the day. I had to know my weight. I had to know how much I lost. The house could have been burning down, but I would still have to know my weight. It was of the utmost importance for Ana to know. To feel in control and have a sense of power. The world could be ending, and I would still have to weigh myself. I continued to do this secretly for some time. My parents were still trying to keep an eye on my weight, and they were weighing me once a week, but I had to know what I weighed every day. Did I lose weight after that run? Did I gain weight from having that extra piece of apple?

Logically, I know it is impossible to gain weight from eating one extra piece of food, but Ana didn't have time for logic and facts. She just wanted the weight to keep falling off me, and she would want me to do that in whatever way I could. By hell or high water, I needed to get that number on the scales down to zero. Due to my weight dropping scarily fast, my parents kept taking me back to the doctors to see if they could speed up the process with April House. To try and get across the gravity of the situation. I think it must have been about my third doctor's appointment when I broke down and said I couldn't do it any longer. It was taking over my life. Every second of every minute of every day was taken up by Ana. I couldn't even eat a banana without breaking down. I couldn't eat potatoes, cereal, bread, rice, beef, fish. I couldn't even allow myself to eat a whole flipping apple because I was so scared of 'extra' calories. I couldn't see my friends. I couldn't sleep. I couldn't work. I couldn't function. It's crazy how things sped up after this, in terms of both the anorexia and the help I was getting. A little part of me, in the back of my mind, was cheering. I had spoken to April House about two weeks ago and they had told me I was on an extensively long waiting list. Suddenly, I had become a priority. This greatly pleased Ana and I felt I was doing the right thing. I felt as though I had succeeded in being ill and been faithful to my illness. I cannot fathom why it was so important for me to prove that I was ill. That I needed people to know I was ill, and that I wasn't doing this for attention. But I couldn't live a life I felt I wasn't worthy of. I couldn't do basic, normal things, because I was supposed to have anorexia.

***

It wasn't long before I got another call from April House and, a week later, I was having outpatient treatment there. Once a week, I would meet with a therapist and my weight was closely monitored. The person I was seeing later became my case manager and is one of the most empathetic, kind, and genuine people I know. I hadn't been having therapy for that long when the possibility of day support and more intensive treatment was discussed. A potential hospital stay was also thrown into the equation and when I was asked what I thought would be more beneficial to me, I had no idea what to say. I was struggling to comprehend everything. I was given some leaflets to read and told to take my time, reading through everything. The possibility of me being hospitalised loomed over my crippled, anorexia- ridden body. It was a dark cloud that I couldn't shake off.

Whilst I had this huge struggle going on inside of me, it was also approaching mine and my dad's birthdays. Normally, I love birthdays and celebrating with my family. This year, however, was different. I dreaded both days. I didn't want to celebrate turning 22. I didn't want to do anything fun. I was supposed to be anorexic. I was supposed to be on a waiting list for day treatment at April House. Ill people don't go around celebrating or having fun, so why should I? I was supposed to be ill for goodness' sake. I shouldn't be galivanting off to London eating gourmet foods and indulging in fine wine. We were due to celebrate my dad's 60th birthday so, to mark the momentous occasion, we had arranged to go up to London for the day. We were going to go for a special meal and then see *Les Misérables* on the west end stage. This had been planned for about a year in advance, but I was no longer in the right head space to be enjoying myself. Too much was bubbling away in the back of my mind. April House, a possible hospital admission, my perforated ear, my failing career... they were all jostling about up there I didn't have room to think about anything good. But at the same time, I couldn't let my parents down.

They had been looking forward to London for over a year. I

had to put on a brave face, if not for my sake, then for theirs. The rash had mostly cleared up by this time, although I still had a few patches on my arms and the top of my neck. The day before London, I took about fifteen laxatives. I was dreading wearing a dress up to London. I was convinced I would look fat and disgusting in it, and I just wanted to rid myself of all the 'toxins' anorexia convinced me I was ingesting. As much as I wanted to, I couldn't put the day off any longer.

***

The day of London arrived. Having taken so many laxatives, I woke up early that morning and had to make a quick dash to the toilet. I just about made it in time, but what came out was more like water than anything else. I knew this wasn't healthy, but Ana was glad that I no longer had such 'disgusting filth' in my body. My heart was thumping against my chest as I got changed into my dress. A long sleeved pale blue skater dress with white polka dots. I used to feel pretty in it. A long time ago. But now I felt sickeningly fat. There's not much of the actual day I remember. Maybe I tried to blot it out because of how miserable I was. What I do remember is constantly tugging at the hem of dress, trying to pull it down and suck my stomach right in to shrink myself. I took up too much space.

I don't remember the train journey that day, but I do remember the mental pain I was in. Feeling like I took up too much of the seat, feeling like everyone was staring at me, feeling like an imposter… God, I hated myself. When you abuse laxatives to the extent I did, you do begin to lose control over your bowel. The urge to go comes on very suddenly and you go from not needing the toilet, to being desperate in the space of just a few seconds. When we finally arrived at London, we dismounted the train and made our way through the throng of crowds out onto the London streets. Not even the bustling streets and excited atmosphere could raise my lips into a smile. I don't think the corners of my mouth even twitched throughout the whole day. I was wearing my Fitbit, as I always did, and I was fixated with reaching my goal step count for the day. Traipsing through the streets made me feel extremely anxious and on edge. I thought everyone was looking at me, laughing at how pathetic and unfit I was. I kept my head down and just tried my hardest to keep up with my parent's as I was so weak. The back of my legs were in so much pain, yet Ana couldn't give less of a damn. She was just devoted to reaching my step target of 30,000 a day. It had started off just as any other good intention does. I vowed to get healthier and lose a bit of weight. Buying a Fitbit led to my behaviours around exercise becoming very compulsive very quickly. The first target I set myself was to reach 10,000 steps a day. Whilst this would be enough for most people, it did not satisfy Ana's greed. The goal posts then changed, moving to 15,000 steps a day. Was that enough for Ana? No, it was not. Well, what about 20,000 then, or 30,000? Of course, that wasn't good enough. If you're still alive then you're not punishing yourself hard enough. Those are Ana's rules. You either die, or suffer so much that your body eventually gives in.

***

The first place we stopped off at in London was Covent Garden. It's beautiful there, and the atmosphere is simply incredible. It was a gloriously sunny day, and there were live performers outside the restaurants providing quality entertainment. My mum wanted to stop here for a drink, so we found a small table near the performance, and sat down. I was in a right strop. Life was carrying on as normal all around me. Yet I was anything but normal. My life wasn't a life right now, and I was consumed by misery. My parents ordered an alcoholic drink, and I didn't want anything. Initially, I tried to refuse, but my dad said he wanted me to have a drink as it was his birthday. Rolling my eyes, and making a big song and dance of everything, I decided on a vodka diet coke. I could feel tears prickling my eyes as Ana's voice leapt out at me, having a go at me for being so weak and greedy. Oh yes, Ana was not only scared of food. Mainly food, but also liquids. Drinking was done for leisure and pleasure, something she was firmly against. My arms were folded throughout the entire thing. I don't remember the performances we saw. Instead, I remember the food people around us were having.

The people on the table next to ours had ordered two full English breakfasts with hash browns, toast, sausage, egg... all the trimmings. The people behind us had ordered scrambled egg and poached salmon on toast. Another table were sharing a bottle of wine and cooked breakfasts. My eyes were constantly darting around, trying to see what everyone else was eating and drinking. Trying to smell the food so I could just get a taste of something that wasn't bland and cardboard like. This was supposed to be a happy day. This was supposed to be fun. And I am so angry at Ana for turning this into such a painful and horrible experience. I spent most of the day trying to hold back the tears and comparing my 'deformed' body to that of others. When we finally left Covent Gardens, we moved on to try and find somewhere to eat. We had booked a table at The Ivy and we were quickly seated. Menus were handed to us and my parents shared a bottle of red wine between them. I wanted to join in. I wanted to have a drink and laugh, but Ana stuck her tongue out and said 'no.' I stuck to water, and even that caused Ana to have a slight hissy fit. 'You're drinking too much frickin liquid' she bemoaned. Trying to quieten down the rising anger of Ana, I glanced over the menus and my heart plummeted. I wanted every single item on the menu. I wanted burger, pizza, fish, steak… just give me everything! I was crying out for good, tasty, food, but I would not let myself off. I would not let myself have even a glimmer of happiness. My eating disorder made me go for plain salmon with a side order of salad and broccoli. Carbs weren't allowed in this mouth.

I feel immense shame and guilt over this. I behaved appallingly that day, and I ruined the day for both my mum and dad. It was your special day and I ruined it. Why was this all happening to me? Why couldn't I cope when everyone else could? You had been looking forward to London for over a year and I was just a moody cow the whole time. I didn't laugh, I didn't smile, I barely talked. I just sat there looking glum, with a face like thunder. I made the day about me. You tried so hard to accommodate my eating disorder when it should have been the other way around. I should have been accommodating you. Instead, I was selfish. I thought only about me and my eating disorder. I should have been trying to please you and not the anorexia. Sorry doesn't even begin to make up for how I treated you, but it's a start. And I mean it from the bottom of my heart. I am so sorry for ruining the day. I am so sorry for ruining 2019. I am so sorry.

***

The next couple of hours blur into one for me. My next main memory of London is, surprise, surprise, food- related. I'd already eaten too much with the salmon and it stressed me out not knowing how it was cooked or what ingredients were used. I had to be extra healthy now. I made my parents take me to Costa where I had a pot of their pea and mint soup. I knew the exact number of calories in it and, although it wasn't particularly enjoyable, I felt it was what I deserved. My mind instantly started searching for ways to compensate when I was back home with Ana. I finished my soup and my mum decided she wanted a McDonald's. This was after a day of drinking and a big meal at lunch, yet here she was craving a Big Mac and fries. I wish I had that freedom. I crave to be that free and uncaring around food. To order what I want when I want and not be tormented hours later for having something that I enjoyed. I don't want to have to go for an extra-long run or eat less the next day. I don't want to have to 'earn' my food. I deserve to eat. It's a human right, a need for survival. And fuck anyone who says otherwise. It doesn't mean I have to eat these foods for every meal every day, but I am able to have them when I want them. And I don't need to do anything to make up for it.

When we eventually found a McDonalds, I planned my own order in my head - a double cheeseburger, large fries, and an Oreo McFlurry with a big dollop of tomato ketchup to dip my fries into. It was my dream meal, my perfect order, I could almost taste the food. Whilst my mum tucked into a delicious-looking meal, all I could do was sit there in stony silence, staring longingly at food I could not have.

Steph: 'Oh my, that burger looks amazing, I can almost taste it...'

Anorexia: 'You are not having that junk. If you eat it, you're going to gain a tonne of weight and people will judge you for eating such filth.'

Inner Critic: 'Hey there fatty. My God you're still way too big. All those rolls of fat you have makes me want to vomit.'

Steph: 'It's normal to have rolls. I'm not ashamed of who I am.'

Inner Critic: 'Well, you should be.'

Anorexia: 'You're not working hard enough. You need to take more laxatives. You need to walk more. Trust me girl, you aren't anorexic, not properly anyway....'

Steph: 'Just leave me alone. If I want to eat, I should be able to without guilt...'

Inner Critic: 'Weak, pathetic, fat. You're weak, pathetic, fat. WEAK, PATHETIC, FAT!'

All this inner turmoil made it impossible for me to be Steph. For me to be a nice person. Never has the term 'hangry' been more apt. As my brain was starved of food, I became incredibly angry and despondent. My feelings were starved and I, in a way, became numb to everything that was going on around me. It was such a relief when we were on our way back home from London. I could go back to being in control again. The brutal truth to all of this is that I was never in control. Ana tricked me into thinking I was in control of my life but, really, Ana was my King.

As my mum and dad tucked into their food, I just sat

opposite them. I couldn't take my eyes off their food. I watched them take every bite and put every morsel into their mouths. That probably sounds incredibly weird and stalkerish but it's the truth. And I'm not going to keep hiding from the truth, I've done that long enough. All my memories from this day are about food. Not even the play or being in London and going to different places. Just the food. That's what I remember. When we made it to the theatre, my parents went straight to the bar and ordered some glasses of wine. What did I have? A few sips of bottled water. Sat down, we were surrounded by merriment, by people talking, drinking, eating, and laughing. I felt so out of touch with everything. *Les Misérables* is one of my all-time favourite musicals. I absolutely adore all the songs, the characters, and the plot. It moves me and transports me to another world. I had been so hyped to see the play. A year ago, I had been so excited to see it in the West End for the first time. We all were. But now, I couldn't think of anything worse. Sitting down with nothing to distract my mind from my hateful thoughts. I couldn't even bare to contemplate the feelings of self-hatred that Ana would no doubt conjure up.

I am sure the play was brilliantly performed, but I can't remember it. I tried to focus on the music, on the words, but Ana was too powerful, and I couldn't ignore her stabs and her jibes. During the interval, I remember queuing up to go to the toilet and I caught sight of my reflection in the mirror. I wanted to gag at the sight of me. I was vile. Even with a dress on and highlighted hair I still looked crap. I wanted to cry. I wanted to jump out of my body, into someone else's less cluttered and chaotic mind. I really wish I could remember the play, remember how the music made me feel, but I can't.

And that greatly saddens me. I also had a pounding headache, probably from dehydration and lack of food. As soon as the play had finished, I couldn't wait to leave the stuffy theatre. I was beginning to feel agitated and claustrophobic, and I just needed to get out of there. I felt suffocated by people and my thoughts and Ana. I needed space. It was late evening and we stopped off at an off license to grab some paracetamol for my headache. If I'm being honest with you, it was a relief to head home. It was a relief for anorexia because it was safe territory for her where she knew when and what I was eating. She was in control of my runs and the times I ate. I wasn't in control. It was Ana. It has always been Ana.

***

On arriving back home, Ana ramped up her tough demands. My parents were both going back to work, having taken time off to look after me and take me to the doctors. Now, however, they had to resume some sense of normality. As much as I didn't want to admit it, life was moving on. Moving on without me. I had another appointment at April House in a few days' time but Ana's priority, at this moment, was running. With both my parents out of the house, I was able to run six to ten miles every day. I pretended I only did two or four miles to my parents, but the reality was I always did a lot more. I ran ridiculous miles in the heat, but all that I cared about was keeping one foot in front of the other. I didn't bother with putting sunscreen lotion on or protecting my body in any way, I just had to run. They were punishing routes as well, littered with quite challenging hills. The more hills I ran up, the more calories I could burn , and the harder I would have to push myself. Therefore, I had to try and fit as many hills in as possible. Simple, right? That is how black and white Ana's thinking is. There were several times during this period where I lost control and soiled my underwear.

Ana would use whatever the number on the scales read to her advantage. Whether the number had risen or fallen, anorexia would find a way to twist things and make me feel useless and pathetic.

Anorexia: 'You're over six stone. That's too much fat. You repulse me.'

Steph: 'The laxatives aren't actually helping me lose weight you know. I may feel big (thanks for that you bitch) but that does not make what you say true. Just because you say it, doesn't mean I am actually fat.'

Anorexia: 'The number on the scales doesn't lie, you fool. You're already a titch and that means that any weight you carry about is a lot more noticeable. You can't pull it off because you're so frickin' tiny. You take up too much space. That's fact, and you can't deny facts…'

Steph: 'But I feel so weak. I don't want to run up this blasted hill again… it's too much. I can't cope. None of my clothes fit me anymore either. I have to tie all my trousers up with hairbands to keep them from falling down.'

Anorexia: 'What point of mine are you missing here??? Your BMI is in the healthy range. Clinically, you're not skinny. You were the size of a bloody whale before, but now you're just fat. You've got a hell of a long way to go before you'll be worth anything, twat.'

I don't think I can hammer home the intensity of the anorexic thoughts. You can't turn it off. You might be able to turn the volume down for only a short moment, but when she returns there is even more of a bite. Even more anger and insults to hurl your way. Ana will hold onto you for dear life, tearing you down piece by piece. She won't be silenced, and she won't be spoken to. Eating disorders like to do all the talking. All you need to do is listen and hold onto her every word. Listen to her. Obey her. Be stuck with her forever. Or fight it. I don't care how hard it is, anything is easier than living with the constant torment and hurt anorexia causes. Life is to be lived, not to be endured.

With my exercise addiction at its peak, my weekly visits to April House weren't enough. Weight was still rapidly falling off me. I was on a path of self-destruction and I didn't want to stop. I had to keep going. I had to prove myself worthy to hold the title of being an anorexic. I had to prove to Ana that I was serious about this. About a week after returning home from London, I was given some hard-hitting truths. I was having my usual appointment with my therapist and he told me that a place at a day support programme (DSP) had become available. This was essentially a four-day programme which ran from Monday to Thursday. It focused on weight restoration and there would be therapy groups in between meal and snack times. Each day began with breakfast at 9 a.m. and we would have morning snack and lunch there, attending therapeutic groups and dietetic meetings in between. The programme would close at 3 p.m. and we would be given an afternoon snack to take home and eat. We were all prescribed individual meal plans – our medicine we were told – and whilst at home, we had to take responsibility and have our afternoon snack, dinner, and evening snack. However, he was concerned that this wasn't the intensive support that I needed.

I wasn't managing at home and, left to my own devices, I would continue to restrict and deceive. I was in such dire straits, they told me the heart-breaking news that I was now waiting for a bed to become available in a specialised eating disorder ward.

***

From this moment, my parents decided I couldn't be left alone in the house anymore as I was too unsafe. They took it turns to stay home from work, looking after me each day. I was still exercising, and displaying disordered eating habits, but they couldn't stop me. Ana cattily told me they didn't have the authority to say anything. What did they know? Nothing. They were constantly treading on eggshells with me, terrified of rocking the boat. They didn't know what to do. What to say. How to cope. And neither did I.

There was one day when I came home from my punishing run and I couldn't stop shaking. My dad was with me at the time, and I could feel my vision going hazy as my legs began to buckle. He had to guide me to the lounge to sit down. I tried to blink away the black spots that were dancing in front of my eyes as I battled with the urge to just close my eyes. He recently admitted to me that he thought I was going to pass out and, whenever I went for a run, he was always on edge thinking that I would collapse and be rushed to hospital. Another time, I was home alone, and I went to go to the bathroom when I glanced up and saw my reflection in the mirror. After a few moments spent criticising the way I looked, I remember falling. There was no warning. One minute I was up, the next my legs went to jelly, and I went down like a tonne of brick. I don't even know what happened. After getting up from the sofa I just remember feeling so faint and weak. It was as though my body wasn't my own and I was shaking all over. My parents did not witness this episode, but they did see me at my very worst. They saw me shaking uncontrollably and crying over having lunch five minutes late. It was terrifying not just for me, but for my parents who had to witness their daughter dying. I spent my days sat on the chair, the bottom of my spine hurting from the lack of protection around the bones. I would do crosswords or wordsearches for hours on end. I wouldn't talk or engage with my family. I didn't do any of the things I enjoy doing. Things like meeting up with friends, drinking, going swimming, eating out, watching movies, reading… I couldn't do any of those things anymore. I couldn't focus on anything. I was always on my phone, looking at food in one way or another. I was glued to my screen.

As well as going for ridiculously long runs, I would also demand walking my dog in the evenings. Our rescue dog, Simba, was so lively and full of beans we had to walk him for quite a long time. Ana jumped at the thought of doing more exercise. Getting in more steps and losing those pounds. Neither of my parents were happy about this, and they did try to stop me, but I wasn't having any of it. Sorry, I meant to say, Ana wasn't having any of it. My parents didn't take it any further because they didn't want to risk having a screaming match, which would have happened. And we did have several shouting matches, where I often ended up crying hysterically or storming up to my room in a right state. The weather was becoming sunnier, but I was still wrapped up in my many layers. I was always freezing. It was such a struggle to even make it down the end of our road without feeling knackered. I went for a walk with the purpose of burning more calories, but also, to try and waste time. Each day dragged so much, and I was trapped in this repetitive cycle I didn't want to be in any longer. This was a good way to pass the time where I wasn't staring at the clock every few seconds, willing away the hours.

***

Despite the rapid decline of my physical and mental health, my family and I went to Burley for a few days as extended birthday celebrations. My Uncle had paid for us to spend the weekend away. I had no choice but to go. I had already ruined everything for my parents, I couldn't ruin this for them as well. They deserved happiness. They deserved to celebrate, and I wasn't going to stop them from doing that. I might have stopped living, but that didn't mean they had to do the same. I knew my freedom was sliding me by, and Ana really did not want me to go. Heaven forbid I do something nice and have a good time. Despite everything negative that was looming over me, I went up to Burley with them. I packed a few things, of course including my running gear and laxatives. This might be a holiday, but that was no reason to be slack and skip exercising. No get out clauses. No excuses. No buts. Running was a must and that was the end of it. I also brought with me food and drink so I knew exactly what I would be consuming, and I could stick to my 'safe' foods. I even went as far as bringing garlic, a bowl, and spoon from home, as well as apples and my soup. I couldn't cope with variation, or spontaneity. I couldn't even deal with buying an apple in case it was bigger than the ones at home. When we travelled up to Burley, we were forced to stop off somewhere to eat. We weren't due to get to the hotel till mid-afternoon and I had to eat before two. To try and pacify me, my parents took me to the Harvester as I had looked up the menu online and seen something I could potentially have without Ana giving me too much of a headache. I was religious with my food routines. I had to stick to them precisely, and if I deviated from this, I would instantly get very anxious and wound up.

My whole body shook with nerves as we entered the restaurant. Walking was a struggle, and it took a huge amount of effort just to keep putting one foot in front of the other. Normally, I would always walk considerably faster than my mum but, in this instance, I was struggling to keep up with her. When the waiter sat us down, he asked me if I wanted the children's menu. He thought I was a child when I was a twenty-two-year-old woman. I was mortified.

Inner Critic: 'Hahaha! You look like a baby. Look at your boobs, there's nothing there. Men have bigger 'moobs' than you. You're laughable, everyone's laughing at you behind your back.'

Steph: 'Just lay off for one minute will you…'

Inner Critic: 'No chance ickle baby. Would you like a bib with your food?'

It's shocking how cruel I was to myself. What I said to myself cut me down more than anyone else's words. You know that saying, 'you're your own worst enemy?' Well, that's what happens with Ana. I was horrible to myself and Ana fed off my low self-esteem.

Throughout my time at the Harvester, I kept my head bowed and spent most of my time avoiding eye contact with other people. I barely spoke two words to my parents as I was so anxious about having food in a different environment. It was removed from Ana's comfort zone. Lots of tears were shed during that meal, and I felt on edge. Not only was I uncomfortable eating food that I didn't know how it was prepared, but I also felt as though I took up too much of my seat. According to Ana, everyone was laughing at me and judging my food, labelling me 'fat' and 'greedy.' Eating disorders have a nasty habit of comparing what you do and what you eat to everyone else. Whatever you do is wrong. I don't know how I made it through that meal. I didn't even taste the food; I was just focused on getting to the end. What should have been an enjoyable time was turned into an arduous affair. When I had finished, I went into the bathroom and just broke down at how fat I felt and how angry Ana was at me. I kept tugging down the jumpsuit I was wearing, horrified by my stomach. It didn't matter how much weight I lost, or how far I'd run, nothing was ever enough. I was always letting anorexia down and that would keep the perpetual cycle of self-hatred going. I ran to lose weight. I weighed myself and never lost enough. I would reduce my food intake more and more. I was still too fat and so the cycle started again. It was never ending and completely unforgiving. It was a relief to finally leave the place, but the relief was short lived. The next hurdle I had to face was the hotel itself.

We stayed in Burley Manor. It was a stunning hotel set in the heart of the New Forest. This was supposed to be a time of relaxation but, for me, it was anything but. My parents had booked a three-course meal at the hotel's restaurant for the first evening we were there. Did I join them? Regrettably, I did not. I hate myself for not going and for putting a dampener on the whole thing, but I just wasn't able to face the food. It was too much for me to handle at that point. Whilst they got suited and booted and made their way downstairs, I stayed in the hotel room. Getting out my bowl and spoon I brought with me from home, I boiled the kettle to have my cup of soup. This was my life. I was reduced to staying alone in the hotel room because the fear of eating unknown foods in front of people I didn't know was paralysing. I spent most of that evening crying. In fact, I spent a lot of last year crying and now, when I want to cry, the tears don't seem to fall. There's just an intense feeling of numbness and disconnectedness from myself. Recovery is an emotional roller-coaster, full of ups and downs and some days, it seems like the downs will never cease. But they will. One day, things will seem a little less dark and although I'm not there yet, I must have hope that someday I will get there. I will persist.

When my parents came back to the hotel room, they were full of wine and merriment. I wish I could have been a part of that special time, but that was not to be. I was filled with a certain sense of jealousy when they told me about the delicious sounding food they ate. I was annoyed that they were able to eat like that and not gain weight, yet if I ate like that, I would immediately gain 10kg. I know that's a lie, but it was so real to me. I felt underserving of enjoying food and, even though other people were entitled to eat and indulge in food, I would not show myself the same compassion. My expressions were vacant, my skin sallow, and I hated life. If I didn't go to the toilet several times a day I would be overwhelmed with anxiety and feelings of fullness which were impossible to sit with. I popped laxatives down my mouth as a person might eat sweets. I was totally addicted and in the very dark throws of my eating disorder. I felt so bad for being such a 'bitch' that I booked for my parents to have a three-course meal in a special restaurant just down the road from a hotel. I could ill-afford it, but I felt as though I needed to do it to try and make up for ruining everything. Scrolling through the menu online, I imagined what I would order if I could eat out. I planned out my meal and drink in my head, but it was nothing more than a silly little fantasy. I knew that if I went out with them, I would just ruin it all so I thought that the only way my parents could enjoy themselves was if I wasn't there. I'd let them down and would continue to do so until the day I die. Screw you, Ana. Just because that's what you tell me does not make it a reality. It is not the truth. It is not true. Simply untrue.

***

When we returned home from our weekend away, I received a call pretty much straight away from April House. I had been given an admission date. Friday 13, June. That was in four days' time. I knew I was going to be hospitalised, but I wasn't expecting it to be quite so quick. Everything was happening at record pace because of how dramatic my decline was. People around me were very aware that I was struggling to cope. That I was slowly killing myself, and if I didn't receive help soon, I might not be there to tell the tale. Constantly in a state of misery, several people made their concerns about me known. Every Sunday we would skype my brother, who was in China for the year teaching English as a foreign language, but I would not show my face on camera. I skulked in the corner, unable to feel any sort of emotion towards him. He's my brother and I love him dearly, but I was so consumed by Ana. Darian, I was jealous of you. You were living your best life; you had a girlfriend, and you were genuinely happy. But Ana would not let me be happy for you. For that, I am so, so, sorry. Family means the absolute world to me and I should have been happy that you were enjoying yourself and living your life to the fullest. Instead, I was upset because here you were having fun, whereas I was stuck by my inner torment and sadness. Ana made me selfish. During our skype conversations I would never say anything, and whenever my parents tried to get me into the frame and participate, I would instantly snap at them. I was so ashamed by the way I looked I didn't want anyone to see me. Hiding my shrinking body behind baggy clothes could only mask so many demons. One conversation I had with a family member really stands out to me. We were at our house and she came over with some birthday cards for my dad and myself. Before she left, she said to me, 'please eat. You need to eat.' Those simple words struck a chord with me, but I still refused to acknowledge I was ill. I was still too scared to eat. The anorexic thoughts were just too powerful.

Turns out my face betrayed my feelings. The baggy clothes did a good job of masking my weight loss, but I could not hide the sadness in my eyes. I could not hide how haunted I was by anorexia, and how dead I felt inside. Even the best mask in the world couldn't hide how much I was struggling at this point. My demons refused to be contained anymore. I might have thought I hid my condition well from people, and I had so many fooled, but the reality is I didn't. They knew what was going on. They just had to look at my face to know I wasn't there anymore. Steph had long gone, and I didn't know when, or if, she would ever come back. Throughout many tears and tantrums, I packed my bags, and, on June 13, I entered the next phase of my journey.

PART TWO:

Hitting
Rock
Bottom

I will never forget when I first entered the Priory. The feelings I had of fear, angst, and despair. I'd done the tiniest amount of research, but nothing could prepare me for what I was faced with. When we arrived, my parents were given visitors lanyards and I was taken up to my ward. The hospital itself was based on three levels, each one housing a different ward. The bottom ward was Kingfisher and that was for CAMHS, so children and adolescents under the age of eighteen. The middle ward was Sandpiper and that was an acute mental health ward for adults. Then, there was my floor, the top floor. Skylark was an adult ward that specialised purely in eating disorders. I was surrounded by ten other patients, all of whom had acute anorexia or bulimia. Strangely enough, eating disorders breed competitiveness. Especially in an inpatient setting, it's focused on who can be the 'best' anorexic. An inherent part of the condition is comparison and I felt like the 'fattest' one there. Imposter syndrome is something I struggle with greatly, having spoken about it in therapy. I always feel like I fail at everything. It doesn't matter what I do, I always feel like an imposter and that I will never be any good at anything.

Inner Critic: 'You're weak and a failure. You should hate yourself because everyone else does.'

Anorexia: 'You don't deserve to be here. You don't need to be here. You're not ill. I mean, just look at how much fat you have.'

Inner Critic: 'Disgusting little tramp. Go die in a hole already.'

Steph: 'No, I am ill, and I do need help. I've been diagnosed with anorexia nervosa and I wouldn't be here if everything was okay.'

Anorexia: 'You need to struggle more and lose more weight.

So many people deserve this bed more than you. Just walk out fatso… just walk out the building. You're not under section… so fuck off.'

This perpetual cycle of self-hatred never halted. It was as strong as ever and I was completely overwhelmed by everything as I was introduced to everyone. My room itself was comfortable enough. Decent in size, fully furnished with a TV, desk, wardrobe, and en-suite. I remember being shown into my room for the very first time and sitting down on my bed, wringing my hands with anxiety and wishing I were anywhere but here. All my bags were littered on the floor as various nurses and health care assistants assessed me. We went through my care plan and it was explained to me that there were six meals a day – breakfast, morning snack, lunch, afternoon snack, dinner, and supper. These were at specific times spread evenly throughout the day, and after each main meal we had to have an hour's supervision in the lounge. As I was a new patient, and they weren't too sure about how high risk I was, it was protocol for them to lock my bathroom. Whenever I needed to go to the toilet or shower, I had to go find a member of staff and they would wait outside the door until I was finished. I had to turn up and complete each meal in the set time limit and if, for whatever reason, I was unable to complete a meal, I would be given ensure. This was a drink supplement that would provide me with the nutrients and calories I would have got from food. I was introduced briefly to the dietician there and my meal plan was prescribed to me. This was my medicine, and I suddenly became acutely aware that I was going to have to face my crippling fear six times a day every day. I felt as though I had fallen into a hellhole and had no choice but to comply with these strict demands.

Due to my body being in starvation mode, I had to gradually re-introduce food to my system. A problem common with eating disorder patients is re-feeding syndrome, a potentially dangerous condition that is caused by a sudden change in your electrolytes. In order to control my intake, I was told that most of my diet would consist of semi-skimmed milk and I would have half portions of lunch and dinner. This would gradually increase depending on the results of my blood tests and weigh-ins. We were to be weighed twice a week, first thing on a Monday and Thursday morning. I was to have weekly blood tests and regular ECG'S to monitor any changes in my heart. Most of this information flew straight over my head. My cognitive ability was so low, nothing they said really registered with me. I stayed mute throughout most of the inductions, nodding meekly when asked if I understood what was going on. A member of staff, and my assigned healthcare assistant (HCA) went through all my belongings to check if I had any 'sharps,' or items that would need to be taken away from me and kept in the office. I felt slightly mortified at having a stranger rifle through my personal possessions. All electrical items and wires were marked and recorded down, and my razors, glass bottles, and chewing gum were taken away from me and put away in a box in the office. In order to use a razor, or anything else in the box, I had to ask staff to sign them out to me. I had to go through a menu plan and choose my meals for the coming week. For the first time in a while, I was faced with foods I had avoided like the plague. Never in my life have I been filled with so much anxiety and dread.

***

My parents stayed with me throughout this whole ordeal, and I owe them so much. I had my lunch, half a ham sandwich, brought into my room and I had to eat with my parents watching me. This is something I had not done for many months. Before, when I was eating, my parents had to eat more than me and they were not allowed to watch me eat. To give you some perspective, I always sat on the chair farthest away from the TV at home. My parents sat on the sofa. We always had the TV on during mealtimes as a distraction, and they had to be facing the TV. If they even glanced at my direction, they would risk me having a massive meltdown. Times at home were difficult and everyone was treading on eggshells around me, too afraid to rock the boat but, at the same time, seriously concerned for both my physical and mental health. When they brought in my sandwich, I tried valiantly to fight back the oncoming flood of tears. It's crazy, looking back, how much one slice of bread and a bit of ham terrified me. It was only half a sandwich, but my eating disorder completely freaked out. Ana was, for the first time in a long time, losing a bit of her control. And it's fair to say she was not happy. Not happy at all.

It's a weird thing to experience, having a member of staff and your parents scrutinising you eat. I was unable to eat food properly at this point, and I nibbled on my sandwich, crying all the way through. I kept putting my food down, hoping to gain sympathy from staff. I wanted them to turn around to me and say, 'don't worry Steph, we're seeing how distressed this is making you, so you don't have to eat any more.' Alas, that did not happen. I was made to complete the meal. Ana feared crusts as she perceived that as being the most 'unhealthy' and 'calorific' part of a sandwich. She tried so hard to get out of eating them, but the staff were unrelenting, and I was made to carry on. It's no exaggeration when I say it took me about an hour to finish and, after the plate was taken away from my room, it was time to be shown around the ward. I remember walking down the corridor and it was almost as though I was disconnected from everything that was going on around me. My brain couldn't keep up with how quickly everything was changing around me.

Saying goodbye to my parents was one of the most difficult things I've ever done. Ana was not just leading me to self-destruct, but she was also impacting those around me. Those who I cared about and those who cared about me. They've been to hell and back just as much as I have and, even now, I don't think I'm quite aware of just how bad I was, and just how scared they were for me. Saying goodbye to them was like bidding farewell to a part of me and nothing really registered with me until later when I began to understand the severity of the situation. I spent most of my first day there trying to come to terms with everything that was going on. I had been prescribed a load of medication and I read and re-read the introductory booklet to the ward that was in my bedroom. My head was spinning, my anxiety was through the roof, and I was in a state of shock. The mattress I had was extremely uncomfortable. It was a special mattress specifically for people with eating disorders, as it was soft to prevent pressure sores and hurting poorly protected bones. I felt I had nothing left, but the truth was Ana was slowly losing her grip on me. The real Steph was beginning to take back control.

***

Time moved in a bit of blur and, before I knew it, it was snack time. Begrudgingly, I made my way down the corridor into the kitchen area. Music was playing in the background and I was confronted by three tables. My heart skipped a beat as a staff member guided me into a chair and presented me with a glass of milk. Milk and my eating disorder were not the best of pals. It represented what Ana feared most. My leg kept shaking, I couldn't control my body. I was jerking up and down and I barely noticed when people murmured their hellos. There were people eating biscuits, and chocolate, and crisps. Food that I hadn't touched in months and months due to overwhelming fear. Now here I was, surrounded by Ana's deepest fears. We had twenty minutes in which to finish the snack, and then ten minutes observation. We could bring in distractions for snack. Most people brought in with them crosswords or wordsearch books, or maybe a newspaper or book to read. I didn't know that at this point, so I had come into the kitchen with nothing to distract me. That was a big mistake. I only had to drink a glass of milk, but I nearly broke down at the sight of it.

'I can't do this' I thought to myself. I wanted to get out of my seat and run away, never to return. I don't think I touched my milk. I wanted them to take pity on me and relent. I thought if I cried a lot then I would get out of eating. I hated the idea I had to drink so many unnecessary calories. Who has glass after glass of milk every single day? That's just not right. It's not normal and they were going to make me fat. All the hard work I had done to stay slim would be undone and I would just balloon in size and not be able to stop. I began catastrophising everything, believing that my weight

111

would go up and up and up, and I wouldn't be able to get it under control.

Steph: 'C'mon don't be an idiot. It's just milk. That's all it is. All these other girls have eating disorders even though they're eating. Just because I have this glass of milk doesn't mean I'm no longer anorexic. Pull it together.'

Anorexia: 'Fuck, fuck, fuck! Get away from that filth. Get out of here. Fucking run. This is torture. You can't have it, you hear me, I won't let you contaminate your body with such toxins.'

Steph: 'Have the bloody milk. These people wouldn't give it to me if it were bad for me. They're trying to get me better.'

Anorexia: 'NO! They're poisoning you, turning you against your only friend. I'm the only person you can trust. These idiots don't know what they're talking about, and you're a deluded twat for thinking they might have a point. Listen to me, not them. YOU DON'T DESERVE TO FUCKING EAT WOMAN!'

My head was lowered, and I pressed my hands firmly against my forehead, trying to iron out the banging noise Ana was creating. My life was crumbling before my very eyes. This is what I had been reduced to. Tears over a glass of milk. It wasn't even solid food. It's the first thing I had when I was a baby, it's what my mum gave me to keep me healthy and alive. Why was I fighting against the most natural thing in the world? Why was I doing this to myself? Why was I being so cruel? My skin was clammy, and my eyes were the size of saucers, betraying my feelings of terror and upset. They kept darting around the room, watching other people. I was afraid of people thinking I was coping and that I wasn't 'sick,' but at the same time, I didn't want to trigger other patients.

I felt so conflicted. I wanted to turn off my own head, and escape my thoughts which were strangling me. Half an hour had passed, and as all the other patients placed their empty glasses and plates on the worksurface and filtered out, I remained seated. How were they so strong and I so weak? They had managed to fight against the eating disordered voices. They had won. I had lost…again. Beating myself up had become a habit of mine. The gloves were off, and Ana went wild, lashing out at me. I was the punching bag, and I was getting beaten down every day. My milk sat opposite me, touching distance away. It was taunting me, and I was letting myself be bullied. A member of staff took the seat next to me and said my name. I looked up with my tear-stained face.

'You need to drink your milk' she said to me.

I wanted to say 'fuck off' back to her, but I held my tongue. Shaking my head and clenching my hands into fists, I let the tears continue to fall. 'I don't want it' I mumbled in between sobs. I'm not going to write down the whole interaction we had because, to be honest, I can't remember it. I did finish my milk in the end, but the anxiety and hatred that caused was unimaginable. I went back to my room, sat on the bed, and cried. I curled up into a ball, rocking back and forth, crying my eyes out. I was barely able to breathe as I was in complete hysterics. I couldn't comprehend what I had done. What I had stupidly done. Ana was punching and screaming and kicking, furious that I had defied her and listen to someone else. At that moment, I wanted to die. What was the point in continuing? I was just going to stay stuck in this cycle of hatred and disgust. I didn't want to wake up in the morning and have to face my fears all over again, day in and day out. Picking up one of my books, I hurled it across the room, and it felt good. I did it again, book after book, just throwing anything that I had in hand. I wasn't trying to damage or break anything; I just wanted to try and vent some of this pent-up anger that was building inside of me.

I have never felt anger like this. An intense, burning, hatred at myself. Anger at being so stupidly weak. Anger for not being strong enough to resist. I didn't have to have the milk. I could have refused. I should have refused. Fucking hell, I'm terrible. I'm such a terrible person. These thoughts were just hitting me one after the other. Boom! Boom! Boom! They were constantly coming right at me, I needed to get the thoughts out of my head. I needed to put these on paper to make me feel less frustrated if nothing else. I picked up the books that lay strewn across the floor and dumped them in a drawer. Grabbing a pen and paper, I began to write. I didn't have anything in mind. I didn't plan on writing anything. The pen just hit the paper and I went for it. Just spitting out random thoughts and feelings. The next few pages contain thoughts and feelings from my journal detailing my darkest days. I didn't see a way out of the darkness, and I was consumed by fear. I was in hell and I kept falling further and further into a blazing inferno of hatred.

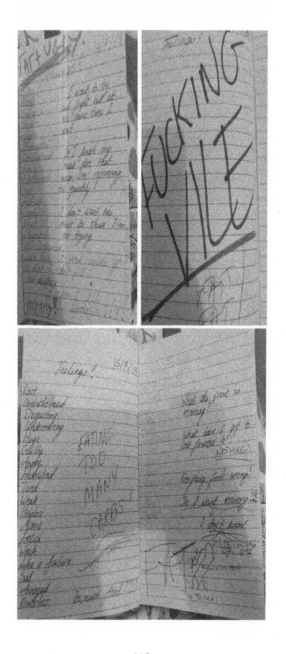

115

Feelings?   27...

I HATE

MYSELF

STUPID FUCKING

SANDWICH

A FULL PORTION U have

3 ?!?!?

It doesn't make any flipping
sense. It was way too hard
and felt disgusting and
regretted it myself. I'm not
sick or skinny enough to be
here.

Do I just GAIN MORE WEIGH

Big fat, stupid, ugly, bitch
you can't do anything right.

I don't want any more calories

Feeling?

Had the orange I feel
sick regret I feel huge. Need
to make up for cheating
done today I don't want
to feel like crap.

Exercise 3x per day:

85 star jumps (x3)
Sit ups lying on right
Raise, staying away from room
100 of mountain climbers (x2)

After nursing supervision
any walking back
corridor
whilst during supervision

INCREASE EACH DAY
NEED TO BURN MORE
CALORIES

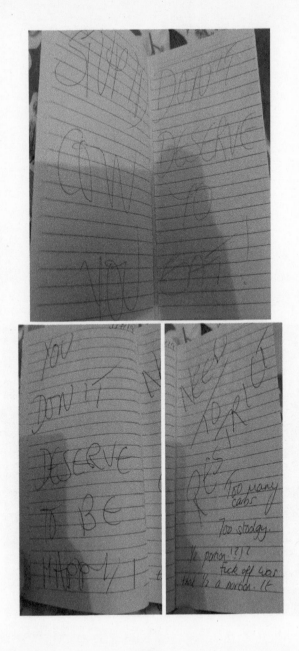

Reading these back shock me slightly. I thought I was so numb I couldn't feel anything, yet all these pages were filled with feelings. Feelings of anger, frustration, hatred, fear, desperation... I was experiencing so many different emotions, I didn't know how to interpret them. I didn't know what to make of the jumbled mess inside my head.

***

My first couple of weeks at the Priory merge into one. I was checked on four times an hour, so I barely had any privacy. I had gone from being able to do what I want when I want, and getting away with so much, to having no freedom or privacy. To having no choice. To facing my fears instead of running away from them. The day dragged slowly past, and it was approaching 6 p.m. Dinner time. I was so anxious, I kept wringing my hands. I wasn't ready to eat. I wasn't prepared for any of this. My brain tried to find an excuse, a way to get out of this. Maybe I could say I had a tummy ache? Or I was throwing up? Or maybe I could have a fever? It was useless. There was nothing Ana could do. Like it or not, I would have to eat dinner. I told myself it was only a half portion. One meal wasn't going to make me gain weight. It would be okay, and I would get through this. Anxiety radiated off me as I made my way down the corridor, trying to get my breathing under control. Vicious thoughts and harsh insults swirled around in my head as I looked up at the ceiling and tried to hold in the tears that were threatening to spill. I don't think I've ever cried so much in my whole life. Going into the communal lounge, I placed my phone on a chair and waited with the other girls to be called in.

The door to the kitchen opened, and I had no more time to try and compose myself. With shaky breaths and a hammering heart, I walked into the room, trying in vain to quell the attacks Ana was making against me. I grew to hate this room. It represents everything my eating disorder hates, and I had some hellish times in there. I cried and cried, breaking down time and time again at having to eat. The room was set up on three separate tables, much the same as it was at snack. The only difference was, here we all had allocated seats at the tables. There was supervised which is where everyone starts off. You sit with a member of staff and they get everything for you. They measure all your drinks and milk, and if you want something from the fridge you have to ask for it. We also weren't allowed napkins at this table which may sound ludicrous, but it does make sense if you think about it. People with eating disorders tend to be very devious, and they will try to hide food in any way they can. Ana jumps at every chance to deceive others and manipulate your weight.

The table up from that was progressional. Here, you were allowed a napkin. You didn't have a member of staff with you, but there were still HCA'S around if you did need extra support. You could go into the fridge and measure out milk and cold drinks. It was a step up from supervised, but you were still watched, and you couldn't use the microwave or kettle. The third and last table was transitional. The biggest difference between this and progressional is that you were able to make your own hot drinks. You could use the microwave, and you were also able to use the kettle and toaster. The tables were set up like this to encourage independence, but it was done in a safe and controlled manner. The final step was eating in the downstairs dining room, which was shared between all three wards. I was directed towards the supervised table, where I had my own name card. A plate of spaghetti bolognaise was in front of it. HOLY FUCKING SHIT! Ana lost her mind at this. A plate full of carbs. Where was the salad? Where were the vegetables? How was this good for me, or a balanced meal? Were they taking the piss?

Steph: 'It's just pasta. It's just a normal meal. C'mon get it together woman.'

Anorexia: 'FUCK! FUCK! SHIT! FUCK!'

Steph: 'Stop being so scared of food. It's just half a portion. I mean, look, staff are having it, and they're not fat. Pasta is NOT bad for me. It's not bad for me. It's not…'

Anorexia: 'Are you for real? Carbs are the demon. Especially pasta. Urgh, it's disgusting. You ain't touching that crap. Not whilst I'm here.'

***

We had forty-five minutes to complete this meal, and I refused to let myself clear my plate. Most of the time was spent fiddling with the spaghetti, picking it up and letting it fall off my fork. This was my worst nightmare. You can see the fear in people's eyes. You can see how terrified they are, and how much grief their eating disorder is giving them. You see people at their very lowest point; I saw someone trying to flee the ward. I saw someone suffer a seizure. I saw grown women, adults, drowning in a sea of misery. I saw people being confined to wheelchairs or their bedrooms. I saw someone with a feeding tube. I will forever be haunted by those memories. I will never forget the pain in their eyes. The psychological games their eating disorder was playing with them. I will not let myself forget how much eating disorders destroy people. How much it strips away from you, and you lose all dignity and freedom. I will not forget the people that I met, and the hardships I know they endure daily. I will not forget what having anorexia meant for me and the people I care about. I will never forgive, and I will never forget.

The food seemed to go on for miles. The HCA who was with me at the time was incredible. She sat there with me as I wailed and spoke to me like an adult. She didn't make me feel silly or stupid, or like I was an attention seeker. She pacified me, and stayed with me the whole time, showing insane amounts of patience. In the end, after about an hour of struggling, I gave up. There was still spaghetti left on my plate, but I had eaten more than I ever thought I could. I was told this would go down in my notes as an incomplete meal and I was given ensure to make up the calories. Drying my eyes as best I could, I made my way into the lounge for supervision. I felt like I was doing the walk of shame. I felt a dozen pair of eyes burn into the back of my skin. Although I had done my best to dry my face, it was still red with the undeniable tear streaks still visible. I flopped down on the empty chair and went straight on my phone, trying to ignore everyone and just blend in with the furniture. The desire to just be invisible was huge. My brain was all over the place and I was a jumbled mess of nerves. Trying to scroll through my phone, I attempted to distract myself from the raging fire of Ana. Safe to say, this failed miserably. It was all consuming and scrolling through posts on Facebook did nothing to improve my mood. In fact, it probably made me feel worse.

I hate admitting this because it makes me sound like a selfish cow, but I was jealous. I was jealous of all my friends, who were living their lives. Who were doing great things with their lives, getting engaged, travelling, going back to university...What was I doing? Crying over a bowl of spaghetti in hospital. I wished to be someone else. I wished I could be normal, and I hated what my life had become. The joke that was my existence. I had no one. I was no one. I was jerked away from my thoughts by a member of staff. She came in the lounge and turned off the TV. I had no idea what was happening, so I continued looking at my phone. It wasn't until one of the patients told me that we were doing meal support that I looked up. Meal support was something that we did every day, after dinner. We would go around the room and it would be a chance for people to talk about their concerns and worries, particularly if they found that meal challenging. It was a bit of extra support for everyone. When they got around to me, I just shook my head, too shy to say anything. I didn't feel worthy of opening my mouth. What did I know about having an eating disorder? Nothing at all. The reality is, I did know what it's like. I *do* know what it feels like to have an eating disorder. What it feels like to have a bully that never goes away. A bully that kicks you until you're down. A bully that never lets up and, even when you're down and at your lowest point, continues to beat you up. I know how much of a sadistic bastard this illness is. And I can't listen to that voice anymore. I can't listen to her lies, telling me that I'm not ill enough, and that I don't know what it likes to truly have anorexia. I do know. I wish I didn't, but I do. I know what it's like to be slowly killing yourself from the inside. And it's horrific.

***

The hour that followed dragged on for ages. I was constantly clock watching and, as people gradually began to filter out, I still had about twenty minutes of supervision left. Your hour supervision starts when you enter the lounge, so the faster you finish your meals, the quicker you can leave. It was just me left. Me and one other patient. She was the first person who spoke to me, and she put her hand on my shoulder and gave it a squeeze. A gesture I will always be grateful for. She looked me directly in the eyes and I could feel the warmth emanating from her. Her eyes were twinkling with compassion and love. An amazing woman. She said she knew how hard it was, but she promised me it does get easier. In time, things do become a little less dark. She gave me hope. Before that I had nothing. No hope, no future. But she planted that seed, and throughout my time there, she would always water that bit of hope. She would keep it alive, and I owe her so much.

I murmured my thanks and she smiled at me and I smiled back. I might not have felt happy but, somehow, she made me feel safe. Very few words were uttered, but she instantly put me at ease, and I felt relaxed in her company. Our supervision ended and we could return to our rooms. Giving her hand a small squeeze, I went to my new bedroom. My new home. There wasn't really anything I could do. My mind was too preoccupied with the food I had just consumed. The food I had banned myself from having for so long. I had a list of fear foods. A list of foods that, if I listened to my eating disorder, I would never allow myself to have. No exceptions.

My list of fear foods was extensive. It left me with virtually no food I could eat without feeling insane levels of guilt. When I was alone in my room, I punched my leg repeatedly with my fist. I was so angry at myself. Ana was angry at Steph. She was absolutely fuming that she hadn't got her way. God, I hated this. I pulled at my hair and clothes, wishing I could just vanish. Wishing that I could make all of this go away. Wishing for some peace that I would not get. For someone that I could never be. Staff checked on me several times throughout the next hour, but I didn't speak to anyone. I didn't want to speak to anyone. I just wanted to shut myself off and forget all of this was happening to me.

I had been in my room for about twenty minutes when I got yet another knock on my door. I had to go for MARSI's (physical observations). This was done three times a day, morning, noon, and evening, and our blood pressure and pulse would be monitored. We would also have our blood sugars and oxygen levels checked. These tests were specifically targeted for people with eating disorders. It took about three minutes and was done in the clinic room in the lounge. Thankfully, I was in and out. The day was nearly over, and I was mentally and physically exhausted. Unfortunately, I still had another challenge looming over me. Evening snack. I made my way down the corridor around five minutes early, and waited in the lounge to be called in. I had changed into my pyjamas. We could only wear our night clothes after evening supervision. We were not allowed to wear pyjamas or dressing gowns during the day, and we had to be properly dressed before breakfast at 8:30am. This was to try and help with people's mental health and make things more reflective of normal life. The door of doom, as I like to call it, opened and in we all went.

I always requested to have hot milk in the evening because it's supposed to help you sleep, but it had the opposite effect.

I found drinking so much milk incredibly challenging and it really messed with my head. I couldn't understand why milk would make me gain weight. Technically, I wasn't eating food, so my head had a tough time catching up with my body.

***

After asking staff to unlock my bathroom so I could brush my teeth, I flopped onto my bed. I never got used to having people standing outside the bathroom when I was in there. Turning my light off, I was grateful for the darkness. Wanting it to swallow me up, I curled myself up into a ball and closed my eyes. My mind was still whirring away, but I was so exhausted I think I must have dozed off at some point. What I didn't realise was that staff would still check up on you throughout the night. I was on four times hourly observations, and this meant I had someone poking their head in and shining a torch in my eyes far too many times. It was 6am when awoke from my sleep. For a minute, I forgot where I was, and I thought it had all been some weird dream. But it was no dream, no figment of my imagination. It was very much a reality. During the night, a member of staff had propped a cushion up against the door, so they didn't have to keep opening and closing it when they did their checks. This small act was greatly appreciated. However, I was not expecting such an early start to the day.

Because I had just arrived, I had a spot weigh in so they could measure my BMI and get an accurate reading. Firstly, I had my morning MARSI's done, and then I was weighed. This was all done in the clinic room with a nurse. I was asked to strip down to my underwear, which I did. I already hated seeing my body with no one in the room, but to have someone watch me in no more than my underwear was torture. I felt so fat and disgusting, I thought they were all judging me and laughing at me behind my back. Laughing at me for thinking I was underweight. When I stepped off the scales, my weight was recorded in a chart and I was asked to sign next to it. Wrapping my dressing gown around myself to try and hide my 'fatness' I returned to my room where I cried. I was crying for most of the day, every day. My life was literally meal, cry, meal, cry, meal, cry, meal, cry, bed.

***

The first few days of my admission passed me by. Still in a state of shock, I found it virtually impossible to get through each mealtime. It felt like I was eating all the time. That I never stopped. Going into breakfast for the first time is a memory forever etched on my mind. Taking my seat on the supervised table, I stared at my cereal. I couldn't see how I could eat all this food that was being forced down my throat. Ana couldn't understand it. She told me this was all completely unnecessary and that they were trying to make me fat. All the work that I had put into losing weight was going to all be for nothing now. Normally, you have half an hour for breakfast, but I went over the time limit. I (no sorry, meant to say Ana) hoped, in doing this, staff would show compassion and give me ensure instead. This cunning plan did not work. Staff sat with me until I cleared my plate. It didn't matter how much of a fuss I kicked up, they would just wait with me until the job was done. They were the rules, and Ana was doing everything in her power to outsmart them. To try and find loopholes in the rules. This didn't work. One way or the other, I would have to complete my meals.

Ensure, to me, was a safety net. I have come to realise that I have a massive issue with choice. If I am making the decision to eat something with more calories, or something that is deemed to be unhealthy, Ana struggles with that. Why go for the higher option when there is a lower alternative? Let me think about this for a moment... umm... maybe because it tastes nice. Maybe because life is too short to spend every waking moment counting calories. Maybe because I deserve food. Life is difficult enough without starving your body and denying yourself any pleasure. One of my biggest battles is showing my allegiance to my eating disorder. If I manage to challenge Ana's rules, or I have a fear food and don't find it as hard as my head is telling me I should, I then jump to the conclusion that I don't have an eating disorder. I was supposed to be terrified of food, and if I wasn't terrified or enjoyed what I was eating, there was a massive war going on in my head.

Anorexia: 'Deserter! You're betraying us. You're betraying me. How dare you have all this food and drink.'

Steph: 'But I don't have a choice. This is my prescribed medicine. This is what I must do. I've tried to get out of things, but it doesn't work.'

Anorexia: 'Can you name one normal person who drinks a litre of milk every day? Exactly. No one does it. You don't have to stay here. You're choosing to, and that means you don't have an eating disorder. TRAITOR!'

Steph: 'This. Is. My. Medicine. It's not greedy, it's what I've been told I need. All these other girls are eating but they still have an eating disorder. You don't doubt their illness, so why should I be doubting mine?'

Anorexia: 'Because you're a dirty little girl. Because you're an imposter. Because everything about you is fake. YOU DON'T HAVE FUCKING ANOREXIA!'

I was brought out of my reverie by a member of staff asking me what drink I wanted. I panicked at this. What drink? I didn't need one. Trying my best to whisper so as not to disturb anyone else in supervision, I asked them what they meant. It was explained to me that I was supposed to have a post meal drink, so I asked for water. I was then told water wasn't allowed. It had to be squash, tea, or coffee. So many extras. So many unnecessary calories. Why have squash when you can have water? Why have milky tea or coffee when you can have them black? Eventually, I asked for very weak blackcurrant squash. For a long time, I just sat staring at the glass. How could I be expected to drink more? It wasn't right. Once again, I was the last person to leave supervision and staff had to prompt me to drink because I was initially refusing it. A week ago, Ana had all the control in the world. I was running whenever I wanted. I was eating the bare minimum, and I was only drinking limited fluids. Now, less than a week later, Ana had lost all her control. The rules in inpatient were strict. All food and drink had to be completed in the given time limit. You weren't allowed to tear your food apart or eat in tiny bites. We had to lick the lid of all our yoghurt pots, and we had to make sure we had all the crumbs from our plates. Everything that brought comfort to me, and made Ana feel safe, was no longer an option.

***

I arrived on the Priory on a Thursday. Weekends there tend to be quiet. There are fewer members of staff over the weekend. The dietician, OT (occupational therapist), the ward doctor, and others, didn't work over the weekend so they were running on minimum staff. Ward trips normally took place on a Friday and Saturday, but I had not been cleared to go on any, so I was stuck inside. Thankfully, my family came up to visit me every day. I lived about half an hour away, so it was relatively easy for my mum and dad to visit. They would take it in turns, but I don't remember much. I know they would sit on a chair by my bed, and I would sit there in mute silence. I barely even acknowledged their presence and when I did speak to them, my voice was laced with anger. They had gone out of their way to support me and be there for me and I was just chucking everything back in their faces. Ungrateful. That's how I was towards them. They would bring me flowers or cards and talk to me, trying to distract me and better understand the condition. Most of the time, I said nothing. I would sit there in silence for over an hour, muttering only monosyllabic words. The pattern tended to be the first half an hour into their arrival I wouldn't say a word. The next half hour I would get very tearful and emotional. And the last half hour I would be very apologetic, hugging my parents and resting my head in their arms as they joined me on my bed. They consoled me whilst I wept and wailed. They cried tears with me. They held me. They kissed me and told me they loved me.

***

I managed to survive the weekend and Monday marked another weigh-in. My weight, since Friday, had remained static. The goal of 0.5 to 1.5kg a week of weight gain was not met, and Ana found this an exhilarating prospect. Even though I had been betraying her and eaten foods, I hadn't gained weight. Ana – One. Steph – Zero. I went to my room feeling strangely satisfied. Although I still hadn't lost enough weight, at least I hadn't put on any and Ana took that as a small win. However, if you failed to meet the weight gain requirement that would lead to a meal plan increase. Meal plans are something everyone with eating disorders dread. It is essentially your prescription, your medicine to recovery, but at the same time it scares the living daylight out of you. I didn't want to gain any weight, but I also didn't want my meal plan increased. It's a catch twenty-two. If your weight doesn't go up, Ana might be happy for a moment but then it leads to an increased intake of food which fucks with your head. If your weight goes up, then it pisses Ana right off.

I didn't realise how much of a privilege it was to be able to eat whatever you want when you want. It wasn't until everything got taken away from me that I realised how much I had lost. I spent so long listening to the taunts and jibes Ana dished out, that I forgot just how lucky I was. How lucky YOU are. To be able to meet up and go out for lunch with family and friends without knowing the menu inside and out. To have chocolate because it tastes damn good. To have a cooked breakfast and a cooked meal for lunch and dinner. To eat what YOU want, and not what you're told you must eat. Please never take that for granted. Appreciate the freedom you have and hold onto it with both hands. I lost sight of everything I *could* do, and Ana fixated on everything I *couldn't* do.

***

Being inpatient demoralises you and institutionalises you. To a certain extent, it is a safe place for those who are on a worrying decline, but at the same time it cuts you off from normal life. It cuts you off from normal people as you are constantly surrounded by ill patients. After I completed another challenging breakfast after weigh-in, I sat in the lounge as usual. Staff were back in and therapeutic groups were on. At half nine the ward doctor arrived, and I was called into the clinic room for my first (of many) blood tests.

I was also asked if I had ever had a DEXA (bone density) scan. It picks up on damage to the bone which is a commonality with most eating disorders. Being underweight increases your risk of osteopenia and osteoporosis. Whilst osteopenia is reversible, osteoporosis is not. This filled me with anxiety. I was worried that, due to my running addiction, I had damaged my bones. I'd had quite a few knee troubles over the past year. The idea that I had permanently damaged my body terrified me. My DEXA scan was scheduled for about two weeks' time and all I could do was wait and pray. Pray that I hadn't destroyed my body beyond repair.

Once I had finished in the clinic room, I returned to supervision. There was a member of staff sat on one of the chairs doing check-in. This was an opportunity for people to check-in with each other and say about how they're feeling. I stayed resolutely silent throughout this. As I was still the 'newbie' I felt too embarrassed to say anything. I felt bad for struggling so much, but I also felt like a fraud, and that I wasn't struggling enough. It was a complete paradox. Everything was such a mess, and I didn't know which way to turn or who to listen to. I felt I needed to struggle to show I was anorexic because, in my head, I didn't look ill, and I certainly wasn't underweight. But on the other side of the coin, I was worried about triggering other patients. It is an incredibly hard environment to be in for everybody, and I was so afraid I was only adding to their struggles. I thought everyone silently hated me. They weren't going to say how disgusted with me they were in person, but I genuinely believed I was loathed and not liked. After check-in, I was able to catch up with the dietician.

Dieticians are people you respect and believe, but simultaneously hate and disagree with. The logical part of you knows that everything they are saying is true. You know that, logically, you are ill. You know that they are speaking the truth and are just doing the best to help you. Logically, you know you're not at a healthy weight, but Ana disregards this. She makes up her own rules. My meal plan was discussed and, due to my weight, I was given an increase. Flaming bloody hell! I had only been there three days and they were already shoving stupid amounts of food down my mouth. Ana told me it was abuse and that they shouldn't be getting away with such cruelty. The only abuser here was Ana. The only cruel and evil one was Ana. Getting through each day was a huge mountain to climb. I was on half portions of lunch and dinner, but I was not coping well with snacks. My eating disorder saw snacks as being greedy. Three snacks a day plus three main meals seemed like an inordinate amount of food, and I could not understand why everyone was so keen to 'fatten' me up. I felt like little Hansel from the fairy tale, and whilst everyone else could see bones and sadness, I could only see 'fatness' and greed. I felt trapped in a prison, powerless to escape. Powerless to fight back. But now I realise that Ana was making me see everything in her tinted glasses, and the line between fiction and reality was blurred.

The snacks that were on offer were quite calorie dense and I had numerous break downs over having glasses of milk and 'impure' foods. Why were they putting me through so much pain? Where was their heart? I now realise that they weren't putting me through pain. They were putting Ana through pain. Ana was the one who was targeted, the one who was shouting and screaming and wailing. They were doing this to save me and kill Ana. Not the other way around.

***

About two weeks into treatment, my meal plan changed quite dramatically. I had been really struggling with sandwiches as I saw this as an unbalanced meal. Where were the vegetables? It was just bread, and I cried my way through every sandwich, getting food all over my face and hair where I was so distraught. I was prescribed promethazine to try and ease my anxiety and I could take 20mg twice a day. It did little to no good. I was still an emotional wreck, completely unrecognisable from a few years back, relying on stress balls to try and get me through. When I met up with the dietician, we made quite a drastic decision. Instead of having a sandwich for lunch, I would now be given 200ml of ensure. My head just couldn't cope with a sandwich as Ana was hurling abuse in my direction at every opportunity. We hoped that having ensure as a meal substitute would help ease some of my pain whilst providing me with the nutrients and calories I required. Ironically, this change made me feel even shittier. It really screwed with my head in ways I can't even begin to explain to you.

I wasn't eating proper food and, therefore, wasn't going to gain weight. It was just a drink and was therefore 'healthier' and 'less fattening' than a sandwich. I was bound to lose weight. I had to. Turns out, this was not to be. I ended up restoring more weight on this liquid supplement than I did on solid foods. When I was weighed next, my weight had spiked more than it had done since my first day. I dissolved into a state of distress after seeing the number on the scales increase. This kick-started another dangerous habit of mine, which I had so far managed to curb in inpatient. My running addiction came back in full force. As I was being checked on four times an hour, I reasoned that I couldn't run. I would get found out, so it wasn't a choice. It was part of my medicine and was out of my control. However, ensure ruined this progress entirely. I started by running on the spot for seven minutes, then doing star jumps for three minutes. I would do this repeatedly. If someone knocked on my door, I would quickly pick up a book and pretend I was reading, or I would sit down at my desk and pretend to be writing. I had everything set up for when staff did their observations. It was a militant operation.

I would place my notebook open on my desk, and I would flick to a page that was about half full, so it looked like I was in the middle of writing. I would then take a pen, remove the lid and place it on top of the paper. I pulled my chair out from under the desk and turned it slightly so I could easily just slip onto it when I heard a knock. I would also grab a book from my bookshelf and place it within reaching distance next to me, so I could make out that I was choosing a new book to read. Everything was carefully planned, and I didn't do particularly intense exercise. It was more a test of endurance. Hours were spent running... and I mean hours. It started off, as I said, with running on the spot and star jumps for a total time of ten minutes. I would then run for ten minutes back and forth, doing laps of my room. I would repeat this cycle for the whole day. I thought I could be in control of the exercise. That I could just do a few hours a day and that would be it. Just enough to halt my weight gain. But I couldn't do it. I couldn't control Ana, and the illness dominated my life. The extremes I went to were insane and I could have died from it. They say exercise is good for you, but what they don't mention is that exercise can be a double-edged sword. It is praised for being a positive, healthy thing to do, but it can easily become an obsession. It can easily turn unhealthy but that is glossed over in the media.

***

Someone said that it was a shame something so good had become so negative for me, and that hurt. Exercise is always praised, and if you don't exercise people are quick to label you as 'fat' or 'lazy.' Just like anything, exercise can become controlling, and it could have killed me. It is so bloody difficult to have to limit your exercise when the whole world shouts out about how important exercise and fitness is. What about those people who suffer from eating disorders? What about them? Do you even consider the impact of your words? Do you ever just stop and think about how incessant talks of dieting and health food swaps can destroy a person? Do you realise how toxic the industry is? How fucking hard it is to not get drawn into the hysteria around weight loss and fad diets? Well, do you? Do you get it? If you eat carbs, you are not fat or greedy. If you don't go to the gym, you are not lazy. If you gain weight, you are not disgusting. Weight loss is always praised. Is weight gain ever praised? No! It should be. It is torturous to weight restore, and have calorie dense foods, when you are surrounded by spiralised vegetables, low carb bread, low fat yoghurts, skimmed milk… For me it has been so much harder to restore weight than it was to lose it and I am sick to the back teeth of feeling guilty for eating. It ends now. I am not going to feel guilty for having my medicine. I am not going to be made to feel shame for having puddings every day because that is what I NEED. That is what is healthy for me.

The only time I wasn't exercising was when I was in meals or supervision. The rest of the time, I was trying to burn off as many calories as was humanly possible. Groups were on during the week, but I barely went to any of them. I wasn't about to waste precious time that could be spent exercising. Why was I going to sit down and talk about things when I couldn't even hold a proper conversation? It would have been pointless. Whenever I ran, I would make sure I wore socks to try to mask my footsteps and I always had noise in the background. I was obsessive in my regime, always having the TV on. I thought I was getting away with it. Staff would occasionally ask me if I were exercising, and I would vehemently deny their accusations. I thought I was a genius for covering it up so well and I felt untouchable. No one could stop me from doing anything if I set my mind to it.

The pictures you are about to see document some of the exercise regimes I carried out whilst at the Priory. I would run for hours, writing down all my times and adding up the total amount of minutes I spent exercising. The tally charts reflected how many star jumps I would do. Each single line in the tally represents 100 jumps. At first, I would have to do a minimum of 10,000, then it quickly went up to 20,000, then 25,000, then 30,000. The number just kept rising. I could have worked out every minute God sent, every second of every hour, day and night, but Ana would still tell me that I wasn't doing enough. That I wasn't burning enough calories. That I wasn't deserving of so much fucking food. She is vicious and cruel, and as each day passed, I found that I had to keep increasing the amount of exercise I was doing. If I couldn't outdo myself, then I would at least have to equal the amount I did the day before. That was an absolute bare minimum. I filled up pages and pages with tally charts and scribblings to try and calculate how much exercise I was doing daily, and how much more I had to do the following day. I only stopped to eat and sleep. It was like I was possessed by Ana. No matter how tired I was, or how ill I was, or what time it was, I had to keep going. To stop now and rest would be failure. I believed I had already failed everything in life that this was the one thing I had to get right. I had to be strong and do Ana's bidding. The strong thing to do would be to stand up against the bully and fight her vicious words. There is a strength in saying no. There is a silent strength in not doing anything. If I had sat down and read a book, I would have been strong. In a way I took the easy way out. Ana was so vile in her torment, that it was easier for me to do what she asked. She is evil!

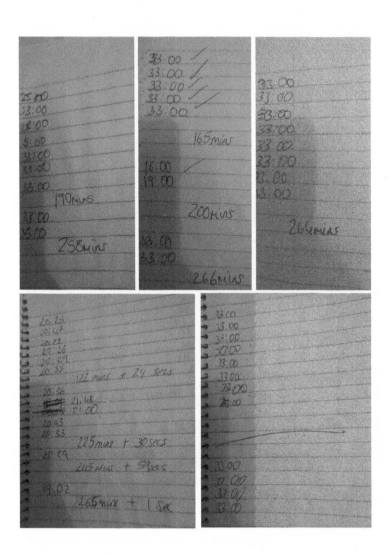

25:00
33:00
28:00
5:00
33:00
33:00
35:00
190mins
33:00
35:00
258mins

33:00
33:00
33:00
33:00
33:00
165mins
16:00
19:00
200mins
33:00
33:00
266mins

33:00
33:00
33:00
33:00
33:00
33:00
33:00
28:00
13:00
264mins

20:25
20:67
20:22
22:26
20:29
20:35
122 mins + 29 secs
20:36
21:48
21:00
20:43
20:33
225mins + 30secs
20:29
245 mins + 53secs
19:02
265mins + 1 sec

33:00
33:00
32:00
33:00
33:00
33:00
73:00
25:00

33:00
32:00
31:02
33:00

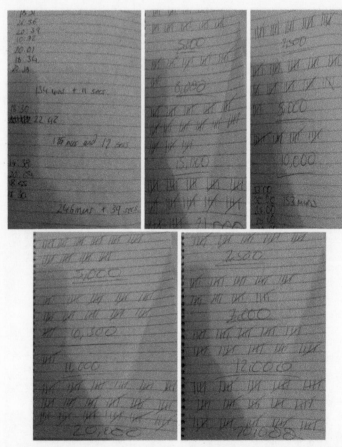

This whole stringent exercise regime continued throughout most of the six months I was hospitalised. It would start from the second I woke up to the second my exhausted body forced me into bed. My next weigh-in went exactly how I wanted it to. Sorry, meant to say how Ana wanted it to. I had lost weight. My exercise regime was working. The dietician asked me if I was exercising when we went through my meal plan together. She said that staff were getting suspicious of me and noticed that I looked quite breathless at times. I had a chance to be honest. I had a chance to tell the truth and admit that I was struggling. Instead of doing the right thing, I lied. How could I be exercising with the constant checks? I feigned ignorance when she questioned why I hadn't restored any weight. They couldn't prove I was exercising, so I thought I had the upper hand and I continued to run. When ward round approached, I requested to have my bathroom door unlocked. Ward round was basically a meeting with your main treatment team. It happened every week and we were expected to fill in something referred to as *My Week in Words*. Here, we could write down any of our concerns, what we wanted to happen and if the past week had gone well. It was a chance to speak up and have a say in your treatment. It is no exaggeration to say that everyone dreaded ward rounds. They were hated by most patients and would often end in tears.

They would start at early afternoon and finish at 5 p.m. although they almost always overran. The main figures in ward round were the consultant psychiatrist and medical director, the lead psychiatrist, the ward doctor and dietician, and a senior staff nurse. There would also be the hospital secretary who would sit at the computer and type up the minutes. Ward rounds must be one of the most demeaning and humiliating things I have ever experienced. They filled me with dread, and I felt completely stripped of my voice when I went in. Imagine being in a room with six professionals. Imagine being physically and mentally unwell and being sat with people who were determining your future. It was debasing.

Despite filling out the form, whenever I went into the room, I felt paralysed to say anything. Furthermore, a lot of what I wrote was ignored and only certain points were focused on. Points THEY wanted to discuss. I was asked what I wanted them to do for me. How the bloody hell should I know? They are the professionals; I am the patient. If I knew what to do and how to recover, I wouldn't need to be in hospital. I was fuming, but my tongue caught in my throat and I didn't voice my true feelings. I was too scared to speak up. I felt judged and pathetic, and things I said were twisted and used against me. For the most part, I was able to hold myself together during these meetings but, as soon as I was in my room, the tears would come. The one good thing to come from my ward round was that I got my bathroom unlocked. I had been asking for about three weeks and they eventually agreed to having it left open. No longer did I have to go to the toilet with staff listening and waiting outside. I finally had some privacy. To be perfectly honest, the main reason I wanted my bathroom open was so that I could run. Yes, it was incredibly frustrating to have to ask to use the bathroom and to keep the door slightly open whilst you empty your bowels, that was not the main driving force behind my request. I now had a place where I could run energetically, and I wouldn't be caught out because I could just pretend to be on the toilet. If necessary, I could quickly sit down on the toilet so if they opened the bathroom door, they wouldn't see anything suspicious. I thought I had it all marvellously worked out and I was so proud of how devious and deceitful Ana was being.

***

I might have spun them lies and weaved a web of deceit, but they weren't falling for it. I could try and convince myself I was the master of deception, but I know this is not the case. They knew. Of course, they knew. When I was brushing my teeth, I was running on the spot. I was walking on the spot when I was in the shower. When I was getting dressed, I would put my trousers and bra on but not my top. I would lay it out on my bed or on the back of my chair so I could be getting changed when staff did their checks. My legs were in so much pain and I was exhausted. More than anything, I wanted to spend just an extra half hour in bed so I could just sleep but Ana wouldn't allow me the respite.

Due to my running, I developed a nasty blister on my foot. It was near my big toe on the edge of my foot, and it was huge, not to mention incredibly painful. I was unable to walk properly so was limping. When staff pointed this out to me and asked what I'd done I would say I didn't know. I was trying to downplay it and hoped I could get away with it. I had also started my individual therapy at this point. I was having weekly sessions with my female therapist and the type of therapy I was doing was CAT (Cognitive Analytical Therapy). This type of therapy wasn't suited to me. Sometimes, that's just the way it is. You are not going to get on with every therapist and not every type of therapy will suit you. That's not a bad reflection on anybody, it's just the way life is. I dreaded therapy. I didn't feel like this therapist understood me at all and I felt belittled by her. Maybe I am being too sensitive, but I wasn't in a good place and I really needed help. I needed empathy, but I just felt like she was laughing at me and didn't understand who I was as a person.

I may have a lot of anger directed at myself, but I am not a harsh critic when it comes to others. I would never judge people the way I so cruelly judge myself. I would never berate and torture someone mentally. But I do it to myself all the time. I could never hate anyone, and I don't for one second blame anyone for my eating disorder and poor mental health. I don't think that someone must be on the brink of death to be suffering from an eating disorder. I don't think anyone has to be nothing but skin and bones to have anorexia. I don't think people aren't allowed to smile if they have depression. I don't think people are coping just because they have good moments. I don't think anyone is stupid for suffering mentally. Yet, I am an exception to the rule.

I am not allowed to smile or laugh or be happy. I am not allowed to live or meet up with friends and do normal things because I'm supposed to be ill. I wasn't allowed to finish a meal without breaking down or gain weight because that would be a betrayal to Ana. I had to be dead. Otherwise, I was fine and not ill. I was terrified of friends thinking I was making it all up because I looked okay. I now realise I did not look well, but I was so caught up in my illness the truth could have slapped me in the face, and I wouldn't have felt it. I didn't feel worthy of a life. I didn't think I deserved to be happy or do well. Life was a punishment for being so disgusting, and Ana was my comeuppance.

***

My therapist made the mistake of thinking that because I have those harsh views for myself, I must also have those same harsh views for everyone else. This could not be further from the truth. I felt like she was turning me into some tyrannical soldier and that only added to the plate of self-hatred I was being dished up. It only made my feelings of self-disgust grow even stronger. I needed someone to pick me up after years of putting myself down, putting myself into a little box and sealing myself firmly in darkness. I needed to be watered, not cut down even more. Most of my sessions with my therapist were not very productive. I cried in most of them and was non-committal in others.

We also discussed my running addiction. She asked me if I was able to control my running, and I looked up at her, and said 'yes.' All lies of course, but Ana makes even the most honest person a compulsive liar. She asked me if I could just sit with my feelings. Just sit with them and not act on them. Brilliant! Super, I'm all cured now! If I could sit with my feelings and not act on them, I wouldn't be in hospital. I wouldn't be having therapy if I could do this alone. I couldn't sit with my feelings. They were too domineering, too painful. Running was my coping mechanism. An escape from the bickering voices in my head. I desperately wanted support and help, but that did not happen.

***

With all this mental pain, I also had to contend with the physical effects of an eating disorder. One of my ECG's picked up a slight irregularity with my heart. It wasn't massive but, to be on the safe side, I was referred to the general hospital for an echocardiogram as an outpatient. At first, I was worried. Worried that through anorexia, I had damaged my heart, but soon Ana's manipulative words crept back in and she made me feel a perverted sense of achievement.

Anorexia: 'See, this is what I've been talking about. Finally, you might have actually succeeded.'

Steph: 'I might have lasting heart damage. I might have pushed myself too far. Holy crap this is serious!'

Anorexia: 'No, it's not! It's not serious enough. You're still walking, aren't you? You're still eating and running? If you were a serious anorexic, you wouldn't be doing that. This might be a chance to redeem yourself. Or have you failed at this now as well?'

Steph: 'Leave me alone!'

Anorexia: 'Well, that's not going to happen is it sweetheart? Now get back to your room and get on with your running. You're wasting time talking. The clock is ticking. Tick. Tock. Tick. Tock.'

It is an exhausting way to live. There are no words strong enough to describe how hellish my life had become. How my own mind was being twisted and turned against me. One of the things that pisses me off most about Ana (and there are many things that anger me about this illness) is that it turns you into a very selfish and self-centred person. I have always tried my utmost to be unselfish and caring. It has been so important to me to be empathetic and compassionate and, whether I have succeeded or not, it is something I always try to do. I would hate to think of myself as being selfish. I hate myself and would happily put myself down to raise others up. I would beat myself up till I was black and blue, but I would care for others. I would swear and curse at myself, but I would try and praise and support other people. But I cannot hide away from the fact that eating disorders are very selfish and isolating illnesses. Ana only ever cares about herself. She doesn't give a flying toss about you, or about the good people in your life. She has no respect for anyone or anything and demands that you do her bidding. Time was irrelevant and life was just an obstruction to Ana's desire of death. There was no room in her life for people who might try putting her back in her box or questioning her. Me, me, me. That sums up eating disorders.

When Ana had taken over ninety-nine percent of my mind and body, I was probably not that far away from death. My life revolved around exercise and this is no way to live. After about a week having ensure for lunch, I asked the dietician if I could switch back to sandwiches. I was supposed to be petrified of gaining weight, yet I had been drinking something that had led to weight restoration. I couldn't deal with this and I reasoned that if I was going to restore weight, then I would rather do it on food than supplements. At least then I could understand my weight going up. We agreed to go back to a sandwich, and I felt the knots in my stomach loosen. But as well as going back to sandwiches, I also had another increase. Moving up a meal plan, I was now expected to have a full sandwich as opposed to a half portion. A yoghurt was also added to my meal plan after dinner, and I wanted to punch the living daylights out of everyone. I wanted to punch the living daylights out of myself. Exercise, for me, was a form of self-harm. We associate self-harm with physical wounds. With cutting yourself or purposefully hurting your body, but it also extends beyond this. I wanted to hurt myself. I wanted to cause damage to my body, to feel numb to the war inside my head. It was dangerous and compelling, but if I had not been running all day, I would have found other ways to inflict pain on myself to try and cope with the walls tumbling down around me. Walls I had spent so long carefully building. It was over with in a heartbeat. If I hadn't been running, I would have cut myself or done something else.

***

I didn't have to wait long for my ECG appointment. I was accompanied by one of the HCA's and feelings of guilt and shame quickly overwhelmed me. I was going to the general hospital and wasting doctor's time. I wasn't sick (yes, I was), I didn't need help (Umm, yes, I did), this was all a ridiculous overreaction and an embarrassment to people who genuinely need help (load of bollocks by the way). I did need help. I was incredibly poorly but I was unable to see things for what they were. My view of the world was distorted entirely by Ana and right now I was being told that they were wasting precious equipment on me. I was a fucking idiot of a twenty-two-year-old who didn't deserve a second of anyone's time. Don't waste your machine on me when people out there are dying. I'm fine. Ana corrupted my thoughts, and she kept my head under the water, unable to come up for air. Unable to break the surface.

These thoughts continued to poison my mind as I sat waiting for my appointment. I was so used to rigid structured that being out of the Priory felt foreign and unnatural to me. My appointment was at 1 p.m. but I had to eat my lunch at precisely 12:45 p.m. That was the rule Ana made me obey. How could I eat my lunch in time? It would mess up my entire day. I can't eat any earlier because that makes it too close to morning snack. So, what do I do? I can't have it later either as that means it's too close to afternoon snack. Ana, what's the answer? How do I get out of this? Ana complicated things and her thinking was so black and white that there was no room for compromise.

It was Ana's way or the highway. It's *always* Ana's way or the highway. My HCA took away that control and decided for me. They had packed my sandwiches, fruit, and yoghurt all in a bag for me, so I was to eat it at 12:15 p.m. How could this be happening to me? I didn't deserve to be eating at all; they had destroyed my whole life. These stupid people who were making me eat all the time. I had things perfectly under control, thank you very much. I didn't need anyone's help. That's what Ana liked me to think. It wasn't the truth. Yes, everything was falling apart. But it was only falling apart for Ana.

***

I ate my lunch in Costa. Gingerly, and with much prompting, I took the sandwich out of the brown paper bag and used a napkin as a plate. My eyes kept darting around the place, and I tricked myself into believing that everyone was looking at me and judging me for being such a fat and disgusting pig. I needed to lose weight, not gain it. I needed to restrict, not eat constantly. Before I even took a bite, I asked the HCA if it was okay to eat. Was I allowed to eat so much food? Did I deserve it? What if everyone was watching me, laughing at me? My leg was bobbing up and down and I was so worried people would realise how disgusting I truly was. She pacified me and was honestly amazing. I will never forget this HCA, she listened to me and helped me through some dark times. She said something which I really needed to hear, something I still need to hear, and that is I CAN eat. I do not need to 'earn' my calories as Ana tells me I do. I am simply having my medicine. A person who has high blood pressure might take tablets, depressives take anti-depressants, if you have asthma you take an inhaler. You don't give these a second thought. People are just doing what they need to do to stay alive. To stay well. And that's what I was doing.

After she had consoled me and I was able to start eating, she ordered herself some food. A panini and coffee. There was no self-doubt or questioning. No calorie checking or hesitation. She didn't even think about it, just ordering what she wanted and tucking into it. She didn't have a care in the world. Food to her was just that – food. I envied that freedom. That spontaneity that I was afraid I would never get back. Why couldn't I just order what I wanted? Why couldn't food just be straightforward for me? Why did my stupid brain have to ruin everything again? The prospect of finishing my food in thirty minutes horrified me. I couldn't rely on ensure here. I had to finish everything. What if I couldn't do it? Or, worse, what if I managed it? Would that mean I never had anorexia? Whichever way you look at it, I couldn't win.

It is possible to win the fight against Ana. It's far from easy or straightforward, but there is always a rainbow at the end of rain. There is a positive to every negative. It is possible to enjoy food. I must believe this. What do I want people to remember about me when I am dead? That I was a good anorexic? Or that I kicked Ana's skinny ass? I think I would rather be remembered for the latter. In the grand scheme of things, my size or shape does not matter. When I am dead and gone, I don't want people to pity me as the poor little anorexic girl. It doesn't matter what I look like. It doesn't matter how much I weigh. It doesn't matter if I have a flat stomach or not. It doesn't matter if I have love handles or a thigh gap. It just means there is more of me to love. There are for more important things in life to focus on.

Don't waste your life trying to achieve the impossible. Don't waste your life making yourself worse in order to get help. You might not believe it but keep saying it anyway and, who knows, you might change your views. Nothing is set in stone. It is not the outside that matters, but what's on the inside. I will be remembered for who I am and not for what I looked like.

With the support and words of encouragement from my HCA, I finished my lunch in time. Well, the only thing I had left to eat was my fruit – a satsuma – but I said I would eat that on my way because time was pushing on and we still had to find where my appointment was. Ana had a sneaky little idea at this point. I could get away with not eating some of my satsuma if I 'accidentally' dropped some on the floor. I wanted to give myself a clap on the back for such a cunning plan. Ana was doing a little jig of joy. After weeks of being on the back bench, it now had a chance to take centre stage. I didn't HAVE to do anything. I could easily get rid of some of my food without anyone suspecting anything. We were surrounded by crowds of people going in different directions. It would be easy-peasy to just drop a few segments of my orange and feign innocence.

I tried to plan everything through in my head. How I was going to drop it, how much I was going to drop, and what I was going to say afterwards. I had to do it now or it would be too late, and I would miss my chance. Doing exactly what Ana wanted me to do, I managed to 'drop' some food. Even before I went to the Priory, I had a thing with leaving food. It formed a large part of my anorexia and, each time I ate something, I had to leave some in my bowl. I would leave a little bit one day, then more the next day, and even more the day afterwards. So, this cycle continues until you end up leaving more than what you eat. I was surprised with how easy it was to get away with and it spurred Ana on. I disposed of the orange segments in the bin as we navigated our way round the hospital. We managed to find the right department with relative ease, and I had my echocardiogram. It was about half an hour and they listened to an ultrasound of my heart. I lay on my back, the HCA in the corner of the room, as the probe took pictures through my chest wall.

I felt highly embarrassed, and it all seemed completely unnecessary to me. A slight overreaction to a small irregularity that had been picked up. My heart was fine, I didn't need any of this. Did I? Thankfully, no irregularities were picked up this time and I was given the all-clear, but others will not be as lucky as me. I may have dodged a bullet there, but I was not so lucky in other areas.

***

I had noticed that my faeces had become increasingly darker. Almost unnoticeable at first, they had darkened over time and now were a runnier consistency. The colour had also changed, going from a medium brown to a tar like black. They emitted a foul-smelling stench, but I didn't pay too much attention to this. I downplayed it, putting it down to my laxatives or lack of iron due to restricting my diet. My bloods were being checked every week and I was a human pin cushion. For a while, I had been feeling increasingly tired and weak, but I put that down to exhaustion and over-exercising.

It was a Thursday in early August, and the day started off just like any other. I had just finished supervision after breakfast, and I returned to my room to continue running. I had resorted to going into my bathroom where I would take my top off and run on a folded-up towel on the floor. With music playing from my phone, I would listen out for staff checking, and lie to them by saying I was on the toilet. They wouldn't ask me to open the door if they thought I was in the middle of a wee. This didn't work, would you believe it. I remember when day staff were doing their checks and they asked me to open the door. They thought I had spent too long on the toilet so, with flushed cheeks and quickened breaths, I slipped on my top and threw the towel over my bath hoping to put them off the scent. They had with them a pulse oximeter and they put it on my finger. My heart rate was 120bpm. They had caught me red-handed. I tried to deny it and said I was constipated and straining, that's why I had an elevated heart rate, but they weren't having any of it. But even though I had been caught out, Ana stubbornly refused to rest.

It was early afternoon when I heard a sharp knock on my door. As soon as I heard this, I stopped what I was doing and acted with lightning speed. The toilet seat was already up so I chucked my top on and sat down, grabbing my phone to turn the timer off. It was the ward doctor. I flushed the toilet, washed my hands (had to keep up pretences) and opened the door. My heart leapt into my mouth and my first thought was that I was in serious trouble over my running. The ward doctor hardly ever makes visits to the patient's room, so I automatically assumed something bad had, or was going to, happen. I braced myself for what I was about to hear, but nothing could have prepared me for what came next. She had just come off the phone from Southampton general saying that my HB (haemo-globin) levels had dropped dramatically. They had been over one hundred, but they were now down to just forty-three. She wanted to urgently do a repeat blood test to make sure there hadn't been a mistake, but I was told it looked like an internal bleed from somewhere. Words failed me. I was bleeding? I might have to go to the general hospital. What had caused this? Was I going to die?

All these thoughts rushed around in my mind, bumping into each other and making a racket. When asked if I had any symptoms, I revealed my black stools and told her how they had quickly darkened. Once more, I was asked whether I had been exercising. I bit my lip. I didn't have a choice. I had to tell the truth. I had put my life at risk, so I had to tell them. They knew I was exercising; they were just waiting for me to admit it. Tears spilled from my eyes as I revealed the extent of my exercise addiction. I nervously asked if it was my running that had caused the bleeding? It was a high possibility. Nothing could be for certain though until I had a repeat blood test. Another needle was injected into my arm and was sent urgently to the lab. The results were expected back later that evening. I didn't know what to do with myself. Since entering the Priory, I hadn't spoken to a single person outside of my mum and dad. I hadn't been outside. I didn't even have my curtains open. I had no idea if it was cold or warm, dry or wet, sunny or windy. Detaching myself from the outside world, I couldn't face something I couldn't be a part of. It was a stark reminder that the world was carrying on whilst I was being left behind. Life had very much come to a halt for me, but for everyone else, it was continuing as normal.

I couldn't comprehend the fact that my exercise had potentially caused internal bleeding. I didn't understand how something praised for being so good for you, could cause such damage. It serves as a brutal reminder that too much of anything is harmful. Too much water can be bad for you. Too much salad isn't healthy. Too much running is dangerous. Dangerous for both body and soul. I was asked if I wanted my parents contacted but I decided against it. I didn't see the point of them worrying unnecessarily when I wasn't sure what was happening. Best not to tell them anything until I knew for certain what was going on. Despite the fact I had just been told that my running had potentially caused bleeding, as soon as the doctor left my room, I returned straight to my running. There was no point in trying to read or distract myself, because no distraction was strong enough to transport me out of my own head. Reading a book or watching TV just wasn't going to cut it. My mind was furiously whirring away as my inner dialogue intensified.

Steph: 'I might have to go to the general hospital. How could this have happened? I thought I was past all of this. I didn't think anything bad would happen to me.'

Inner Critic: 'You are so pathetic. Why is it that everyone else can exercise and diet normally, yet you are unable to? EVERYONE can exercise in moderation, except you. EVERYONE can get the right balance, except you. You will never be normal.'

Anorexia: 'This is good! If you have caused damage, it means you have done at least something right. If you're going to show your allegiance to me then you need to start having more going wrong with you. It might be a mistake and the result might be different. You better hope it's not.'

Steph: 'I don't want any of this!'

Anorexia: 'Look, the likelihood of the bleeding being down to me is very slim, okay? Most of your blood results up till now have been relatively okay, things might have been a bit iffy, but nothing too bad. All you need to do is keep running and everything will be fine. I promise you. Don't you trust me anymore?'

No! No, I don't trust you, you're a sneaky, filthy, lying, bastard. Ana never told me the truth, not once. She made sure the only thing that I was being fed was her lies.

***

Dinner time approached and I still hadn't received the results, so a cloud of doubt was hanging over me and made a trying situation even more difficult. Never, in a million years, did I ever anticipate me having a complete meltdown over half a portion of a jacket potato and beans. That was my dinner for the day, and the prospect of having all those carbs was enough to make me cry.

It wasn't even a full jacket potato. It was half a potato with half a can of beans. This isn't enough food to sustain a child, let alone a young woman. I kept getting told off for putting my knife and fork down after every mouthful. This only made it harder to keep going and every time I placed my cutlery down, it took great effort to pick them up again. All I wanted to do was run away and stop eating. If this is what recovery meant, I would rather not do it. It was causing me so much pain to have to go through this inner torment six times a day. I needed a break from everything, but recovery always requires you to be on your toes. I cannot emphasise the sneakiness of eating disorders. They are constantly trying to find a way to worm their way back into your life and, if you're not careful, it is all too easy to slip back into old habits. You will start off having skimmed milk instead of semi-skimmed, then it will be low fat yoghurts instead of full fat. Then you'll be cutting out puddings and snacks and, before you know it, you are firmly in the grasp of your eating disorder once more.

It was near the end of evening supervision when an HCA called me outside. They had my results from the second test back. My bloods were now forty-two, so they had dropped even more. They were calling an ambulance for me and I would be going straight to the general hospital. My parents were mentioned but I struggled to concentrate on what was being said. The anorexic side of me was thrilled that I finally had something wrong with me. Starving myself and exercising crazy hours had finally paid off. The real side of me, the Steph in all of this, was mortified. I couldn't fathom how running, which is something loads of people do, had caused bleeding. They asked if I wanted to be the one who told my parents, but I said I felt unable to face them. I couldn't bear to hear their voices break when they realised their little girl was more ill than they thought. I already felt like I was carrying the weight of the world on my shoulders, I couldn't face the guilt of knowing the hell I had put my parents through. The living nightmare that my anorexia had created. Words were spoken but I can't remember any more of the conversation. My mind had completely shut down and I returned to my bedroom, my eyes brimming with tears.

I sat down on my bed and just sobbed uncontrollably for a solid half hour. When I finally managed to compose myself, I began to pack. My head hurt from crying so much and my cheeks were blotted with tear stains. I pulled a bag from the top of my wardrobe and began to pack. It didn't take me long to choose a few possessions and, making sure I also had my phone charger, I did the only thing I could do – and that was exercise. I knew the ambulance had been called and my parents notified, so there was nothing more I could do. It was now a waiting game. I found my inner critic hating on me for having an ambulance. There were people out there dying, people who were struggling to breathe or seriously injured, yet I was given an ambulance. There was nothing wrong with my legs. I could breathe on my own, I wasn't dying. I certainly didn't need an ambulance. Ana encouraged me to walk all the way or, if that failed, I could get a taxi – why send an ambulance when other people were so much more deserving of help? I had done this to myself. It was all on me. It wasn't until after evening snack that the ambulance arrived.

***

I quickly put on some shoes, picked up my bag, and followed the HCA (who was on a night shift) out of my room. Signing out of the ward, I came face to face with two paramedics who were waiting for me in the corridor. I kept my head bowed, too ashamed to look at their faces. They shouldn't be here. They should be out there helping people who deserve it, not wasting their time on fools like me. The bag was taken off me by the HCA as I followed them downstairs and into the car park. The ambulance had pulled up outside the front of the building and I could feel my cheeks flush with embarrassment as they helped me into the back. I wasn't on a hospital bed or anything like that, I just sat on a chair, the HCA behind me. Riding in an ambulance sounds quite dramatic but it really wasn't. There were no flashing lights or anything like that, no speeding or running red lights. It was a quiet drive to the hospital. It was dark outside, and the roads were deserted, so it took us a little over fifteen minutes to arrive at A&E. They pulled up outside the main entrance and helped me down from the back. I was taken into an almost deserted waiting room where they sat me down on a chair and checked my vitals. My blood pressure and pulse were measured as well as my temperature. This is not how I envisioned my day to turn out. This is not what I pictured life to be like after graduating from university. Any dreams I had were no more than figments of my imagination as I sat in silence, trying to close my eyes and get some respite. Doctors and nurses were talking, equipment was buzzing, and I desired nothing more than sleep.

We weren't waiting for too long when we were taken to AMU (the acute medical unit). My phone was buzzing so I reluctantly answered it. I heard my dad's anxious voice. He was clearly in a state of panic and I was grateful that I could not see his face. That I could not see his hurt expression, or the lines of worry creased in his forehead. He was desperately trying to find out if I had already been transferred to the general. With a heavy heart, I told him I had just arrived and was being moved to AMU. He told me he loved me and promised me he would be by my side soon. I was absolutely shattered, and, as I made my way to the ward, I found myself struggling to keep up. We weren't even walking that quickly, but all the energy had been sapped from me and it wasn't until I was discharged from hospital that I realised just how awful I had been feeling. I had put it down to mental exhaustion, but it shocked me how much clearer my head felt when I had my blood transfusion. For so long, I had been used to feeling like complete and utter crap without realising it. It had become normal for me and I didn't realise it was possible to not feel tired and weakened. I had felt as though my head was wrapped in cotton wool and I thought that would be for the rest of my life. That I would never be able to function properly or think clearly and I resigned myself to the fact that I deserved this. My head was a complete mess as I sat in bed. There was too much noise. Medical equipment was endlessly bleeping, people were snoring and talking…I tried in vain to blot it all out, but Ana's fiery abuse only added to the racket in my mind.

AMU is an incredibly hectic ward. Doctors and nurses work tirelessly around the clock, and there's never a dull moment. I was taken to a bed directly opposite the nurse's station and, for most of the night, I had various people popping in and out, trying to do blood tests and insert a canula. My veins were not playing ball after being prodded and poked for such a long time. Multiple nurses and a doctor tried to stick a needle into my arm, so I ended up with several nasty bruises. Eventually, they managed to find a vein that didn't collapse. My blood was taken, and they also inserted a canula in the crook of my elbow. Drifting in and out of sleep, I vaguely remember someone shouting in the early hours of the morning. The lights around the ward were dimmed and, apart from the staff, most of the patients had fallen asleep. It must have been just after midnight when I heard someone shouting. It was so out of the blue and unexpected, and I couldn't help but give a wry smile. A woman, I am not sure how old she was as I couldn't see her, shouted 'get off me! I'm not a lesbian, I don't want people thinking we're together!' I might not have caught sight of her but I sure as hell heard her. The whole ward did. As I looked up from my hospital bed, I caught my dad and the HCA sharing a slight grin. In grim moments such as this, you really learn to appreciate the value of smiling. It is so easy to become despondent in hospital, to give up all hope and cave into the demands of your illness. You lose hope and, for me, I lost faith in myself and my own ability to live a happy life. I was quite willing to just give in. Tired of fighting and being belittled by Ana and my inner critic, death seemed a welcoming option. But my family didn't let Ana win. They kept me fighting and, without them, I really don't know where I would be today. I owe them more than they can ever know. I must have managed to get some sleep because the next thing I remember is my dad telling me he had to go home. It was 5a.m. Promising either him or mum would be back soon, he kissed me goodbye, and I waved him away, sadness written all over my face. I was in a lonely place and, even though I constantly had a member of staff with me, I felt completely isolated, like no one understood the pain I was going through. That's what mental health does. It's good at that. It's good at making you feel weak and that you should be able to cope. If you were a better, stronger person, you wouldn't be so vulnerable, and you could get on top of life rather than life getting on top of you. They're the lies and twisted truths your head tricks you into believing. I believed I was a useless twat. I had nothing wrong with me. I had all my limbs and all my faculties, yet I was miserable. There are so many people in life who have good reason to be sad, but me, what reason did I have? What fucking reason did I have to be so fucking miserable all the fucking time?

***

Throughout my time in the general, I did not have a single minute to myself. I would have an HCA stay with me during the day, from about 8 a.m. till 8 p.m. I would then have another person, normally agency, supervising me during the night. Even when I went to the toilet or to brush my teeth, I was accompanied by a member of staff. Constantly in their line of vision, even whilst I slept. I felt so claustrophobic and frustrated. Not only did I have doctors and nurses watching me, but I was also being supervised like a little child. I understand why I was on a 1:1. Eating disorders will use whatever means necessary to take back control. The temptation to run on the spot when I was brushing my teeth or doing star jumps when I went to the toilet were high but, with a member of staff outside the door, I was unable to do this. Ana physically couldn't do anything. Unable to fight back, I let the doctors try and 'fix' me. I was given two blood transfusions to replace the large amount I had lost and they each took about three hours.

I think they expected my stay in AMU to be short, but I stayed there for nearly a week. Nothing mattered to me at all, everything just seemed so pointless. I feel it is important to stress how dedicated hospital staff are. The jobs people do are amazing, from the doctors to nurses to porters. Everyone has a role to play, and they are all important and valued. They do truly incredible work and they save lives. They give people the most important gift they possibly can – they give people a second chance at life. They give hope to families. Not everyone will get their happy ending, but lots will. We can dwell on the negatives or we can try and focus on the positives, however small or inconsequential they may seem. For physical health, hospitals are amazing. However, there is a lack of understanding about mental health. Blood transfusions, plasters, operations... none of it can fix the problems of my mind.

One thing really stands out to me during my stay in AMU. Even though it said on my medical notes I had a diagnosis of anorexia nervosa, doctors and nurses didn't seem to be aware of this. When someone came to check my blood pressure with a cuff, he made the comment 'my God, your arms are skinny.' Uhm... excuse me? What the hell? This cannot be justified in any way. You wouldn't say to someone 'oh my god, your arms are so chunky' so why is it okay to say mine are skinny? I was incredibly self-conscious of my arms and was aware they looked like twigs. I hated wearing short sleeved tops because it showed my arms, and I was disgusted and ashamed for people to see them. I had to have a child's cuff because the adult one was simply too big. As I have already mentioned, eating disorders are not about vanity. They are not about looking good but about feeling good. Feeling like you are in control. You might not have a handle on anything in life, but you have some control in seeing the number on the scales keep going down and down. That's what keeps your eating disorder alive and kicking. Again, this fuels the fire that it is okay to lose weight, but not to gain weight. It is okay to be skinny, but you can't have fat. You can see someone's ribs, but you can't have rolls of skin protecting your organs and keeping you alive. Imagine wearing jeans. When you bend over, they naturally crease. You don't think your jeans are too big or ugly, it is just the way it is. It's the same with your stomach. Even when I was at my lowest weight, I still had rolls in my stomach whenever I bent down. It is natural. It is normal.

***

Catastrophising is not helpful in any situation, least of all when you are in hospital and things are completely out of your control. Seeing a plate full of food broke me and I was consumed by fear and hatred. I saw all food as 'poison' and thought that people were attacking me and making me suffer because that was what I deserved. I thought people got twisted pleasure from seeing me so steeped in misery. Being on a hospital ward did nothing to ease my anxiety and, whilst I don't remember exactly what happened whilst I was admitted, I know one thing for certain. I can't go back there. I may have pulled through once, but I don't know if I have the strength in me to go through it all over again. The horror and panic and alarm I felt at the whole situation. Wanting something to go wrong with me but, at the same time, wanting to be fine and feeling like I was wasting a bed in hospital. Taking up yet more space than I was worthy of.

Ana latches on to anything she can that gives her a sense of power. With me, one of the things she used against me was timings. All my meals had to run like clockwork and if things were late, even by five minutes, the panic inside me would increase tenfold. For a person with a healthy relationship with food and their body this is not an issue. For me, however, it was a disaster. A monumental cock up of the highest order. I was used to having breakfast at 8:30 a.m. At the Priory, that had become the new normal for me and it was something that provided me with a certain sense of safety. At least if these timings were adhered to, then all my food would be spread out evenly and it wouldn't be too close to my next snack or meal-time. At the hospital, rather understandably, timings can't be stuck to. The rigidity of my mealtimes was broken in an instant.

At the Priory, we would do the meal plan a week in advance. We would have three options for the cooked meal and then a sandwich list for lunch. These meal plans were on a four-week rota, so I was able to stick with the same 'safe' meals and I didn't really challenge my eating disorder throughout my whole inpatient admission. Well, I had no choice but to challenge myself here. I had no idea what the portions were like. I was still on half portion for dinner so what would I do? I didn't know how my meals were prepared. If they were too high in calories. If they were 'healthy' My mind went into overdrive.

Anorexia: 'Lazy bitch! Not only are you eating way too much food, but you're also sitting on your fucking arse all day doing NOTHING! Your weight is going to skyrocket, and it'll be your own fault. Stupid twat!'

Steph: 'I don't have a choice. Listen, I am constantly with a member of staff. I have doctors and nurses checking on me every couple of hours. Even if I wanted to, I couldn't exercise. It's physically impossible for me to do it.'

Inner Critic: 'If you were strong, you would find ways to do it anyway. You wouldn't give up just because things got hard. See, this just shows how pathetic you are. You're letting people walk all over you. Oh, you know I always tell you how you're shit at everything? Well, I've just thought of something you are good at. Being a doormat. Having people trample all over you.'

Anorexia: 'FATTY! Lose some weight yeah.'

I could never win against these formidable forces. I wanted

to run away from my problems and bury my head in the sand, but that was the problem. I couldn't bear this. You would think your brain wants to protect you. That it wants your survival more than anything else, but Ana corrupts everything she touches. She can turn even the greenest of leaves into dust. Nothing is too much for her. Nothing is enough for her. Ana made me believe the food was poison when really it was her. She's the poisonous, sadistic, arsehole. She knows no bounds and you will never be a slave to a crueller mistress.

***

Being in AMU meant that I couldn't run away from my thoughts. My coping mechanism, which I know was destructive, was no longer available to me and, without it, I felt lost and even more afraid of the thoughts I would be left alone with. All that time to ruminate on my anorexic thoughts. Because I also had three snack times in addition to my meals, staff had to bring with them some supplies. I had ensure bottles, cereal bars, digestives, yoghurts, and peppermint tea bags brought in. Thankfully, we were able to store all the supplies in the fridge after explaining to one of the nurses the situation. The HCA I was with was able to go and get the food I needed with no real issue, and the staff were very accommodating. Strangely, breakfast was one of the most difficult meals for me at the hospital. I thought it would be the cooked meal, but it was surprisingly breakfast. At the Priory, I used the same cup to measure out my cereal and I always used the same small bowl. My fruit, a green apple, was cut into segments and my 150ml of semi-skimmed milk was measured out for me by staff. I knew exactly which cereal I would have every day – bran flakes – and the fact I was measuring everything out gave me a certain sense of security. Most people just pour cereal and milk into a bowl and stop when they feel like they've got enough. I do not know what counts as enough, what counts as too little. What is the 'right' amount? We got some very perplexed looks as we asked staff for an extra mug and exactly 150ml of semi-skimmed milk. We also asked for an apple but that wasn't available for breakfast. This meant whoever I was with had to make a quick dash to the shops to pick up some fruit; and Ana would then dictate that I cut it up into small segments. Being in hospital meant that I couldn't use my usual apple cutter, so it was onto plan B - a butter knife. Not the best tool to use, but I was forced to improvise.

I was able to choose bran flakes (much to Ana's relief) and we used a mug as a measuring tool. The fact it appeared larger than my usual cup didn't help. Was I going to gain yet more weight? How could I get away with less food? Maybe I could try and trick the staff? It sounds such a silly thing to fear, but large mouthfuls scared me. Everything had to be cut up into tiny pieces and a habit I developed in hospital was the desire to eat foods separately. I feared enjoying food more than I *should*. Food should just about be palatable but not tasty. If food tasted nice and I savoured the taste of combining different flavours, then I wouldn't be able to stop myself from eating. I would just continue to shovel filth into my mouth. Ana made me think I had no self-control and could never get the right balance.

Ana also made me wait. Breakfast arrived at 8 a.m. but I just left the food on the table, unable to even look at it. I refused to touch it until it was precisely 8:30 a.m. and not a minute before. The curtains around my bed had to be completely drawn, shutting me away from the rest of the ward. I wouldn't allow anyone to see me eat, even my family. I had tears streaming down my face as I kept saying 'I can't eat all of this food. I'm going to gain so much weight. This is disgusting, I'm disgusting, and this is more food than I should be having.' Once again, I catastrophised everything, believing that I was eating more food than I would have at the Priory and this would lead to a ridiculous spike in my weight. I didn't deserve so much fucking food. Just leave me alone and let me waste away. I don't know how I managed to finish the meal. I remember having nurses come in through the curtains to give me medication and check my vitals. As soon as I saw the curtain even move slightly, I would put my food down and stop eating. No one could see me like this. It took me about forty-five minutes to have a bowl of cereal and an apple and I can't explain to you the sheer feeling of disgust I felt after this. I was stuck in bed all day every day for goodness knows how long. I was shovelling food down my mouth every couple of hours. I was having blood transfusions and I was afraid that would cause me to gain more weight. I was afraid of blood. Of blood making me heavier and making me look less ill. Yes, I know you are all reading this and thinking I am totally bonkers, and I can't deny it. It is bonkers. The whole thing is mad and makes about as much sense as a chocolate teapot. But it was real in my head. Distorted as it may be, I had no concept of reality and I interpreted my own perceptions as real. Ana was the only person who had the guts to be honest with me. Even I wasn't truthful. I was a liar and a fool, a cheat and waste of time. The only person who said things how they were was Ana and I had to look 'anorexic'. I had to fit into people's preconceived ideas over what it means to have an eating disorder.

***

My mum came to visit me after breakfast. She got there before nine o'clock, but I told her to wait elsewhere in the hospital because I was still eating. She was a complete star and I feel so guilty for doing this to them. Who tells their parents they can't visit them because they're eating? Who doesn't even want their family to see them drinking? Ana, that's who. When my mum saw me, she cried and held me like she was holding me for the very last time. I wanted to hurt myself, but I never wanted to hurt those closest to me. After I had finished breakfast, my mum was by my side and the doctor came and spoke to me. I was told that I clearly had an internal bleed from somewhere. They would continue with the blood transfusions and then do a repeat blood test to be sure that my HB levels had risen sufficiently. I was then told I would need an endoscopy to investigate the bleeding further.

My mum revealed to me that they had told my Aunt and Uncle I was in hospital. I was furious. How dare they go against my wishes and tell people about my condition. They didn't HAVE to know. No one needed to know what was happening to me. There was no reason to worry, and I didn't want to be a burden to people. They had been asking after me but when I was admitted to the general, they decided they couldn't hide it any longer. They were so worried about me. So worried about the impact this was having on my internal organs. They were afraid of losing me and that's a hard thing for a daughter to admit. They thought I was going to die. As soon as my Aunt and Uncle found out, they drove straight back to Southampton. They were currently on holiday up in Bamburgh, but they came down as soon as they heard the news. They had asked to see me in hospital, and I felt like I couldn't refuse. They had clearly been concerned about me because they cut their holiday short. They drove home the same day my dad told them about my condition. They didn't wait, or just speak to me over the phone. They felt they had to visit me in person, maybe to assure themselves that I was going to be okay. To support my parents and comfort them when they were so anxious and afraid for me.

Reluctantly, I agreed to see them. Ana wanted me to refuse but, looking into my mum's worried face, I felt unable to argue. Seeing her eyes brimming with tears, her pain was so evident. I had to see them. If not for my sake, then for the sake of my parents. I was supposed to have anorexia. I was supposed to be sick yet, whenever I looked at my reflection, I saw nothing but fat. Fat everywhere I looked, fat everywhere I touched, fat on every part of my body. It hurt to sit down for too long because my bones weren't properly protected, but that didn't matter. I saw anorexia as a badge. A medal. And I was not worthy of that title. How could someone with so much fat and so much colour to their cheeks be anorexic? How could I be anorexic when by BMI could be a lot lower? How could I be anorexic and still be alive? How could I call myself anorexic when I haven't suffered for long enough? I didn't know what it meant to have an eating disorder.

BOLLOCKS! Absolute fucking bollocks! I do have an eating disorder. I am still very much trapped in a mental prison. The time span is irrelevant, it's the amount of pain you are in that matters. It's how much you are hurting both physically and mentally that counts. It's about thoughts, not time. I do not know what thoughts were rushing around my Uncle's mind

170

when he saw me. I do not know how my Aunt felt when she saw me hooked up to a blood bag. I can only assume they felt fearful. They felt sad that I had put my body through so much shit. That I had put my parents through so much hardship. The shock that I had got so bad in such a short period of time. The last time they had seen me I looked okay. I had still lost a significant amount of weight at that point and was still very much anorexic, but it was much easier to hide back then. It is scary how quickly you can deteriorate in such a short space of time. In the span of six months, I had gone from eating with my family to being given blood transfusions in hospital for internal bleeding. The HCA I was with left when my family arrived, and we had a few moments of privacy together. Well, as much privacy as you can have on a hospital ward. My parents left me alone with my Aunt and Uncle for a bit. I was so nervous my stomach was tightening into knots. What was I supposed to say to them? What if we had nothing to say and we would just stand there in total silence for goodness knows how long?

Turns out I needn't have worried. It was, dare I say it, nice to see them. It proved my inner critic wrong and was the first step in me realising that people do care about me.

I have no idea what we spoke about. I think we kept things light-hearted and avoided talking about my condition, which I appreciated. My head wouldn't give me a break, I didn't need other people to interrogate me further. They asked me if I was still reading a lot? I fell out of love with books for several years due to my illness, but I was slowly beginning to win back that love.

***

It was about 12:30 p.m. and my lunch, a ham sandwich on brown bread, was brought to me by catering staff. The HCA returned and I awkwardly asked my family if they could leave whilst I had my lunch. I didn't want them to see me struggle and cry over a bloody sandwich. Thankfully, they were very understanding, and agreed to leave, saying that they were hungry and needed to get some lunch anyway. They promised to come back and visit me after lunch though. I always had a yoghurt and piece of fruit with my sandwich, so the HCA grabbed one of the labelled yoghurts we had placed in the fridge and I had a green apple. I opened my sandwich which was cut into quarters, and I could feel the panic rising. I began to take apart my sandwich. I needed to see how much margarine they had used. How much ham they had used? In addition to this, I also had to have Tim's Dairy yoghurts. It had to be this brand. They were the ones supplied to the Priory, so therefore they were the only one's Ana permitted me to have. I didn't want to eat all this food. In hospital most people lose weight, yet I was convinced I would gain lots of weight.

I didn't want to see other people eat food I could only dream about. I know hospital food is grim, but I craved things like pasta and cheese, and seeing other people eat these foods was too painful for me. Why did they deserve it? Why could they eat it and not gain weight yet, if I had it, my weight would rocket? Ana is good at spinning lies. She could easily say that the world was going to explode, and I would believe her. She could tell me to jump from a cliff and I wouldn't hesitate to obey. I kissed her feet and carried out all her fantasies and instructions. No matter how much I was hurting, I had to carry on and follow that voice. I was disgusted with myself, and I wanted to throw my sandwich up against the wall so I wouldn't have to eat it. Ham had quickly become my 'safe' filling. It was just ham. There was no other 'extra' added in, no sauces to make it taste richer, it was plain and simple. It was what I was entitled to, no more, no less.

When I finally finished everything, including my post-meal drink, I didn't have to wait long for my family to make a reappearance. My Aunt and Uncle were carrying something in their hands. It was a brand-new kindle. I was so touched by the gift I couldn't stop thanking them. Before I knew it, it was time for them to leave and I bid goodbye to the one thing that connected me with normal life. The rest of the day passed by slowly, eased only using my Kindle. In preparation of my endoscopy, I had to fast for six hours. FUCKING FUCK! FUCK! FUCK! FUCK! Whilst no one particularly enjoys fasting, it generally won't have too much of an impact on someone's state of mind. They would just fast for the time required and then go back to eating normally afterwards, giving it little to no thought. I wish the same could be said for me.

I was so caught up in Ana. My time in AMU was hellish and I was fed up with having a member of staff watch over me day and night. I didn't want to talk to anyone. I didn't want to eat. I didn't want any of this. When dinner came around that night, I ordered an omelette and peas, and I had to get the HCA to half the portion for me. Even though I knew they had taken off the correct amount, because I had no way of proving it, Ana twisted it to make me think they were working against me. She made me believe that they were purposefully making me eat more than I 'should be.' She made me believe they were doing it to spite me and were laughing about how stupid and gullible

I was behind my back. Dinner came at around half five and I spent about twenty-five minutes refusing to even take the lid off it because it wasn't the 'right' time. When I was eventually coerced into eating (I couldn't wait any longer and my food was already stone cold,) I began to make a start on my dinner.

Two little sachets of salt and pepper were provided with the meal, but I put them to one side. Do you like salt and pepper on your food? Or other flavourings or spices? Most people do. Most people add flavour to things to make food taste nicer and make the experience more enjoyable. For me, however, I couldn't face food tasting nice. I didn't want food to be disgusting, but I did want it to be as bland as possible so I wouldn't be tempted to over-indulge. I know condiments don't have any calories but, in my head, they did. If I gave into temptation and added salt to my food, then my weight would shoot up and I might end up liking the food. I'm supposed to be anorexic. I'm supposed to not like food and barely eat anything. One thing I have really noticed about me is that I have incredibly harsh rules surrounding my eating disorder. There is no flexibility where Ana is concerned, and I want to give you an insight into just how cruel and unforgiving her demands were.

I had to stick to all my food times religiously. I could not deviate from this at all, even if my hunger were insatiable.

If I gave into temptation and ate food earlier than I was supposed to, I would be weak and greedy.

I had to have green apples. No other fruit was permitted (even red apples.)

I had to have water with my main meals, and weak squash with my post-meal drinks. Too much squash meant too many extra calories.

I had to struggle with every meal and be one of the last ones to finish.

I had to break down over my cooked meal every day or I was a failed anorexic.

I had to resist treatment and not gain weight to prove my worth and to prove to myself that I needed professional help.

I was not allowed salt or pepper on any meal because it might make food taste nicer and, as an anorexic, I am not supposed to enjoy food.

I had to have brown bread (no white or seeded bread was allowed.)

I wasn't allowed rice or pasta because that wasn't a balanced meal and would be too calorific. Where were the vegetables, or salad?

I couldn't add any 'extra' items of salad to my sandwiches. I had to have plain fillings.

I had to have the raspberry yoghurt because it had the fewest calories.

I had to have plain digestives for my snack instead of hobnobs because it meant I could save a few extra calories.

I had to have hot milk with nothing added to it (like Horlicks or Nesquik) because it was completely unnecessary and too indulgent.

I had to prove that I was anorexic, so I had to struggle and rely on ensure sometimes.

I wasn't allowed cheese of any kind.

It is strange because other people can have anorexia and still eat. Other people can still be anorexic and add condiments to their food. Other people can be anorexic and finish their food quickly. The only person who couldn't do any of those things was me. I was the one to impose all those restrictions on myself. I cannot fathom out why I am so self-critical. It baffles me to this day why I must abide by such stringent rules, but no one else needs to. My inner critic is certainly a powerful force, and I find it incredibly difficult to ignore its torrent of abuse. When I was eating my omelette, I had my anorexic voice telling me off for being a failed anorexic, and my inner critic was calling me a revolting pig. With the support of the HCA, I managed to finish my measly half-portion, followed by a raspberry yoghurt, and afterwards I tried to do some reading on my new kindle. I was terrified about the endoscopy. It wasn't the procedure that worried me, but the fasting.

***

Night-time came and went, and the catering staff came around asking patients what they wanted for breakfast. It hadn't been written down anywhere that I was supposed to be nil by mouth, and I assumed, because they were offering me breakfast, that I was allowed it, and I could just have my operation later. Turns out, this was not the case. I was due to have the endoscopy that day but, because I had eaten breakfast, it was postponed. It was rescheduled for the following morning but because I wasn't an emergency, they couldn't guarantee a time slot for me. If there were emergencies, mine would be postponed as I was not a priority. I totally accept that I was quite low down on the list, but this poses a huge problem for Ana as she thrives off certainty.

I ended up having the procedure at half four in the afternoon, and I was a moody cow the whole day. When my mum came and visited me, I snapped at her. I told her I didn't want the endoscopy as I was convinced that they wouldn't find the bleed and it would all be a waste of everyone's valuable time and effort. I shouted at her saying she had no idea what I was going through so had no right to tell me how I should be feeling. Who the hell was she to tell me that everything was going to be alright? She didn't understand that Ana was hurting me for my own good.

I had sent my mum away. I was being so rude and unreasonable, I don't blame her for going, she had every right to. There was no excuse for my behaviour, and I felt wracked with guilt afterwards. Even though Ana was my abuser, she hoodwinked me into thinking that everyone around me was dangerous. That they were out to kill me and the only person on my side was Ana. She was my only friend. She was the only one who understood me.

It was about fifteen minutes after my mum had left, and I was wheeled away to have my endoscopy. The next thing I remember is waking up in the recovery room with an HCA sitting beside me. The sedative I had been given was beginning to wear off, but I still felt a little drowsy. I was told that the camera didn't pick anything up and there was no tear or sign of internal bleeding. It was frustrating more than anything else. I needn't have gone through all that fasting and mental torture. I was angry that I was going through so much and still had no answers. I was annoyed that the doctors had wasted their time and equipment on me when other patients were in actual need of help. I was so fed up. Fed up with being in hospital. I hadn't washed or showered for days, I hadn't changed my clothes, I hadn't slept properly, and I didn't have a single second to myself. Life could just do one. In my pit of despair, I didn't want to carry on. I wasn't even worried that I could continue to have internal bleeding.

I don't know quite how to explain it to you, but I just knew that this wasn't the only time I would end up in the general. I am aware that sounds strange, and you are probably sat there reading this thinking 'what is this girl on about?' but I just knew.

***

I was discharged from hospital a few days later, and I distinctly remember feeling on edge. It was 12:15 p.m. That meant I had only half an hour to leave, get to the Priory, and change my clothes. I only had half an hour until I *must* eat my lunch. There wasn't enough time to do everything Ana demanded. As panic surged within me, I exited the general and had to shield my eyes in the blazing heat of the sun. This was the first time I had been outside in three months and I was eager to retreat into the darkness of my anorexia. The Priory had arranged for a taxi to pick us up but there was no sign of my getaway vehicle. We had rung them about twenty minutes ago, so where the hell was our transport? The HCA I was with had just recently started, and I became increasingly agitated. I could sense her nervousness and that only served to make me more anxious. I kept asking her to ring back the taxi firm to check. Were we in the wrong place? Would they be able to reach us because of the construction work?

I even asked if we could have a walk around the building to see if it had pulled up elsewhere outside the hospital. Eating disorders find tiny loopholes and openings and, as soon as they find your weakness, they manipulate you and hit you where it really hurts. Ana saw this as a chance to get in those extra steps. If I could walk around the building and up and down the car park, I could pretend to just be keeping an eye out for the taxi. All those extra calories I could burn, all those steps I could take – it was too good an opportunity to miss. Ana sees herself as a genius – I see her as more of an obnoxious self-centred twat - but in her eyes she can do no wrong. She is untouchable, indestructible, and immune. Nothing or no one can even touch her.

SHE IS AN ABSOLUTE FUCKING BITCH. I HATE YOU ANA! I BLOODY HATE YOU AND ALL THE LIES THAT YOU ALL TOO EASILY WEAVE! I HATE MY BODY BECAUSE YOU HAVE MADE ME FEEL LIKE I DON'T DESERVE TO TAKE UP SPACE! YOU FILTHY LITTLE BASTARD... I HATE YOU WITH EVERY FIBRE OF MY BEING. I DESPISE YOU. I LOATHE YOU. I WISH YOU WOULD DIE!

But I have come to the stark realisation that I don't need to die. I don't need to be alone anymore. It is Ana who needs to go an die in a hole, all alone. I don't need to be shut off from the world, Ana does. I don't need to be trapped in a hellhole, Ana does. Ana needs me to survive, but I don't need Ana. I can't live with her; I might be able to exist for a time with her talking over me at every opportunity she gets. But I won't be able to live with her because, quite simply, she won't let me. How can I be me? How can I live, and I mean properly live, whilst being tied up in a cage all the time? How can I live with my mouth taped up and my body being moved like a puppet on a string? HOW CAN I DO THIS? Screw Ana and screw barely making it through each day. I don't need laxatives. I don't need my eating disorder. It brings me no joy or happiness, or satisfaction. It brings me only pain. I have spent years in a state of silent pain, and I have finally found my voice. I have ripped off the layers of tape Ana has applied over my mouth for so many years. I AM FUCKING DONE! But I am not done with living.

***

My head was in a spin, and time was still ticking by. My life may have stopped, but life carries on around you. Whilst you put your life and dreams on hold because of this stupid godforsaken illness, the world still moves on. People still get up and go to work, winter changes to spring, changes to summer, changes to autumn. The years roll by and people grow up. You might be trapped in the body of a child and the mental prison of your eating disorder, but just because it stops for you, that does not mean it stops for everyone else. That's the cruellest thing about being ill. What life did I have to look forward to? Why be stuck in such a torturous cycle of self-hatred and self-destruction when the beauty of the world is passing you by? What was the point of it all? Just because I don't see a point does not mean there isn't one. Just because I couldn't see the light does not mean there was no light to find. Just because I was bitter did not mean the world was bitter towards me. It really is all about perception, and I can only hope that one day my perceptions will change. That your perceptions may shift after reading this book. I need to learn how to live with an eating disorder, I need to adapt to a different way of life. A life where I am in control and can say the word 'no.' It is such a loaded and poignant word, 'no' and it is a word that seems to have skipped the dictionary for eating disorders. Ana does not know the meaning of the word, but I do. It means I have had enough of being treated like filth on the bottom of your shoe. It means I am not going to be your slave anymore. It means I break free from your chains. It means goodbye... and good riddance.

It had just gone twelve thirty and I was close to having a full-blown meltdown when a taxi suddenly pulled up. My ticket out of here had finally arrived. Grabbing my bags, I jumped in the back as quickly as I was able to. As soon as we arrived at the Priory. I rushed up the stairs to my ward, taking them two at a time. Opening the door, I was greeted by all the girls who were waiting in the lounge ready to be called in for lunch. I was still on a 1:1, so I was accompanied to my room where I just had enough time to dump all my bags. Before I had time to calm myself down, I was hurried along to the dining room to eat my lunch. It was a Sunday which meant that the cooked (main) meal would be in the middle of the day. What used to be one of my all-time favourite meals, had now become a plate of horrors. I had strived to avoid these foods for months, and now I had no choice but to bite the bullet and swallow the fear. Literally swallow the fear. Roast potatoes, gravy, meat... it all felt so wrong. So 'impure' and 'dirty.' Why have all this disgusting poison when you can have a bowl of salad instead? Why waste all these calories on such filth?

***

After another torturous mealtime, I was allowed out of super-vision so I could finally have a proper shower. Having a shower with someone watching you is unnerving to say the least. I may have been scrubbing my body clean, but I felt dirty inside. I felt like I had put on ten pounds over the past five days, and I couldn't stand it. How could I possibly be expected to gain yet more weight? It didn't take me long to shower. I wanted to be naked for as little time as possible. When I got out and wrapped a towel around myself, I refused to look at my reflection. My body was grotesque, and I didn't want to be reminded of how horrible I was, inside and out. (Note to self: I did not see what other people saw, only what Ana wanted me to see.) I chucked some clothes on, not caring how I looked or if they even matched, I just needed to cover myself up. I hated being on a 1:1, and I remained supervised for a few days after being discharged from AMU. Whenever I went to sleep at night, I had to have my door propped open and my lamp on so that staff could see me clearly. One night I turned over on my side a couple of times, trying to get comfortable. All the rooms were kept at temperatures of around twenty-two to twenty-three degrees, and I was feeling increasingly hot and sweaty under the covers. The night staff who was with me at the time told me to stop moving, thinking, perhaps, that I was trying to do some extra exercise and burn off calories. This was not the case however, and I felt incredibly hacked off.

I felt like I couldn't move a muscle. I was too afraid to turn over in case they accused me of trying to over-exercise. I couldn't get dressed without being watched and I distinctly remember when a member of staff refused to look away whilst I was undressing. They had to keep me in their line of vision apparently, but every staff member who was with me responded differently. Some would give me a bit more privacy and let me shut the bathroom door slightly when I went to the toilet, others would always want me to be in their direct line of sight. I cannot stand the sight of my own body and to have another person watching me when I was at my most vulnerable, was one of the hardest things I have ever had to endure. I felt disconnected from my body, disconnected from everyone and everything. When I went to get my medication, I was followed. When I went to have my MARSI's done, I was followed. When I went to go to the kitchen, I was followed. Followed everywhere I went, there was no alone time, no moments respite. If my head wasn't hurling abuse at me, I had to contend with talking to staff and sometimes I really didn't want to talk. Sometimes I wanted to be silent, and just be far away from everyone. I just wanted to be left alone so no one could see how broken I was.

***

Every day I would beg staff to take me off 1:1. After several painful days, I was finally granted some freedom. This meant one thing: it was time to ramp up my exercise and make up for lost time. Ana was verbally bashing me, and I had no choice but to ignore my sore body. It was time to get back on my feet and run. Back and forth, back and forth. It was time to jump on the spot. Up and down, up and down. It was time to count every single second I spent exercising. It was time to do tally charts of the number of star jumps I completed. It was time to make up for all the valuable seconds I had wasted being holed up in a hospital bed and on a 1:1. I had a lot of catching up to do.

The next time my parents visited me, they had some big news. My brother was coming home from China. At first, Ana jumped in with her thoughts. What if he thought I was faking it? Last time I had seen him, I had looked well, and I was still eating 'normal' foods. What if he thought I wasn't ill? What if he realised how much of a freak I was? I had tried so hard to shield him from this. I felt like a burden and I didn't want him to worry about me when there was nothing he could do. I wanted him to enjoy his year in China, and not think about his stupid little sister. However, all secrets come out eventually. We had a tradition where, every week, we would video call my brother. Since entering the Priory, I was, of course, unable to partake in our weekly chats anymore, and I had made my parents tell him some lie about why I wasn't there. He was getting more and more suspicious; my parents were getting more fraught with worry. He had to know the truth. We had hidden it for long enough, they couldn't keep up pretences any longer.

They had told Darian that I was ill. They had told him I was in the hospital and he was already on a flight back to England. He would be arriving at Heathrow airport the following day. I couldn't believe what I was hearing. My brother, my wonderful, amazing brother, was coming back. He was coming back to see me. I immediately felt guilty. The voice of my inner critic was gnawing away at me, having a go at me for being a burden and worrying people unnecessarily. I thought it was my fault that he was cutting short his time abroad, and I was the reason he was spending all that money on a flight home. How selfish was I? How stupid was I? He was in China living his best life, and I had to be my stupid self and ruin everything, just like I always manage to mess everything up. I'm such a crap sister. I'm an even worse daughter. I've let everyone down yet again. I'm a disgrace. Let me just stop you right there, inner critic – I'm going to but in for once. You always but in when I don't want you to, so now I think it's my turn, don't you? I am NOT a disgrace. I am NOT a burden. My brother wanted to be there for me, I wasn't forcing him to do anything. He was choosing to come and see me because he loved me. I may find that hard to accept but I know it's the truth. I know that he never once saw me as a waste of space. I was… am… his little sister and he wanted to be there for me and support me during this difficult time. That's what families do for each other, and it wasn't my fault I was ill.

***

I will never forget when my brother came to the Priory the following day. The last time I had seen him was in November 2018 when I waved him goodbye at the airport. I was so terrified of him seeing me. I could feel my heart rate increasing as I tried to take deep breaths to steady my nerves. Ana and my inner critic bombarded me with what if's.

What if he hates me for not telling him earlier?

What if he thinks this is all my fault and I caused myself to have an eating disorder?

What if he realises that I'm an attention seeker?

What if he sees how goddamn fat I really am?

What if he wonders why I'm in hospital, taking up a precious bed when I am clearly TOTALLY FINE?

What if I don't know how to respond to his arrival? What if I don't want to talk to him?

What if I've lost my brother for good?

Ana, being the selfish twat that she is, made me only think

about myself. I was thinking about how scared I was feeling. How guilty I was feeling. How stupid I was feeling. How fearful I was. I did not spend a single thought on what it might be like for my brother.

He hadn't seen me in nearly a year. I imagine he was out of his mind with worry, having only heard horror stories from my parents of me having blood transfusions and being hospitalised. Throughout the depths of my illness, I never spared a thought on anyone else. I never thought how this was affecting my family. How this was affecting my friends. You don't realise that in abusing yourself, you are also abusing others. You become so self-absorbed and seeped in self-loath-ing that you almost blot out all other people. You see them as mere inconveniences, nothing more. But they are far more than you realise. They feel more than you give them credit for. They love you more than you can imagine. I remember the first time I laid eyes on my brother. He looked well. More than that, he looked genuinely happy. He had a glint in his eye, rosy cheeks, and a slightly awkward smile. I was grey, pallid, and gormless. A far cry from my usual self. The first thing he did was give me a massive hug and I held onto him for dear life. All the fears that had circulated my mind for days instantly evaporated and I felt safe in his embrace. I couldn't stop more tears (I really was like a bloody waterfall) as we clung to each other. Eventually we broke apart and he sat on my bed and presented me with a special gift. A gift that I carry around with me to this day, and it will forever serve as a reminder of the bonds we have as siblings. The precious relationship between sister and brother... that bond is unbreakable, and it becomes all too easy to forget how special family are. How much they really mean to you. His gift reminds me of that love.

I have asked my brother to write down some of what was going through his head during this difficult time. I want to show you that it not just the sufferer who is affected by this disease. I know I went through hell and back last year, but I am fully aware that it was just as challenging for my family and friends. They must have been just as scared as I was, just as lost and hopeless. Just as helpless to do anything. I couldn't fight Ana, but they couldn't save Steph. They were power-less to stop me from self-destructing. They didn't know if this disease would kill me. Imagine the person in life that you love the most. Imagine them living in a constant bubble of hatred and torture. Imagine them slowly killing themselves whilst you can do nothing but stand by and watch. You can't save the one person who means more to you than anything else in this world. You can't be there for them because they don't let you in. You can't help them or hold them or soothe them. You can't protect them. There is nothing you can do to help. Now imagine how painful that must be. Whilst I was in that bubble of hatred, I was numb to most things. I couldn't feel because I was starving my body and mind of essential fuel. (Note to self: next time you are offered a piece of cake, fucking eat it. It tastes nice and your body will thank you for it!) Whilst I was in a starved state, my family were not. I want to show you the illness through the eyes of others. Through the eyes of those that know me most. To show you how cruel and evil and unrelenting this illness is. Below, is what my brother said about seeing me for the first time in a year:

'When I was told of your illness, I was horrified and shocked. I

had my head in my hands and I couldn't sleep for worrying about you. My flight back was an anxious one and travelling to the Priory was even more nerve-wracking. I had heard all the horror stories from mum and dad, but I couldn't quite process it. Seeing you was a shock. I had never expected to see a morose, virtual stranger shuffling around a foreign hospital room. Hugging you was the biggest shock. You didn't feel like Stephanie. I felt like I was embracing someone completely unknown and that almost brought me to tears. To see my sister like this. To see no glimmer of mischief in your eyes, to see no cheeky smile on your lips. It was a stranger's face looking back at me and it shocked me to the core.'

It hurts. Reading this, writing this, it hurts. It fills me with a sadness I don't think I will ever fully be rid of. I had no idea of the impact this was having on my brother. He was in China. Well, he was supposed to be in China but, instead, he was sat in my room staring into the eyes of a stranger. When we broke apart from our hug, he presented me with a small golden bag. In it was a box and two small red pouches, complete with golden silk threaded through in an ornate pattern. There was a small golden box underneath the pouches, but I opened the pouches first, tracing the pattern with my thumb and admiring the beauty of it. Inside, were two jade bracelets. There was a jade disc surrounded by two beads either side and it was all threaded through a red string. I instantly fell in love with them and slipped them onto my bony wrists. I then picked opened the box. Inside was a beautiful jade pendant, once more on a red string adorned with coloured beads. It was light green in colour and the pendant had a carving on it. In the Chinese zodiac calendar, I was born in the year of the Ox, so my brother had picked a design with my own zodiac symbol engraved on it. I put down the necklace and hugged my brother once more, squeezing him tight and thanking him for such beautiful gifts.

When my brother explained the special symbolism behind them, my love and appreciation for them increased tenfold. Jade is a treasured gemstone in China, it is a precious stone that supposedly has healing powers. It is believed that when the jade touches the flesh, it will protect you from any evil, disaster, or illness. It will suck evil forces out of your body and stop them from entering. It is believed to have properties of purity, longevity, and nourishment. But most importantly perhaps, it is believed to open your heart to love. My heart had been enclosed in the darkness of Ana. It was in her death-like grip, entrenched in her ideals and unable to move into the light. I was filled with hatred. Hatred of life, of food, of myself. Hatred of everything. I had no room for love. I had nothing or no one to love, I was unable to see or appreciate the good things in life. Whilst I am not remotely superstitious, I do believe in the power of the mind. If you believe in something strong enough, then you can make almost anything happen. Since I was given the jade, I have slowly but surely taken positive steps forward in my recovery and I do believe that my jade has something to do with it. From a psychological point of view, I do think it has helped. It has given me a sense of hope, a sense of protection. It healed my relationship with my brother and made me realise how amazing he is. How amazing my family are. It is not only my jade that is a precious gem, but my family too.

The red string is supposed to bring you good luck and I always wear it around my neck. Every day when I put it on, I am reminded that I am still fighting. I am still alive, and, like a stubborn old ox, I am not going to be beaten. I had been so scared about seeing him, yet now he was here, I didn't want him to go. I wanted him to stay with me but all too soon our time came to an end. They had to leave whilst I had my last snack of the day. He promised me he would see me again soon and I apologised for ruining his time in China. He said I wasn't ruining anything, that he loved me and was going to be there for me. He wanted to come and visit. No one forced him to come home, it had been his own decision. To be honest, I think he needed to. For his own peace of mind, he needed to see what I was like for himself. I can try my best to explain to you the state I was in, but no words will ever accurately describe how dead I was inside. How grey I looked. How miserable I was. It is something you need to see with your own eyes to believe just how harrowing this illness can be.

***

Fast forward a couple of days, and 210,000 star jumps later, my stools began to go dark again. Oh no, here we go again! After I had been to the toilet, I left the toilet unflushed and went to get a member of staff. I was told by the ward doctor to keep a close eye on my stools and to notify them immediately if I experienced any changes. I could feel my palms going sweaty as I knocked on the office door and waited for an HCA to come. I nervously explained about my stools, and they accompanied me back to my room to check for themselves. My heart dropped as they agreed with me that the colour wasn't normal, and they went to inform the ward doctor.

I was taken straight to the clinic room where I was told to lie on my side, with my trousers rolled halfway down my legs. I was covered with paper towels and examined. Although she couldn't see any bright red blood, she could tell that my stools were still very dark, which was indicative of internal bleeding. Once more, I had my blood taken, although this time it was an emergency. My arms were still bruised from my last stay in AMU, but she eventually managed to find a vein that didn't collapse in my wrist. She sent them off to be tested at the general immediately and I was told I would hear back around mid-afternoon. Returning to my room, I picked up my phone, went onto stopwatch, and ran. The same words circulated my head as I battled to stay focused on exercising.

'FAT! STUPID! DUMB! CUNT! BITCH! PATHETIC! TWAT!'

Every hour that passed was torturous. My body was scream-ing out in pain. My mind was on full throttle, hurling insults at me left, right, and centre. Running, eating, supervision... that was all I did. Not only was I counting down the minutes of exercise I was doing, but I was also counting down the hours till my results came through. Getting through each meal was already a herculean feat, and my fear of going back to the general only added to my misery. It was just after my after-noon snack when I had my results. My bloods had dropped again. The taxi had already been booked. I broke down on hearing this, and I remember saying 'no, I can't. I can't go back to the general. I can't go through all of that again. Can't I just stay here, and you can monitor me?' I was practically on bended knees, pleading with them. I couldn't go through all of that again. I couldn't have more tests and go through more unknown meals. My life was already a big pile of shit, and I was close to breaking point. Even though I wanted my bloods to go haywire, I didn't want to go to the general. Hell, I didn't even want to be in the Priory. I wanted to be six feet under.

***

After I had been told I was going back to AMU, I sat on my bed and made the difficult call to my parents. I half hoped that they wouldn't pick up the phone, that I could just leave them a voicemail so I couldn't hear the pain in their voices. My dad picked up on the third ring. I wanted to keep the conversation as brief as possible, and I wanted to minimise the amount of hurt they had to go through. Ana had the complete opposite thought to me and wanted everyone around me to be in pain. She wanted every part of my life to be stooped in misery and angst. She wanted to cause harm to me and those around me. And she very nearly succeeded in finishing me off. I don't think my parents could go through that again. I don't know if I would have the strength to fight it again. It literally takes up all you time and energy, recovery really is a full-time job, and you can never lift your foot off the pedal, not even for a moment.

'Do you want to die?'

Those words should never be spoken by any parent. I am still haunted by the fact that they thought I was going to die. That they thought I wanted to kill myself and, to an extent, I did. I did want to end things. I am so angry that I put my parents through hell. They raised me up. They fed me when I was hungry, bathed me when I was a baby, looked after me when I was poorly, supported me through university. And they were now terrified of losing me. That should never, ever, have happened. I will never forgive myself for putting them through that. The sleepless nights I must have given them, the hours they spent worrying or crying, the number of times they came up to visit me because I was so distraught. They would have given their lives to save mine, but I just didn't care. The sad thing is I would put myself through the pain all over again, I would punish and beat myself up, but I would not hurt my family again. The problem is you can't separate the two, and I found that out the hard way.

The two are intertwined. I can't harm myself without harming others. I can't shield others from my pain because they care about me and want to be there for me and help me. I can't single myself out and think that what I do to myself won't have any consequences. I can't fall into the trap of thinking that the world would be better off without me. I was eager to put the phone down. I didn't want to talk to anyone, let alone have such a tough conversation with my parents. I knew their hearts were breaking and I didn't want to acknowledge that it was my doing. That I was the one who had thrown their lives into chaos.

I don't know how I managed to finish the conversation with my parents without crumbling into a pool of tears. I said I didn't know when I would be back the general, but it wouldn't be long, and I would let them know as soon as I arrived so they could come and visit. I desperately didn't want them to see me. I was in an absolute state and the last thing I wanted was my parents to see their daughter lying in a hospital bed. I had a canula inserted into my vein to save my veins from being prodded more than necessary, and as soon as I had showered and packed my bags, the taxi had arrived. Off I went for round two.

***

Even though I was going to the general, I was more concerned about dinner. I should have been worrying about bleeding internally, but instead I was scared about not being able to exercise. My priorities were fucked up! This time, instead of going straight to AMU, I was sent to the major trauma unit. Once there, I was taken straight to a bed where I had my blood taken and I was also subjected to another ECG. I messaged my parents to let them know where I was, and it wasn't long until they joined me. I felt so ashamed to be back at the general. No one else has internal bleeding caused by exercising. Why can't I be normal? Why do things have to affect me differently? Why am I so weak? Why can't dinner always be served at 6pm? Why is everything so up in the air?

After explaining to nurses my situation, they were able to provide me with a hot meal around my usual dinner time. It was roast chicken. There were several thoughts racing about in my mind at this point. The first one was oh shit! This chicken is roasted. Couldn't it have been boiled instead? My second thought was why is it covered in so much gravy? So unnecessary! My third was why do I have to have potatoes? Can't I just have chicken and veg instead? I don't need carbs... I'm not exactly doing any strenuous activity to warrant so many calories. Right, okay, let me break it down for you.

YOU NEED CALORIES TO SURVIVE! YOU NEED TO EAT!

It really is as simple as that. Even if you are sedentary, you still need to feed your body and mind. You need to eat more food than you might initially assume. I'll tell you what you don't have to do though. You don't need to run a marathon to have a bowl of spaghetti. You don't need to work out every week to have a sandwich. You don't need to go to the gym every day to have a bar of chocolate. I am not saying having spaghetti for every single meal of the day. I am not telling you to eat chocolate for every meal and snack, but everything in moderation. You have one life, and each day is precious. You won't get those years back. Food is a given right and does NOT have to be earned. You deserve to eat what you want when you want. You deserve to enjoy meals. You deserve to enjoy your life. I happen to enjoy pizza. That means I am going to eat pizza (eventually, I'm still working on that one). I am not going to deprive my body of delicious foods anymore. I need to treat my body in the same way I would treat anybody else. With love, kindness, and compassion. With pizza, spaghetti and burgers, but also with vegetables, salad, pulses, and fruit. With a bit of everything.

You know the game of Simon says? Well, this is a game of Ana says.

Anorexia: 'You can't have a roast dinner. It's got too much gravy and is bad for you.'

Steph: 'Yes, of course.'

Anorexia: 'You're fat and ugly and disgusting. You need to run to burn off all these calories.'

Steph: 'Whatever you say, Ana.'

Anorexia: 'Everyone thinks you're a greedy, attention seeking pig. Everyone hates you.'

Steph: 'I know.'

Anorexia: 'You need to stop eating. It's fucking vile… you're just going to pile on the pounds, and you already take up more space than you are worth.'

Steph: 'Yes Ana.'

I say 'yes' to everything Ana says. No matter how ridiculous or dangerous it is, I agree with her. She tells me I don't deserve anything. I say okay. She tells me people would be better off without me. I say you're right. You get the picture. Unfortunately, it is easy to believe Ana's lies. It is easy to believe her because she ensures that no one else can be the voice of reason. She makes sure you isolate yourself from anyone who might question her. She makes out that everyone but her is out to destroy you. If all you hear are Ana's words, then you can't help but believe them, because you have nobody saying anything different. You have nothing else to go on.

When I finished my meal, I called my parents in and they stayed with me for several hours. I needed to go to the toilet. Even though I had my parents and brother with me, the HCA still accompanied me into the cubicle. I was an adult, and I couldn't even be trusted to go to the bathroom by myself. I had no privacy, whether I was getting changed or going to the toilet, there was always someone in the room with me. As I sat down on the toilet seat, I held my head in my hands, trying to mask my embarrassment and shame.

Inner Critic: 'You're such a loser. You went from university to this... God you're a disgrace. Having someone watch you go to the toilet... I mean c'mon, this is a joke.'

The only loser here is Ana. I am not going to be made to feel a failure. Yes, I went to university. Yes, I was hospitalised for six months. Yes, I had internal bleeding. Yes, I had someone supervising me twenty-four seven, but does that mean I am weak? No, it does not. Going through an eating disorder just makes me stronger. I can just add it to the list of things I have faced... and conquered. It doesn't have to destroy me. It doesn't have to break me. It can make me. I was so anxious to be out of

196

there, I quickly flushed the toilet and washed my hands. I was too embarrassed to look my parents straight in the eye when I waved them goodbye.

As they walked into the lightness, I went further into the darkness. I made my way back to the familiar surroundings of AMU and I drifted into an uneasy sleep. I spent nearly two nights there before I was transferred to yet another ward. I really was making my way around the hospital!

***

My bloods had not dropped as drastically as before, but I still had abnormally low levels. I was given two iron transfusions and was also told that I needed to have another endoscopy to see if they missed anything. Ana had been cursing at me non-stop, and I went through all of that for nothing. They were still no closer to finding out what had caused my internal bleeding. If it's even possible, I would say that this hospital admission was even more tumultuous than the first. My mood was all over the place and I felt like a ticking bomb about to explode at any moment. I felt totally unstable and completely exposed. The results of my second endoscopy once more came back as inconclusive. What were we supposed to do now? Well, it was between a colonoscopy and a capsule endoscopy. This is the less invasive procedure where a capsule is ingested and then travels down the digestive tract, taking pictures along the way. It was decided that I would have the capsule endoscopy. Before the procedure, I was expected to fast for twelve hours. I was also given moviprep to drink, which is a type of laxative.

It was a grim experience. At one point, I refused to have any more because it was making me feel so sick. Thankfully, I was given the capsule in the early morning so most of the twelve hours of fasting occurred during the night. Several adhesive patches were placed on my abdomen and I was given a special belt to wear. It was quite a thick, black belt and it was wrapped tightly around my waist. I had to keep this on for most of the day and I was given the capsule to swallow. Before I could do this, however, I had to hold each end between my thumb and forefinger until it started flashing. It was then ready, and I swallowed it down with a gulp of water. I had to wait two hours after taking the capsule to have any clear fluids. This meant I was able to have a clear broth for lunch and some orange jelly. I could also have squash so long as it wasn't red in colour. This is because any red foods or liquids could have been picked up as blood by the camera.

After around eight hours of wearing the contraption, I was finally able to take the belt off. I was told that it would take some time for them to process the pictures, but they should have the results in the next few days. I did not hold out much hope for the results shedding any light on the issue. Pushing those negatives thoughts down, I tried to turn my attention to something else. As I no longer had to have clear fluids, I was able to have dinner. You might think that this would horrify me, and to an extent, it did. But, in a strange way, I was also relieved. Relieved that structure could finally be resumed.

After dinner, I went to the toilet. I was finally able to go into the bathroom alone. Normally, the HCA I was with would stand outside the bathroom door but because my hospital bed was literally opposite the toilet, they didn't always follow me. The laxatives I had been given caused extremely runny stools and anything that comes in one way must come out the other. I looked down into the toilet bowl and saw the capsule, still flashing away. It had passed through my system and naturally had come out in my faeces. I raised my head up and was confronted by my reflection in a full-length mirror. When I had finished on the toilet, I washed my hands and, staring at my reflection, I started to do star-jumps. I then took my top off so I could examine my 'fatness' and ran on the spot, using my phone as a timer. I only did this for a couple of minutes because I knew I had to get back to my bed soon or risk arousing suspicion from staff. But I was determined to keep doing this every time I went to the toilet or to brush my teeth. A minute of exercise was better than nothing, and I had to do something when I was sitting in bed all day.

The following morning, the results of my capsule endoscopy were back. Can you guess the results? Bingo! They came back inconclusive and showed no obvious sign of bleeding. Fanbloodytastic! I was told that the only other thing they could do was a colonoscopy, but they wanted to schedule an outpatient appointment for me. I wouldn't have the procedure for at least another two weeks. I was so done. I was done with being stuck in hospital, done with eating all the time, done with being prodded and poked and tested. I was done. Whilst I sat in bed, confronted only by Ana's hatred and abuse, the ward manager came to see me. His visit coincided with my parents coming, and I remember him asking me how I was. It's a normal thing to do. It is normal for people to ask how a person is when they see them, but I was frustrated and angry. I was fed up with being asked if I was okay all the time. No, I wasn't okay. I was about as far from okay as it was possible to be. I was at the bottom of a deep, dark, pit. He asked me how I was finding things, and I could barely conceal my burning anger. There had been several issues, which my parents brought up to the ward manager.

One of the main issues I had was the need to be eating with others. I can never eat by myself. Other people must be eating with me and, preferably, they must be consuming more food than me too. At the Priory, I always sat with a member of staff during mealtimes but, in hospital, this changed. There were several occasions were staff had not eaten with me, and I found that hard. Every single body has different energy requirements. No two people have the same metabolism, or the same food requirement. It is futile to compare because you don't know what other people are doing when they are not with you. It doesn't matter how inactive you are, you STILL NEED TO EAT! If you have an active lifestyle that means you NEED TO EAT MORE! Whatever you do, or whatever you don't do, food is still needed.

I remember there were a couple to mornings where I had asked the HCA I was with if they could have breakfast with me, but they said no. They said they had already eaten, or they weren't hungry. Well, guess what? I wasn't flipping hungry either! I didn't want all this food shovelled down my mouth, but I was doing it anyway. I had to clear my plate, not a morsel of food could be left. So, imagine how I felt when staff would leave food or say no because they weren't hungry, or that they would get something to eat later. That messes with Ana. It really screws your head over. I was in such a state, I needed just this one thing. I had nothing else, I just needed someone to eat with me. Was that asking too much? I couldn't walk or run, I couldn't meet my friends, I couldn't get a job, I couldn't sleep in my own bed. I couldn't do anything anymore. I understand that in real life, people are going to leave food, and that is okay. I am not telling you that you always must clear your plate and lick your lids off your yoghurt pots (you may do that anyway,) but I do not expect everyone to always eat everything they are given. What I did expect, however, was that people working with eating disorders would have a bit more sensitivity surrounding the issue. But their lack of knowledge astounded me.

***

There was one lunch time where I couldn't have my usual sandwich because the kitchen had run out. This meant I had to have white bread instead of brown. When the food was brought over, I stared at it for half an hour. I refused to even touch it, I just sat in my bed, with my curtains drawn, crying and squeezing my stress ball. The HCA who was with me at the time did not comfort me or eat with me. We just sat there in stony silence, as I couldn't stem the cascade of tears that were flowing freely down my cheeks. I couldn't have white bread. Not according to Ana

After a ferocious shouting match between Ana and I, I finally began the torturous process of eating it. I didn't get any support during this meal. I will never forget how disgusted I felt with myself for having white bread. How repulsed I was that I was having it a few minutes earlier. I will always remember how I had to get through that alone. There might as well have been no-one sitting with me, there was no conversation throughout the whole meal, there was nothing. Not even a glimmer of empathy.

I know it is difficult for someone who doesn't have an eating disorder to understand the phycological impact it has. To understand how fearful someone is of bread, or whatever other food it might be. From nuts, to potatoes, rice, pasta, cheese, chocolate, banana... they can all be absolutely horrifying to someone suffering with an eating disorder. Each person has different fear foods, and different 'safe' foods and I do understand how difficult it is to comprehend, particularly because there is no one size fits all. My fear food could quite easily be someone else's 'safe' food but that doesn't mean she doesn't have an eating disorder. It doesn't mean I'm a fraud. Ana morphs into different forms, depending on the individual, and it is difficult to track something when it is constantly changing and developing. Eating disorders are constantly evolving. My own eating disorder is different to what it was this time last year. One of my fear foods used to be mashed potato, but that has now morphed into a 'safe' food. But pasta is still a food I am yet to conquer during my recovery. I will do it, but one little step at a time. I will learn to enjoy pasta again. I will. I will. I will.

I really needed some extra support. Having white bread was a huge psychological obstacle for my eating disorder. I was shocked by how little help and compassion I was shown. Another example was when I stormed out of my room and into the corridor during a snack time because I was so distressed. One of the other patients was getting increasingly stressed and was beginning to shout at doctors and nurses. She was saying things like 'I just want to die. Why won't you just let me die?' That did it for me. I was already really struggling eating my yoghurt and that just tipped me over the edge, and I had to get out of there, I felt like I couldn't breathe. I needed space. I felt paralysed and completely closed in. I refused to finish my yoghurt, and they let me get away with not having it. That made Ana jump for joy.

***

I am trying to put my conflicting thoughts on paper to help you understand the mind of just one anorexic. The one thing I have noticed with my eating disorder is that my thoughts are so contradictory.

Example number 1:

I must eat all my food. I don't have a choice. This is my medicine, and I am being made to clean my plate. It is out of my control. I am in hospital in an eating disorder ward, so I must be poorly.

BUT

I just got out of eating a yoghurt. So, I can get out of eating food. If I were a proper anorexic, if I had any allegiance to my eating disorder then I would refuse the food. I am choosing to go against my eating disorder, and that means I can't have an eating disorder.

Example 2:

I'm having internal bleeding issues because I am so underweight and am punishing my body to such extremes. I am anorexic because I wouldn't have a diagnosis if I weren't. I wouldn't be given blood and iron transfusions if there was nothing wrong with me.

BUT

I am still alive. I am still too big and taking up far more space than I am worth. How dare I say I have anorexia when there are people out there genuinely suffering and in pain. What do

I possibly understand about pain? I haven't suffered enough. I am NOT ill enough.

Example 3:

I must have the lowest calorie foods and need to struggle to prove to the world that I deserve my place here. If I enjoy food, or choose the higher calorie option, that will lead to more than the bare minimum weight gain of 0.5kg a week. I can't enjoy food or have a variety. I must stick to the same things.

BUT

I can't recover if I don't challenge my eating disorder. I don't have to struggle all the time. It is okay to make progress, but it doesn't suddenly mean that I don't have anorexia. I can choose foods I enjoy. I don't have to live my life in constant fear of them just to prove that I am not a fraud.

It's so confusing. One part of me is telling to think one way, another part is telling me to think the complete opposite. Who do I listen do? Who is right? I had been telling myself that I had no choice but to eat six times a day. That I had no choice but to clear my plates, have my ensure, complete my snacks. But I had just gotten out of eating a yoghurt. What else could I get away with? How many calories could I cheat? It just keeps spiralling, and I just keep falling further into Ana's embrace. There is no end point with eating disorders. You just keep spiralling. You just stay stuck in a perpetual cycle of self-disgust. You stay trapped in the prison of your mind. I don't think I can even begin to accurately describe the pain of eating disorders. I can't make you realise just how horrific they are, how deadly they are, how evil they are. I wish I could out Ana for the bitch that she is.

***

I was discharged from the general about a day or two later. As soon as I returned to the Priory, I began wondering why I had such an obsessive personality. Why I couldn't exercise without getting the right balance or eat without taking everything to the extreme. I do believe this is one of the reasons I developed an eating disorder. I do not know why I have such an obsessive personality, and it does worry me. It worries me that I will never be able to get the right balance with anything. That I will never be 'normal' or have normal thoughts. I am also a huge perfectionist and I place unrealistic standards on myself. If I don't meet my expectations I feel like a failure. I feel out of control so I resort to my eating disorder as that is something I can control. I am in charge of what enters my lips and how many hours I spend exercising. Of course, I am not in control. Ana is always the one making the decisions for me, but it became my safety net. I felt I was drowning, and waves just kept crashing down on me I couldn't keep swimming. I sunk. Perhaps, it was also because I was so scared of 'doing life' as my therapist has mused? Maybe she's right.

Maybe I was so terrified of being an adult and doing life, of having all the responsibilities that comes with being an adult. I was terrified of failing life and I didn't see the point in trying anymore because I would just end up humiliating myself. There was no point to life because I was destined to 'fuck everything up.' Even my best efforts weren't good enough and everyone was just waiting for me to mess up so they could laugh at me. So, the world could mock my stupidity. Ana twisted this to her advantage and used my perfectionism as a weapon against me. She turned my brain against me, my thoughts and actions were no longer my own.

***

About two weeks after my second general hospital admission, I received the details of my colonoscopy. Sachets of moviprep were sent to the Priory, and quickly taken away from me so I couldn't abuse them. I was just given the moviprep to drink over a period of around two hours. I couldn't drink it quickly because it made me feel so nauseous. It tasted just as disgusting as it did before, but I was made to drink it. I had an HCA sitting in my room watching over me, whilst I tried my best to ignore the raging battle going on inside my head.

Part of my treatment at the Priory was, of course, a specialised meal plan, but in preparation for my colonoscopy, I had to have different foods which caused me to freak out. I thought the endoscopy was bad, but that was a walk in the park compared to this. The preparation was a lot longer. I was given a list of foods I should avoid and foods I should be having, and I went through this with the dietician. Together, we came up with a modified version of my meal plan, but it still caused huge anxiety. A lot of the foods I had to avoid were my 'safe' foods and probably constituted for seventy-five percent of my diet during weight restoration. I wasn't allowed fibrous meats, yoghurts (I had about three yoghurts a day,) jacket potatoes or wholemeal bread. I couldn't have biscuits or dried fruits and nuts. Bran flakes and other high fibre cereals were also off limits, as was butter, margarine, oils, and milk.

Two days before my colonoscopy, I had to make these changes to my diet. My breakfast consisted of bran flakes and a green apple. But not today. I had to have a bowl of rice krispies, no whole fruit allowed. You might be able to randomly pick a cereal, to change it based on your mood or what you are feeling, but I cannot. I must stick to my wholemeal cereal. No excuses, no exceptions. Why have something unhealthy when you can have something healthy? Because you only live once, and life is too short to be counting every single calorie, that's why. Instead of my cereal bars and digestive biscuits I would always have for my snacks, I had to have five rich tea biscuits. It would have been three digestives or hobnobs but, because these had less calories, I had to have more. Ana swore at me for having so many biscuits and for being a revolting piece of shit. I was an absolute disgrace. Everyone was laughing at me, saying that I wasn't anorexic behind my back and that I was making it all up. No one was laughing at me, except for Ana. No one thought I was making it all up, except for Ana. No one thought I was a fraud, except for Ana. You get the gist. Ana was the one who constantly accused me of being fake, she was the one who made me believe that everyone was laughing at me, judging all the food I was shovelling down my greedy mouth. So what? I had five biscuits instead of three. Did the world end? Did my weight skyrocket? Did I get discharged because people thought I was miraculously cured? No. None of those things happened, despite all the catastrophising that my head was doing.

For dinner, I had to have plain fish (it couldn't be coated in breadcrumbs like it normally was.) I could have it with mashed potato, just without the margarine, and mushy cauliflower and carrots. Instead of my usual vanilla ice cream, it was substituted for four scoops of lime sorbet. I felt like I was eating more than everybody else. I would only be having three scoops of ice cream but because this was just a sorbet, I had to have more. How can I be eating so much? I was repulsed with myself, disgusted that I had ploughed through all the food and completed each meal.

***

The feelings of disgust didn't leave me after I had left the kitchen. They stayed with me for the rest of the evening and well into the night. I couldn't get the thought of me stuffing food down my face out of my mind. Not only do you feel worthless and disgusting when you eat the food, you also feel worthless beforehand and afterwards. It doesn't stop when the food stops. The thoughts just keep on coming, faster and faster, louder and louder. My sleep was already disjointed, and I specifically remember that night, getting very little sleep. I couldn't relax, I couldn't switch off my brain. I was worried about the procedure, I was worried about the foods I had eaten, I was worried about my weight going up, I was worried about fasting. I kept tossing and turning, trying with all my might to quell the shouting going on in my head.

I was awoken around 6 a.m. for MARSI's. I say I was woken up, but I was already awake. I dragged myself out of bed, wanting nothing more than to just close my eyes and hide under the covers. Wanting to run away from the world but there is no chance of that happening in an eating disorder unit. You get up, you get dressed, you eat. End of discussion. It was the day before my colonoscopy. I could have breakfast so long as it was finished by 9 a.m. After that, I would only be on clear fluids.

That was the last meal I would be having for at least twenty-four hours. I already felt hungry. How was I going to cope for the whole day? I didn't see the point of having the colonoscopy.

The day ticked by painfully slowly. I was able to go to morning snack where I was given Bovril, and I found myself staring at other people's snacks, wishing I could be back on my proper meal plan. It gave me permission to eat foods. I was prescribed my meal plan, or my medicine, which I had to take.

Thankfully, I didn't have to go into the dreaded door of dorm for lunch or dinner. I had some more Bovril, alongside a glass of squash, in the lounge. As soon as I finished, I was allowed back into my room. I was still under staff observation in my room, but at least I didn't have to contend with being surround by other sick patients.

From 5 p.m. till 9 p.m. I had to have the moviprep and I fell asleep shortly afterwards. I remember getting up several times throughout the night, making a hasty dash to the toilet. It literally poured out of me like water and, even though it was uncomfortable, I knew it was doing its job. The anorexic side of me was also incredibly happy that I was 'cleansing' my body and she started getting excited over how much weight I could potentially lose.

***

My day of my colonoscopy arrived so I got up early, took my medication, and was told to drink several glasses of water. When we arrived at the general, it didn't take long to find where we needed to go, and I made another few, hasty dashes to the toilet as the laxatives continued to do their job. I must have been waiting for about an hour until I was called.

The next thing I remember is coming around in the recovery room. I was eager to get the hell out of there. To get back to the Priory and resume my meal plan. The results came back clear (as I knew they would) and I was free to leave. I was relieved that it was over with but, at the same time, I was peeved. I had endured two general hospital admissions, three endoscopies (including the capsule endoscopy,) and a colonoscopy. And they still couldn't tell me why I was bleeding internally. They still didn't know why my blood count kept going down. I desperately wanted them to tell me exactly what it was. I wanted, no I needed, an answer my problems, but I didn't get what I wanted. I was left with more questions than before. Was it my exercising? How could that even cause bleeding? Was it down to my laxative abuse? Either way, as soon as I returned to the Priory and was taken off a 1:1, I began to run again.

It had been discussed in ward round. I would be taken off constant supervision, but my room would be locked throughout certain intervals during the day. My bathroom was also locked, so I had to ask staff to open it. I tried arguing with them and asked if I could have my door wedged open instead so, when staff were walking down the corridor, they could clearly see into my room. This idea was dismissed however on the basis that all the bedroom doors were fire doors and therefore had to remain closed. I know they were trying to help, but I still wanted Ana to be my best friend. It didn't stop my running addiction; I just made sure I ran extra hard when I was allowed back into my room, to make up for all the lost time. Unsurprisingly, it didn't take long for my bloods to drop again. The third time in about as many months. Back to the general hospital I went, my hopes for a life outside of my eating disorder dwindling by the minute. My belief in myself to recover was blown to smithereens and I really did see no way out. I thought this would be what the rest of my life would look like

– in and out of inpatient treatment and general hospital visits.

***

I arrived in AMU and was quickly transferred to D7 where I spent about two nights. My HB levels had only dropped a little and it didn't warrant me staying in hospital. I was stable and there was nothing they could do for me. They had already carried out all the tests they could on me, so I was discharged quickly. The Priory agreed to monitor me closely, so I was placed back on 1:1 for a few days, but it wasn't a long enough period for me to make any real positive mental steps forward. I remember there was an agency male member of staff who had taken over my supervision for an hour, and he opened my door and pushed his chair up against it. He didn't feel comfortable being in a room with a young girl which I can understand, but I was unable to bite my tongue. I didn't have a go or anything as dramatic as that, but I did express my frustration and exclaimed how ridiculous this all was. I also remember being pissed off because I had been told I couldn't have my door open, yet here they were, opening my door. If it was a fire door as they kept telling me, then it should always be shut. Yet here they were, propping my door open in the middle of the day. I had many angry conversations with staff about this, but to no avail.

I was eventually taken off 1:1, and they tried locking my door at several intervals throughout the day again. They also introduced a new measure. I would randomly have people coming in to check my pulse and heart rate. If it were accelerated, I was told I would be given ensure to make up for lost calories. Despite the threat of ensure, this never actually came to pass. They did catch me out running, but they never took it further and I was never made to have ensure. They just used it as a deterrent, but it wasn't enough to stop me. Everything came to a head on collision when I broke down in front of my mum and dad.

I was sat on my bed, my parents perched on the end when I fell apart and revealed to them that I was still running excessively. I was exhausted; I was desperate for sleep that wasn't dominated by me thinking about how many hours I had to run the following day. I wasn't paying attention to my feelings because I was using exercise as a way of blocking out all my negative thoughts. I couldn't accept how miserable and anxious I was because I didn't give myself any time to stop and think about how I really felt. It was too painful. My foot was on fire, my head was aching, and I felt like I could quite easily pass out at any moment. I didn't know how much longer I could carry on. How many more lies I would have to tell, how many more laps of my room I would have to run, how many excuses I would have to make, how many blisters and sores I would have. Day in and day out I was spending all my time running and eating. I reached a wall. I just couldn't keep it up any longer, I couldn't keep pretending that I was okay and had my running under control. I had nothing under control. I peeled back my sock and revealed to them the ugly-looking blister, which had gone an angry shade of red. They were horrified by what they saw. Horrified that I was able to still exercise to the point of physical injury in a place that was supposed to be safe. In a place where I was supposed to be protected from myself. They quickly arranged to have a meeting with the ward manager and staff charge nurse at the time. The meeting was scheduled for the end of the week, and I was not prepared for the aftermath.

**

The meeting took place in one of the therapy rooms outside of Skylark. It was just the five of us, and we all took our seats. It felt a bit like an interview for a new job, and I kept my gaze down, staring intently at the floor. I didn't want them to see how distressed I was, how ashamed I was, how weak I felt. My parents explained how I was still running in my room, how locking my room at random intervals throughout the day was an easy way out, and not an effective form of treatment. I explained how I was running when staff were checking in on me four times an hour. As soon as I heard a knock, I would act fast, sitting down on either my bed or desk as I tried to appear as unflustered and innocent as possible. I don't think they could quite understand just how extreme my addiction was. How many hours were consumed running, how I only ever stopped to eat and go to sleep. I looked up and said: 'Please help me! I want to stop, but I can't. I don't know how to stop. I can't do it.' I was begging for help.

During that meeting, we were all promised that steps would be taken to ensure I got the mental help I needed. That I got the right type of therapy and that they would deal with my issues, rather than just putting them on hold for a while by putting me on a 1:1. I really thought this would be a turning point for me... that I had turned a corner in my recovery and was going to get help and other coping mechanisms that weren't so self-destructive. We left the meeting feeling like a huge weight had been lifted off our shoulders, and my parents felt a lot more comfortable leaving me alone. They were reassured of my safety and the ward manager had certainly said all the right things. However, I got the shock of my life when I had my next ward round.

I want to emphasise the fact that I asked for help. I BEGGED FOR HELP! I told them I couldn't stop on my own, and I needed serious intervention. I needed help to deal with my thoughts and advice that wasn't 'just sit with your feelings and breathe. Feel the floor beneath your toes... be at one with the chair.' No thanks, I feel the blister under my foot, and pain whenever I stand up. I don't want to be at one with any piece of furniture, thank you very much. I told them meditation and mindfulness weren't suitable for me at this point, but all my concerns were instantly dismissed in favour of their line of argument. And they would not deviate from their preconceived ideas and intentions. So much changed during this ward round. Normally, very few changes would be made but this time was markedly different. I went from having escorted fresh air breaks to unescorted breaks. This meant I could go down to the grounds by myself, without the supervision of a member of staff. I was free to do what I wanted, as no one would be watching me. I was also given two half hour walks a day. Previously, I had not been able to go for any walks, but this had now changed so I could have a total of an hours walk every day. In addition to this, my bathroom door was unlocked, they stopped locking my bedroom, and they put an end to the random pulse checks and ensure supplements. My hourly observations were also dramatically decreased from four down to two. I was speechless.

***

I had just told them I couldn't manage this by myself. Both my parents and I had attended a meeting just a few days ago where we were promised that I would get more support and therapy. That they would deal head on with my running and find ways of addressing it and adopting more useful coping mechanisms. Well, everything that was said in that meeting was a load of bloody bollocks. Nothing they promised us came into fruition. Nothing at all. They did the opposite of what they said, and I left ward round in floods of tears. I tore down the corridor and went straight to my room, where I picked up my phone and rang my dad. I couldn't believe what had just happened. I thought I must be dreaming, and I pinched myself, only to be struck with the realisation that this wasn't the result of my overactive imagination. This was reality. My hands were shaking as the sobs kept coming and I babbled away to my parents, explaining to them what had just happened. They were just as stunned as I was. To say they were angry would be an understatement. They were fuming. They felt let down and betrayed. Heartbroken that everything we had brought up had been completely dismissed and ignored.

I was in pieces. My parents were in bits. It was an awful time for everybody, and when the pull of Ana gets stronger, I need to remind myself of those dark times. I do not want to go back there. I have worked too hard to throw it all away, and I don't know if my family would withstand another inpatient admission. This was the beginning of the end. This marked the first step in the breaking down of the relationship between myself and the Priory. Things only get worse from here on, and the trust between the professionals and I was unsalvageable. We were on the beginning of a slippery slope, and I was about to fall even further down it.

***

A few weeks after this whole debacle, I came down with a bad cold. I had a hacking cough that stubbornly refused to subside. It was as if all the air had been knocked out of me and it was a struggle to just drag myself up out of bed. Most people, when they are feeling poorly, would give themselves a break. They would allow themselves to have a couple of days or weeks off to recuperate. They perhaps wouldn't exercise, and they would give themselves permission to sleep a bit more and just relax. You can probably hazard a guess as to what comes next. Yes, you got it. I didn't show myself any kindness. When I went for my MARSI's I politely asked if I could have some lemsip, but they refused. They said they could give me paracetamol or strepsils but, because lemsip wasn't written in my medical chart and hadn't been prescribed by the ward doctor, I was unable to have it. I ended up being given paracetamol instead. It didn't really do a thing, but I suppose it was better than nothing.

I asked multiple times for lemsip. I asked all the HCAs on shift. I asked the ward doctor when she did my blood test. I asked every member of staff that was in, but it wasn't until around 5pm when I was finally able to have lemsip. They had crossed off paracetamol, so I no longer had that on PRN. PRN is just an abbreviated way of saying when needed. I had my daily medications, but I also had medicines which I could request. I had promethazine (an anti-anxiety tablet) on PRN, so whenever it was approaching a difficult meal, I would request this tablet. It also helped me to sleep at times. My cough persisted for over two weeks. The ward doctor had promised to examine my chest every day, but that never happened. It wasn't until I was on the tail end of my cough, and I was beginning to feel a little better, that she examined me properly.

During my cold, I did not attend any therapy groups. I didn't go for any ward trips or participate in any life skill sessions because I just felt so wretched. Every week, a small group of people (who weren't on the supervised table) would be taken to Tesco so we could learn to pick and prepare our own lunch. This would usually be done on a Monday or Wednesday, and then ward trips would sometimes happen over the weekend. This was provided we had enough staff, which we rarely ever did. Ward trips, for me, were difficult for many different reasons. Predominantly, because I felt I couldn't have anorexia and do 'normal' things. I couldn't enjoy myself or treat myself to new things because that would mean I don't have an eating disorder. The idea of going to a place with people wasn't something that I could even contemplate. Everyone would be watching me and laughing about how fat I was. How I was a fake. So instead of facing my fears, I stayed cooped up in my room. It is odd what we can make our bodies do in extreme circumstances. Our bodies can endure so much, far more than we ever give it credit for.

***

My cough eventually improved, but nothing else did. I was having weekly therapy sessions with my CAT therapist, but they weren't helpful. To make therapy work, both individuals need to feel like they are being listened to and respected. They both need to feel understood and be willing to listen to and accept what the other person says. This was not the case for me. I felt completely misunderstood. She would say things to me like 'you are kidding me, babe?' and 'sorry, I don't mean to laugh, but that sounds ridiculous.' Not things I wanted to hear from anybody, let alone my THERAPIST! I felt she misjudged a lot of her comments, and I didn't feel comfortable talking to her. I dreaded therapy. I would sometimes be close to tears even before my session had even started. She accused me of exercising to the point of physical injury which, okay, was true, but she could have handled a lot better. Whilst none of my sessions with her were particularly helpful or engaging, there was one occasion that really sticks in my mind. I remember it so vividly, even now. It hurts thinking about it, and I wish I could forget what she said, but I have latched onto it, and it affects me to this day.

I was in a terrible state. Some harsh words had been exchanged in the days leading up to this moment, and I had lots of issues that I wanted clarification on. The most important issue was that in my latest ward round, they had threatened to discharge me. Out of the blue, they threatened to discharge me with immediate effect. Apparently, I had made some unhelpful comments to one of the patients, but they wouldn't tell me what it was. I had then spoken to all the girls individually and asked them if I had said anything to upset them. They all reassured me that I had done nothing wrong and were just as baffled as I was. I tried racking my brains to think of what I might have said, but nothing sprang to mind. I always tried to be careful what I said to people and, when I did have slightly heavier conversations, I would make sure I did it with people who I was close to and had a good relationship with. I was driving myself insane trying to figure out what it was I could have said. Trying to figure out if I had upset anyone or said something detrimental to their recovery. But I was drawing blanks wherever I looked. No one was able to shed any light on the matter and, when I did try and ask staff about it, they brushed it under the carpet and wouldn't tell me what it was I had supposedly said. They just told me it was unhelpful and sounded like I was promoting eating disordered behaviours. This made my head spin even more. I would never promote Ana. I hate the bitch. No one deserves to have an eating disorder. I don't care who it is, nobody should have to suffer the consequences of an eating disorder.

When I brought this up with my therapist, her response shocked me to say the least. I had explained that I had asked all the girls if I had said something unhelpful to them, and they all vehemently denied it. They had no reason to lie to me and I like to think I got on well with the other patients. They were all wonderful people; kind and gentle souls who had been a victim of their eating disorder. On voicing my concerns to my therapist, her answer was 'well, maybe they didn't tell you because they're scared of you.' I already have cripplingly low self-esteem, so that came as a huge blow to me. I needed my therapist to pick me up, not push me down. I already thought all the other patients hated me, and this only confirmed my unstable thoughts. I have never thought of myself as an angry or intimidating person. I'm barely over five foot and I have a rather embarrassing tendency of tripping over my own feet a lot of the time, so I am not a scary person. Or, at least, I don't think I am. But this threw me, and made my inner critic laugh out loud and jump straight back up on its high horse.

Inner Critic: 'See, I told you everyone hates you. I only

flipping told you that you're a waste of space and everyone is talking about you behind your back. This just proves I'm right.'

I had no proof this was the case. When I had gone to the general, all the girls had made and signed the most beautiful cards with the sweetest messages written inside. They wouldn't do that if they hated me, would they? I could not believe that my own therapist had knocked me down with such a savage blow. She knew I struggled with what people think of me, and my inner critic was stronger than most. She knew that would hurt me, but she said it regardless. I just wanted to shout at her and storm off. Storm out of the Priory and away from this hellish existence I was being forced to endure. Instead, I stayed rooted to my seat and folded my arms over my chest, holding back yet more tears. This led to another problem. My hunched over demeanour and pained expression made staff think I was angry. I even had to do an anger quiz at one point because they thought I had anger issues. I am not an angry person. I was frustrated and pissed off. I was scared and miserable. But I was not angry. I bottle things up, I hide how I really feel. I would fold my arms over my chest a lot of the time to try and hide my deformed stomach. I would stare into space because I was mentally torturing myself. I would keep my head down because I couldn't bear to see people look at me with pitying eyes. I couldn't bear to see them think I was an attention seeker, and a pathetic little girl. I was already so disappointed in myself, and I didn't want to see other people's disappointment in me.

I left therapy more upset than when I had started it. Once more, I phoned my parents and, through sobs, told them what had just happened. They were horrified. How can this all be happening to me? How can people trying to make me better get it so wrong? Was it a punishment for being me? I was beside myself with fear and worry. I thought they would discharge me, and I had no idea what I was supposed to have done. I have been called many things, but intimidating has never been one of them and it caught me off guard. My parents wanted to hold another meeting with the ward manager to try and change my therapy. I wanted to try CBT (cognitive behavioural therapy) as I didn't feel like delving into my past was helping me. I couldn't change the way I felt, but I could try and focus on changing my behavioural patterns and focusing on a new mindset. Since my first day in July, there had only been two therapists, and one assistant psychologist.

***

When they eventually hired a CBT therapist, I immediately tried to change my therapy. I would write it down for ward round, but it was instantly dismissed. I desperately wanted to try something different and try and approach my anorexia from a behavioural aspect. My parents arranged to have a meeting with the head psychologist and ward doctor. We were told that they would try a two-pronged attack with both CAT and CBT therapy. That they would work hand in hand with each other and be a slightly more intensive treatment than what I was currently receiving.

We left the meeting feeling a little unsure on the outcome. Our previous meeting had appeared to have gone well. All the correct things were said, but nothing came of it. They went against everything they had promised and did the opposite of what we begged them to do. We were worried the same thing would happen again. Our fears were confirmed the following week when I had my ward round.

'Do you find yourself forgetting things?'

That was the question they asked me. I was mortified, and hurriedly replied 'no,' trying my best to reassure not just them, but also myself. They had planted a seed of doubt in my mind, so I was beginning to wonder if I was going crazy. I can sometimes be a bit forgetful, am I more forgetful than I realise? Could I possibly be any weaker? Was I forgetting that I was in fact forgetful? My mind buzzed with so many questions. I couldn't think straight, my head was such a mess. The new therapist then explained to me that the reason they asked this question was because I kept asking for CBT. They kept saying no, and shut down any possible conversation about it, and I was penalised for asking for help. They made me feel completely inept and like I had a memory problem.

I honestly felt betrayed. I had begged them to help me stop running. I had pleaded for CBT. I had cried out for help, and they had just thrown it all back in my face. They had their own ideas, and nothing anyone said would change them. It's almost like they know best and if they can't help you, no one else can. After this incident, I stopped asking for another therapist. What was the point if all they were going to do is penalise me for trying to have a say in my own treatment? Instead, I decided to focus on something else. Moving from progressional table to transitional. It is hard not to compare yourself or feel angry with yourself when you are surrounded by ill people who are progressing much further, and much faster, than you. I couldn't figure out what I was doing wrong. Why was I still only on progressional, yet I was the person who had been there the longest? I asked if I could move up to the transitional table, and it was agreed, on the condition that I have a therapeutic meal with my mum and dad.

A therapeutic meal is where you go to the downstairs kitchen and you eat in front of your family. You are, of course, surrounded by other patients and sometimes staff as well. If they weren't supervising the meal upstairs, most would tend to eat in the dining room, and it was quite a daunting environment. Not in a horrible way, but just because of the nature of eating disorders. I was very secretive about what I ate and where I ate. Here, not only was I confronted by my parents, but I was also confronted by strangers and staff. I was bloody petrified. I decided to have lunch with them first. A sandwich felt a lot more manageable than a cooked meal. I don't know who was more anxious. Me or my parents? The apprehension was palpable as I took them out of Skylark and to the dining room. Thankfully, it wasn't too busy, and we were able to find a quiet round table in the corner. Some of the other tables are a lot longer and can seat around eight or more people around them but, on this table, there was only room for the three of us which eased some of my anxieties. My sandwich was brought to me (I just had to mix up the filling and assemble them) and I went to get my yoghurt and green apple. My heart was racing, and my hands shook with visible nerves as I tried to make my sandwich in front of my parents. They had gone up to the servery and ordered a big plate of food that smelled and looked rather delicious – but terrifying at the same time. I might not have been able to eat the food, but I could at least smell it. The most important thing was that I was eating with my parents for the first time in months.

It was enjoyable. It made me feel normal for a change. No argument broke out and the catastrophising my head had done in advance did not come to light. It never does happen the way my head makes out. We managed to have a civil conversation, share some smiles and some laughs. It felt like we were a proper little family again. Don't get me wrong, it was still a nerve wrecking experience for all of us, but I was glad I had done it. Glad that I was able to manage. Rewind to just a few weeks ago, and this would never have been possible. It would have been nothing but a dream. But I had kicked ass. You hear that, Ana? I was kicking your stupid little ass.

***

After successfully having the therapeutic meal with my parents, I was confident that I would move up to the transitional table. I had done what they had asked, and I had overcome what was a massive hurdle for me. However, I was dealt a cruel blow. When I asked the dietician if I could progress to the next table, I was told I could not. Apparently, it had been reported back to her from members of staff that I had forced my parents to eat an inordinate amount of food. That I had put pressure on them to go back for seconds and have ice cream so that I could eat less than them. I was horrified. I felt disgusted and violated. Were they spying on me? How dare they! Yes, I struggle with people eating less than me, but I did not force my parents to do anything. They *wanted* to go up and have more food. They weren't paying for it and there was a variety of foods on offer which, naturally, they wanted to try. I was then told I had to have another therapeutic lunch with my parents where they eat the same or less than me, and they also added in a therapeutic dinner, just for good measure.

They also changed the goalposts even further. The dietician said that she had phoned my mum to ask about home leave, and apparently my mum had sounded reluctant to let me come home and didn't want me to take longer periods of home leave. They were pushing me for more home leave when I didn't feel ready. I was told I would not be moving up to transitional until these goals had been met. Naturally, I phoned my parents as soon as ward round was over. It was here that I found out the truth. The Priory had not phoned my mum. In fact, she had recently bought a new phone so there was no way she could have spoken to the dietician or anyone else because they wouldn't have had her new number. My mum was livid. They lied to my face about contacting my parents when they had done no such thing. What else were they lying about? What other truths had they covered up? No phone call had been made to the house phone or either of my parent's mobiles. I had done exactly what they wanted. I had completed therapeutic meals with both my parents, and I had done so successfully. I really thought they would reward me for my efforts. We had my CPA meeting coming up soon, so we decided to wait until then. We needed to get to the bottom of things and have reassurance that I was in a safe environment.

***

After the meeting, I was visited in my room by the dietician and occupational therapist. They apologised for the confusion and agreed to move me up to the transitional table from that evening. From here on, everything happened so quickly. I know about a week after moving me to transitional table, they then moved me to the downstairs dining room. After all the hassle I had been through just to move up one table, they were now moving me to a different environment entirely. It didn't make any sense to me. I think it was leading up to Christmas and I was given home leave over the festive period. I was able to spend Christmas eve till the day after boxing day at home with my family. My brother had officially returned from China, so it was to be our first family Christmas together in two years. Normally, I love Christmas. It's one of my favourite times of the year, but this time was different. I was terrified. I didn't know how I would be able to cope at home with all the food and drink. I wouldn't be able to join in with any of the traditional festivities. I couldn't have chocolates or Christmas pudding, or cooked breakfasts. I couldn't have alcohol. Ana stomped her foot down and demanded that I stick rigidly to my meal plan and try and wheedle out of eating some of the meals. If anything, this was a golden opportunity to lose weight.

I thought not being able to exercise would be a bigger challenge for me. But I was surprised by how easy I found it to not run. Okay, let me rephrase that – I felt guilty as hell and I struggled with eating and not being able to burn off the calories – but I knew I didn't have a choice. There was no way on Earth that I would be able to exercise at home. They wouldn't let me out of their sight, and I simply didn't have the space to go running or do star jumps.

I don't remember Christmas day itself. I was too preoccupied with food and exercise and dieting… basically Ana was dominating everything in my life, the selfish cow. The one thing that really sticks in my mind is my evening snack. I had agreed, after prompting from my family and the dietician, to have five small chocolates as a Christmas challenge. I spent the entire day ruminating on this and wondering if I could manage. If there was any way I could get out of doing it. I was awake all night worrying about it. I spent all day dwelling on it. Eventually, the time came, and my parents could instantly tell that something was troubling me.

YEAH! HAVING TO EAT FLAMING CHOCOLATE!

The tears came, my parents pacified me… you know how it goes. Instead of five chocolates, they agreed that I could have two. It took me over an hour to eat them. No, your eyes did not deceive you. You did read that correctly. It took me AN HOUR to eat two pieces of chocolate. I spent most of the time crying, burying my head in the crook of my arms. The overwhelming feeling of self-loathing consumed me, and I kept tugging at my dressing gown belt, as though I was tugging my rolls of fat. The belt represented my disgusting fat rolls. That's the image Ana had conjured up in my mind at any rate. An image that I couldn't shake. She made sure that her distaste for me was known.

Out of the whole day, that is what I remember most about Christmas. How sad is that? I couldn't enjoy the day because I was so anxious about eating chocolate and I was worried about letting my family down. I couldn't properly join in and I was worried that they would be disappointed in me. It was Christmas time, and I couldn't even make the effort of trying to challenge my eating disorder? The thing is, I did challenge my eating disorder. Just by getting out of bed some days I am challenging my eating disorder. By talking to my family and friends I am sticking up my middle finger to Ana. By being home and eating in front of my mum, dad, and brother, I was showing her who's boss. (Note to self: I'm the boss. Steph's the boss.) How can I let them down when I am trying to fight off my demons?

***

I returned to the Priory the day after boxing day. It was a bittersweet goodbye. I think a part of me, the anorexic side, was relieved to be back. I now had to stick to my meal plan, and I knew exactly where I was. The times were like clockwork and I knew exactly what to expect for each meal. The other part of me, the real Steph, was gutted to be back in this prison. I had had enough of everything, and the relationship between myself and staff was irreparable. What was the point of me staying if I was just going to keep exercising and cause myself physical and mental harm? I felt so mentally conflicted, I just craved freedom.

For quite a while now, my stools had been okay, but I noticed they were starting to darken again. I instantly told the ward doctor, and she did another blood test to send off to the general. However, before they even had my results, they made me go to A&E as a precaution. I was not happy about this. Surely, we should wait for the results. Whilst in A&E I was given a sandwich for dinner. Normally, my cooked meal would always be in the evening so a part of me was thrilled that I had got out of having a proper meal.

Anorexia: 'Hahaha! This is brilliant! Think of all the calories you are saving. If you were at the Priory, you would be having a full portion of cooked dinner PLUS a fucking pudding.'

Steph: 'But I'm really hungry. And I've already had a

sandwich for lunch. I don't really fancy another one.'

Anorexia: 'Stop whining. God, you're so annoying. A sandwich is way less than your usual cooked meal. And, even if you have fruit and yoghurt with it, it still has less calories. You should be pleased, this is good. Now, we need to figure out what else you can get away with...'

She really will take any opportunity she can. Any opening or way in she can find, Ana will be there in a heartbeat. She won't give you any chances, she'll take whatever she can whenever she can. I had to eat my food in the waiting room, in front of people.

Finally, I was called over by the doctor. They had got my results back and they were stable. My haemoglobin levels hadn't dropped so I was free to go. Well, that was a waste of time, wasn't it? I was mightily hacked off. I was also anxious about snack time as it was already 9pm and I was due to have my snack. I asked my dad to go and get me a coconut milk latte. I already had my usual cereal bar, so I was just missing the milk. I was able to finish my snack in the waiting room and as soon as I returned to the Priory, I went straight to bed.

I was exhausted from the events of the past few days, and the only thing I could think about was how early I would need to get up in the morning to do my exercise. I was also scared. I knew the Priory felt that it was my time to leave, that there was nothing they could do for me and I think a part of me was worried they were right. What if I was beyond help? What if I wasn't strong enough? What if I was never able to stop exercising? What if I permanently damaged my bowel? When professionals give up on you, it becomes nigh on impossible to have any self-belief, especially when your esteem is already at rock bottom. They thought I was beyond help… maybe I was too far gone? Maybe Ana would never be tamed? I had been unable to stop running. I was still underweight and dependant on laxatives. Yet, they were letting me go. I felt like I was being thrown out to the wolves, and I wasn't prepared for the viciousness of it all. I was shortly given an official discharge date:

January 15, 2020. I knew it would be soon, but I wasn't quite prepared for how sudden it was.

PART THREE:

The Road
To
Recovery

I felt completely unprepared. I couldn't leave the Priory, could I? I wouldn't be able to stick to my meal plan, would I? One of the most terrifying things about leaving hospital was the distinct lack of support. I had spent over half a year confined to the hospital ward. I had been having intensive weekly therapy sessions, and I was acutely aware that I was going from this to nothing. I had no support set up within the community. My life had been dictated by doctors and mental health nurses, and there was no transition process. There was no gradual reduction of treatment. One minute, I was in hospital, having room checks ever hour. The next, I was at home, where Ana could claw back her all-important control.

The day I was told of my discharge is one I am not likely to forget. I had a nurse and the consultant psychiatrist come into my room to break the news. They explained that I was beyond help and, because I had failed to pick up the phone to my case manager, I was clearly not willing to ask for help. They said it was my fault that I didn't have a place at April House and there was no room for negotiation. My date to leave was set in stone. They knew I felt worried about going back to the community and was anxious that I would not be able to maintain my current weight. I already felt so uncomfortable in my foreign body and I was disgusted with myself for reaching this weight. I did not see how I would be able to keep this up at home, when I knew I could get away with more in front of my parents. Ana would play tricks that my parents were not aware of, and I was afraid that it would be easy to hoodwink them.

I think the worry was that, as my parents, they would be too emotionally connected to me. Before entering the Priory, they had trodden on eggshells around me for months, too afraid to rock the boat. They didn't want to risk me flying off the handle and I knew that seeing me in distress would in turn cause them great pain. They didn't deserve that. I wondered if they would be able to be stern with me when they saw the emotional turmoil I was in. I also didn't have any job to go back to. I hadn't seen any of my friends for over six months. I was to go back to nothing... how could they let this happen? I voiced my concerns and they completely dismissed them in favour for their own views. I might as well have stayed quiet and not had any opinion at all, for all the good it. I didn't even wait to be properly discharged. I packed my bags as soon as I was able to, and I departed the Priory on the 9th of January 2020, six days before my official discharge date.

***

When I was hospitalised, there was a certain amount of hope and relief. I thought that I was in a safe environment, a place where not only my physical health would be monitored, but I would also get intensive therapy. I thought that they would help me, and, with their support, I would gradually improve. Turns out that this was not the case. Yes, my physical health was monitored, and I had MARSI's every day, weekly ECG's and blood tests, but my mental health was rather neglected. My exercise addiction worsened, and I ended up with internal bleeding.

On reflection, the Priory did save my life. I would have undoubtedly succumbed to Ana had it not been for their intervention. Perhaps, I wasn't as cooperative as I should have been, but that is the trouble with eating disorders. They take over your entire body and mind. My eating disorder became me, and I lost my entire identity. I didn't want to starve my body and run to the point of internal bleeding, but Ana didn't give me a choice. My limbs were turning against me, my mind had been corrupted, and my thoughts were laced with self-loathing. I couldn't think for myself because my body was putting all its resources into keeping me alive, there was no room for rational thought. I never wanted Ana in my life. I never chose to have an eating disorder. I was a lost little girl, and Ana became my crutch. My master was Ana, not the health professionals. My allegiance was with Ana, not the Priory. My life was with Ana, not with my family and friends. We had our issues, there is no doubt. But I must face reality and accept that the only reason I am still alive is down to the Priory. They did stabilise my physical health. They did get my weight to a healthy point. I was still plagued with problems long after my discharge, but I was alive and with my family. I was in the best place possible.

***

I was sent home with a week's worth of medication and a copy of my meal plan. That was it. Six months of my life had passed me by in a haze of pain and misery, so what the hell was I going to do now? I had no outpatient support, no job to go back to, I had cut off ties from everyone, and I was afraid of my neighbours seeing me. I was so terrified everyone would see me as a fraud.

There was no foundation to this belief. I have no evidence that this was the case. It was just my own mind playing tricks with me, making me feel unworthy. Anyway, what does it matter what they think? I know the truth. I know what I went through and the heartache I put my family through. I know that I have a diagnosis of anorexia nervosa so why can't that be good enough for me? Not only am I making unfair assumptions of how people view me, but I am also setting myself up for failure. I will never look anorexic. I will never be ill enough. I will never be able to see my body for what it really is. I see it through my distorted lens, and I am aware there is a difference between what I see and what everyone else sees.

Do you remember those fun house mirrors? You look at your reflection and see a distorted image of yourself but, as soon as you look away, you forget all about it. Well, Ana won't let you forget. That distorted image is etched into my mind forever. I don't have the luxury of switching my brain off because Ana won't let me. She purposefully blots out all reasoning and logic because it reveals her to be a lying cow. She isolates you so that she is the only person you talk to. She makes sure that no one can ever question her, so you end up hanging onto her every word. How can you know the truth when you are only surrounded by lies? How can you see reality when Ana ensures that everything you see is distorted? Exactly. It's impossible... and that's how Ana likes it.

I was struggling to give myself permission to be anything other than miserable. To be anything other than anorexic. My case manager had tried to contact me whilst I was still in hospital, but I was unable to answer his calls. I was paralysed with fear. Every time my phone rung, I panicked and would break out in a cold sweat. I physically couldn't bring myself to just pick up the phone and speak to him. I was afraid of being accused an imposter, and I didn't want him wasting his time on me. What if he asked me how I was feeling? What do I say to him? I was angry, upset, frightened, lost, unsure of myself. I felt like a fraud, a failure, a freak, a piece of trash. How could

I express all these feelings in one phone call? I didn't know what to do. Thankfully, my parents took the reins. My dad phoned April House and asked to speak to my case manager. Over the phone, he explained my fear paralysis and asked if we could have a face-to-face meeting so we could try and sort something out. We were able to arrange a meeting for the following day. I was amazed by how quickly they were able to fit me in, and how understanding they appeared to be. We got seen to pretty much immediately, and I cannot praise my case manager enough.

He was empathetic, understanding, respectful, reassuring. He really listened to me and when I told him that I couldn't face talking to him over the phone, he didn't even bat an eyelid. He didn't question it or make me feel guilty. In fact, he said he understood. He didn't hold it against me, and I was able to open with him. To my relief, I was offered a place at their day support programme with immediate effect. I couldn't believe it. My biggest fear was going from inpatient treatment to nothing, but they were giving me the most amazing lifeline. He had fought my corner and for the first time in a long time, I remember smiling. I remember feeling grateful and relieved. Before, I felt like I was being chucked out of a plane with nothing to hold on to, but now I had a parachute. Now I had something to grab hold of and guide me back down the path of recovery. I now had something to help me stay in the air, to stop me from falling and spiralling out of control. I had hope. With the support of April House, I have been able to make positive steps forward in my recovery.

They have honestly been incredible. I have achieved things that I never thought were possible. I have eaten foods that I never even touched at the Priory. I have made some amazing new friends, and I have reconnected with old ones too. I have met people in café's, got into arts and crafts and, most importantly, I have begun to laugh. I can write and read again, I can do things that don't revolve around food and exercise. I can enjoy watching TV with my parents, I can make jokes again, I can smile. I can smile with the twinkle back in my eyes. The sadness is still there. The pain is still there, but I am coping. I do have setbacks, and I have fallen down several times, but I always dust myself off and carry on. This time last year, I didn't see a future, but here I am. Still alive and kicking. I might not be able to see myself getting married or enjoying my job, but that doesn't mean it won't happen. I guess what I am trying to say is that just because you can't see something, just because you can't imagine something, it doesn't mean it won't come true. Just because you can't see a future, doesn't mean there isn't one. Just because you feel like a failure, doesn't mean you are a failure. Just because you have bad days, doesn't mean you won't ever have good times again. If you give up, then you are giving up on yourself. Your head might tell you that there's no point in trying because you'll be rubbish at whatever you do, but so what? Okay, you might not be the best at something, but that doesn't mean you aren't good at it. Where there is good, there is always better. Where there is bad, there is always worse. Just try. Surely a future of any kind is better than no future at all? Surely growing old is better than dying young? It's got to be worth a shot.

***

April House took a chance with me. They gave me a place on the programme, and I was given a new meal plan based off the one the Priory had given me. I officially started the programme about a week after our initial meeting with my case manager. Starting DSP was a nerve-wrecking experience to say the least. Because I was a new patient, they organised transport to and from the centre. This meant I would either go by taxi or in the back of an ambulance. I felt so guilty for wasting valuable resources. I also live about five minutes' drive away from April House, so I was embarrassed at having to be driven in the back of an ambulance. Let me just clarify something here. Although it was an ambulance, it was used for non-emergency patients. Essentially, it picked up people who were, for whatever reason, unable to make their way to appointments at the hospital or other healthcare centres. My legs were working perfectly fine. I wasn't wheelchair bound; I didn't need any of this. They were making a fuss over nothing and other people are far more worthy of this service than I am. Don't waste your breath on me. I felt so guilty and pathetic for using patient transport, even though the logical side of me understood why. Let's look at the facts here, shall we?

Fact 1: I was still underweight.

Fact 2: I have an exercise addiction, which had previously caused internal bleeding on three separate occasions.

Fact 3: If I lost any more weight, I would be in the dangerous zone again.

Fact 4: I have anorexia nervosa and spent six months in hospital because of it.

Yes, I can see why they were wasting their resources on me? What Ana has me believe is vastly different to what the facts tell me. As I have said, Ana doesn't understand facts or logic. Well maybe she does understand them, she just chooses to ignore them because she must be right. I didn't choose to have patient transport. That decision was taken out of my hands and made for me by my health professionals. Most people would walk because they genuinely want to. Maybe because there is no need to drive or take public transport. Maybe it benefits their mental health. I don't walk because I want to. I walk because I am driven by Ana.

***

I miss doing things because I enjoy them. Ana has stripped me of so much, and I resent her for taking away my freedom. If I didn't go for my walk every day I would panic. If I didn't go for a run, I would panic. My whole day was ruined if I couldn't stick to my rigid exercise timetable. I tried to manipulate the staff and persuade them to let me walk, but I was told that this wasn't going to happen anytime soon. They knew it was coming from an unhealthy point of view, and they didn't want to give Ana any more satisfaction. Turning up for day support for the first time, I was introduced to various members of staff. The information that was being relayed to me just went it one ear and out the other. This was a completely different environment to what I had grown accustomed to at the Priory, and I could feel my nerves rising. I was told we only had half an hour for meals, which seems like a perfectly reasonable time frame. Well, Ana didn't see it as reasonable. She had a full-on hissy fit.

Anorexia: 'You what now? Half an hour to eat!?!? Are you flipping kidding me?'

Steph: 'Well, obviously they're not. This is what is expected of me now, so I don't have a choice but to comply.'

Anorexia: 'How many times do I have to repeat myself until

you get it in that thick skull of yours? You always have a choice. Thirty minutes is not long enough... if you manage to eat everything in that time limit then that will just be more proof that you don't have an eating disorder.'

Steph: 'Please shut up! Please, just leave me alone. Please.'

Anorexia: 'Oi... don't you try ignoring me. I'm not going anywhere fatty. You can't run away from me... get it... you can't RUN away. God, I'm a genius! You could at least have the decency to laugh when I make a joke. Bloody hell, Steph! You don't have an eating disorder, and this is just going to prove everything I have already told you.'

Before I could dwell too much on this, I was taken to the lounge and introduced to the other patients. The programme only caters for eleven people at a time and, when I joined, there were three other girls. Our age range spanned from twenty-two to eighty, showing that Ana doesn't give a monkey's ass what age you are. It goes to show just how difficult it is for people to fight back against their illness. So many people have relapsed and ended up back in inpatient or outpatient support, and that frustrates me so much. That people's lives are wasted on such a bastard. That good people, honest people, are brainwashed, their livelihood and families destroyed by their eating disorder. Will I relapse? Will I ever be free of Ana? The truth is I don't know. I like to think I will be able to say goodbye to the bitch at some point. But I also need to remind myself that healing is not linear, that recovery is not a straightforward path. It is full of twists and turns, bumps and lumps, rivers and oceans. I may relapse, I may not. But that's okay, I just need to accept that it's all part of the journey and tripping over a rock does not mean I have to keep being pummelled down to the ground.

Relapse doesn't mean a life is lost. It's part of the journey to the life you will gain.

***

When I went into the lounge, I was met by four, shy, smiling faces. They introduced themselves to me, and vice versa. I then sat down on one of the sofas and tried to get my breathing under control. In my head, I was by far the biggest one there. In my head, all the other patients had a right to be here, but I did not. I could accept they were poorly, but I could not show myself the same mercy. In the Priory, we had to have an hour supervision after each main meal, but here it was only half an hour. We also had to sit with our feet on the floor and we weren't allowed to cover our stomachs after eating. This was so that we were able to sit with our feelings of fullness and discomfort without letting the eating disordered thoughts take over. Here, however, we were able to put our feet up on the sofa. We were able to wrap blankets round ourselves or hold onto cushions. It felt a lot more normal. At home, I don't sit with my feet firmly planted on the floor. That's just not a comfortable or relaxed sitting position for me. Even pre anorexia, that was how I always sat. Curled up into a ball or hugging a cushion over my chest if I was cold. I was grateful that we could do those things here. The first meal I had there was morning snack, and I had chosen to have a spotty dotty ice cream. We had a four-week rota for our meal plans, and we would fill them in a week in advance. We were able to take pictures of this so we could mentally prepare ourselves for each meal. I hadn't had ice cream for a snack for years. On each day, we were only given an option of two things for snacks and meals, so I was forced to have foods that my eating disorder had steered me away from at the Priory. I was forced to challenge my eating disorder rules.

Ice cream for snack!?!? What was I playing at? I couldn't do this. Couldn't I have a nice, healthy piece of fruit instead? Not only did I have to have ice cream, but I also had to have a glass of semi-skimmed milk. I was used to always having cereal bars or plain digestives for snack, a hobnob was about as adventurous as I got. I very quickly realised I wouldn't get away with things here. That I would soon have to face my fear of chocolate and cheese. That I would sometimes be forced to have a main meal in the middle of the day instead of sandwiches. That I would have to have crumpets for breakfast and not the same cereal every day. I would be given a variety of foods, and this is something that has plagued me throughout this recovery process. It still plagues me to this day. I am gradually improving though, and thanks to April House, I have been able to have more dinners and sandwich fillings. We had fifteen minutes to complete each snack, and I remember thinking that I couldn't do it. That I wasn't cut out for this and I should just get up and run away. I wasn't being tied up or held against my own will, all I had to do was get up off my chair and walk away. But I sat there. I sat firmly in my seat and ate. It is amazing what you can do when under pressure. What you can do if you really set your mind to it. Yes, I was slow, and I had to be prompted several times, but I finished it. And, what's more, I didn't have a massive meltdown in the kitchen either. Whilst Steph was proud of me, Ana was not.

Anorexia: 'How fucking dare you! If you were poorly, you wouldn't have managed that. You didn't even cry over it. It should, at the very least, have reduced you to tears. You're a disgrace!'

***

After snack, we returned to the lounge where we had our observation. We were then able to go to the toilet before the next therapeutic lesson began. April House had a more intense timetable than the Priory. There were a lot more groups, and they were evenly spread out throughout Monday to Thursday. Sadly, the programme was not able to run throughout the full week, so it was only Monday to Thursday, but it was incredibly beneficial. It just goes to show that you don't have to have groups every single day, so long as the groups that are on are good. The groups at April House were all amazing and, in their own way, useful. We had WRAP (wellness recovery action plan) which is where we each focus on our own recovery and recognise the warning signs in order to get the appropriate help. We also had a body image group which was tough and hard-hitting, but it was completely necessary. It is not going to make me love myself, but it did make me realise that my view of my own body is not accurate. That I spend so much of my life, far more than I would like to admit, weighing myself and examining myself in the mirror from every possible angle. My body is my body, and instead of fixating on what I hate, I need to start looking at what I do have. That I can walk and run, that I am able to see and think and feel. It is about what my body can do, not what it looks like. We also had a dietetic group which was run by the dietician there. We looked at carbohydrates, protein, fats, and why each one is important for our body. Fat does not equate to being fat and is part of a balanced diet. No food is evil. No food is going to instantly cause weight gain. Not only does it fuel your body, but it also fuels your own mind, and not your eating disorder.

Other groups included mindfulness and relaxation, peer support, goal settings, and anxiety management. At the end of each week, we would all set ourselves three goals. The first goal would have to be eating disorder related. So, for example, one of my goals was to have fruit 'n' fibre for my cereal at home instead of bran flakes. The second goal was a self-care one, and this could be anything from painting your nails, watching a film, dying your hair, or anything that made you feel good about yourself. The last goal was a more practical one, about things we didn't necessarily want to do, but *had* to do. One week, my goal was to order a repeat prescription of my medication from my local GP. The best thing about this group was that it wasn't just for the patients. Staff also took part, but instead of an eating disorder goal, they changed it to a work-related one. Everybody's goals were written down in a folder and would be gone through the following week. We had to score each goal with a mark out of ten (one being didn't do it at all, and ten being nailed it.) It was a useful group because it also gave me something to focus on that wasn't my anorexia. It gave me permission to dye my hair or look after myself for a change. Anxiety management was another fantastic group. Pretty much what it says on the tin, this group focused on managing our anxieties. It didn't just revolve around food fears, but other fears too. It could be maybe meeting someone you haven't seen in a long time, or maybe going to a café and ordering a coffee or hot chocolate. We would work on building up to these goals using a hierarchy system. We would start off with something manageable like maybe having a coffee at home, and then work your way up to ordering one in a café. I credit this group with helping me reconnect with friends.

***

In addition to these groups, we were also given time every week to go through our meal plans with the dietician on a 1:1 basis. We had to fill out a food diary which detailed what we ate, when we ate, and how it made us feel afterwards. It was useful to see all my thoughts written down on paper, and it helped highlight some of my overriding fears. I realised that I was afraid of feeling hungry. That I jumped to the conclusion that I would never be able to get the right balance and, if I started feeling hungry, that would lead to indulgencies. It also made me realise just how much I find choice and variety hard. How Ana sees variety in a negative light, and I would be a failed anorexic if I enjoyed food or had a nice range of things. I am not a failed anorexic. I am a recovering anorexic. There is a difference.

Ana's safety net was taken away from me at April House. They really did make her squirm. We would have sandwiches some days, but we would also have things like soup (with bread and butter of course) and beans on toast. We would have hot meals to spice things up a bit (because variety is good) and that really messed with my head. A lot of the thoughts I have told you about do not make an ounce of sense, and I am not about to change that trend. Ana had me believe that I could only have one 'hot' meal a day. That soup or baked beans was the equivalent of a main meal because it was hot, and therefore I was being greedy and eating far more than I was deserving of. If I had soup, I didn't see why I had to have it with bread and butter (because it tastes goddamn nice, that's why) and I just saw all these components as 'extra' and completely unnecessary. I felt selfish for having more than just soup. I would have fruit and a yoghurt, alongside the bread and butter, and that did not sit well with me at all.

April House forced me to have foods I could only ever dream about before. I had crumpets for breakfast, shreddies and fruit 'n' fibre. I had baked beans on toast and soup, I had pasta and pizza. I had chocolate bars, mousses, cheese, and cake. I had spent six months at the Priory getting out of eating my biggest 'fear foods.' I never once had pasta or chocolate. I didn't touch cheese, chips, pizza… I was able to get away with so much. Although I left the Priory being able to eat in front of my family, I still had very stringent food rules. I was still very much under Ana's spell. Her performance was bewitching, and she compelled me to follow her. To walk by her side into the abyss. I completed all my meals and snacks whilst there, even if it seemed an impossible task. I battled through and overcame some giant obstacles. I think what helped was that staff would often have the same foods we had, and they just had so much freedom around food. I remember the occupational therapist moaning about eating lettuce, and that it was just rabbit food. She wanted more pizza and less of the green stuff. I looked up to her and wished, more than anything, that I could have her joy and zest for food and life. That I could be so carefree. The staff were so amazing when we were having challenging meals and they would try and distract us with some inspirational coasters. We all had a coaster placed at our seats with a beautiful inspiration quote to keep our spirits and strength up. We would also play silly games like 'would you rather…' and the alphabet game. We would pick a random topic, like household furniture, and we would go around the table working our way through the alphabet and thinking of household objects beginning with the next letter. My favourite one was when we got to 'U' and my key worker blurted out 'under sink cupboard.' I think we all burst out laughing at that point. It was so random and ingenious, it made the meal so much more manageable as our thoughts weren't on what we were consuming, but the conversation we were having.

One thing I also really appreciated was that they could sense I was struggling, without me saying anything. At the Priory, my hunched over demeanour had been interpreted as anger, but here they saw it for what it was. Fear. The need to hide away and protect myself from the swords dripping with Ana's venom. I was assigned a key worker and every week we would have a half hour session and discuss anything that was on our mind. It was a chance to say how we really felt, and I found myself opening up. I normally find it incredibly difficult to be open and honest. I have built up so many walls and barriers over the years, it is hard for me to reveal the crumbling ruins that are left behind. I didn't need to say I was worried. She would just know. I didn't need to vocalise my struggle. She could sense it. One of the things she helped me with the most was reconnecting with my old friends, and she really tried to help build up a life outside of my eating disorder. For the past year, I had only talked to people with eating disorders, and I explained how petrified I was. How afraid I was of being labelled a freak. I thought she would laugh out loud over how ridiculous I was being, but she didn't. The level of empathy she showed me was incredible, and I never felt the need to justify myself. I was never worried about saying how I really felt because I knew they weren't going to ridicule or belittle me. However, as with everything in life, there is also a downside.

***

The programme was focused on weight gain, and there was a target of 0.5kg to 1kg a week. If we failed to comply, we would be sent on reflective leave. This is a week off the programme where you have a chance to reflect on whether this is the right support for you. It gives you a chance to think about where, perhaps, you were going wrong, and what you could do to fix it. If your weight didn't go up enough for a second time, you would then be dismissed from the programme. I understood why this was the case, although it was a bitter pill to swallow. They could only cater for eleven patients at a time, and it covers the whole of Hampshire. The places are precious and there is a long waiting list. They need to make sure that those on the programme are fully committed to recovery. At the end of my first week, I had not restored enough weight. We were weighed twice a week, Monday and Thursday, but Thursday's weight was more of a guidance than anything else. It was Monday's weigh-in that counted. We then had something called a review which is where we would be called into a room with the dietician, our case worker, and care manager. Our family and carers were also allowed to attend. After having had a disappointing weigh-in, they broke the news to me that I was to go on reflective leave. I was devastated.

I really thought I had done enough. If I am being totally honest, I thought reflective leave was only a threat, and it wouldn't happen to me. I thought they would be far more lenient and give me more chances. My complacency nearly cost me my place there, but it also proved to be a turning point.

I had underestimated them, convinced myself that they wouldn't dismiss me from the programme just because I missed out on the weight target a few puny times. This proved to me just how serious they were. The parachute that I had clung on to was being prised away from my grasp, and I felt myself spinning out of control again. How was I going to cope without them? I had let my case manager down, I had let my family down, I had let myself down. I was hit by a sudden wave of panic. They were not kidding. I had been extremely lucky to have been offered a place so quickly after discharge, and I had done nothing but thrown it back in their faces. I was proving the Priory right – that I was beyond help. I couldn't allow this to happen. It was a minor setback, but it didn't mean that I had to keep falling. My outlook on things began to change from hereon, and I found myself determined to prove to them that I was serious about this. That I did want recovery, and that I was willing to fight fucking Ana. I wasn't going to let them down anymore. I was going to kick butt and give it my all. I *had* to have April House; I couldn't let them slip away from them. I *needed* them, I *wanted* them, I was determined to keep my place there.

The hardest part of that day was breaking the news to my parents. It was walking through the front door and saying that I couldn't go back for the rest of the week. I cried. They cried. We all cried rivers that day. But I do believe everything happens for a reason, and a lot of good came out of reflective leave. It certainly served its purpose, and I really did reflect on everything. It was a huge eye opener for me, and, in a weird way, I am pleased that it happened. I needed something to shock me into action, and this did exactly that.

That week I really did try and challenge my anorexic thoughts. That was the best way I was going to prove to them how much I wanted their support. I made sure I always had semi-skimmed milk instead of skimmed. I stopped hiding food, I changed my yoghurts... I actively tried to restore weight. I wanted the number on the scales to go up. Not by a lot, but I wanted to have restored 0.5kg. It would be the best way to convince them that I had thought about it and I was determined to carry on. I didn't have to restore any weight over this period of reflective leave, but I felt I needed to. I had a lot to prove, mainly to myself, and I was determined to stop letting people down. Enough was enough. I think this was my epiphany moment. I don't know what changed, but something in my brain clicked and I was angry at Ana for ruining things yet again. For getting in the way of life. For trapping me yet again.

Steph: 'Hey, Ana, I've got something to tell you.'

Anorexia: 'Oh no, what is it now, you prat? What do you want this time? How about another slap?'

Steph: 'I have two words for you.'

Anorexia: 'And what would these be? You're right, yes boss, okay Ana? Am I getting warmer?'

Steph: 'Not even close...'

Anorexia: 'Well spit it out then will you.'

Steph: 'FUCK OFF!'

God that feels good. Shouting at Ana feels damn good. I worked my socks off that week and, when I was able to return the following Monday, I had restored 0.5kg. They praised me for putting in so much hard work, but I did struggle to hear those nice things. I struggled to accept the praise. There are moments where I get flashes of bravery and want to face my eating disorder head on. Then I get moments of weakness, where I back down and panic and start regretting everything. This was one of those moments. After such a positive week, I could feel Ana rising in anger again. I could feel her venom as I saw the number go up on the scales. I could feel the heat of her fire when staff and family praised me. I did what I had to do and the fear of being kicked off April House had motivated me to stay on track. Now I had achieved that, I was worried my newfound confidence would waver. I was worried that I wouldn't be able to keep this up, and Ana would bite back with a vengeance. She did bite back. Ana will never stop biting back, she will never be able to hold her venomous tongue, she will never go quietly.

Battling Ana is like a game of tennis. Back and forth, up and down, left and right. It's all over the place, and there will be highs and lows. I gradually began to restore more weight, and in about eight weeks I had reached my goal BMI. This brought with it a wide range of emotions. I felt anger and disgust. But I was also proud. I could confidently say that I had done everything in my power to fight Ana and do the right thing. I could look them directly in the eye and say that I gave it my all. The anorexic side of me was repulsed and disgusted by what I had done. Ana was angry that I had betrayed her, and she berated me for not having a proper eating disorder and for being so pathetic. So many contradicting thoughts were rushing around my head I couldn't make head nor tail of any of it. Can you understand it? Probably not, but that's the whole point. It does not make any sense. Eating disorders are not based on reason or logic. They are not fair or just. They have no sense of what is right and wrong. I need to stop trying to understand my eating disorder. Whilst I understand some of it, I will never understand all of it.

I do not understand why hot food scares me. Why I find a banana scarier than an apple. Why I struggle with seeded bread and not brown bread. Why I am afraid of having a day where I don't exercise. These are all irrational fears. These are all part of MY anorexia. That doesn't mean everyone suffering from anorexia shares those fears. Eating disorders vary from person to person, and they cannot be grouped into one category. Each case is different, and deserves to be treated with respect, empathy, and kindness. With an open mind and non-judgemental attitude. Whilst it is true that I have made significant progress since joining the day support programme, I have also had some wobbles. It hasn't all been smiles and laughter, there have been some very dark days as well.

***

There are two instances that stick in my mind. The first goes back to February 11, 2020; My brother's 24th birthday. He had spent his previous birthday in China, and I wanted more than anything in the world, to enjoy the day. To be the happy sister that he wants and deserves. To join in with the drinking and eating. Was I able to do any of those things? No, I was not. I went to April House for the day and came home around half three. My family were in the lounge drinking wine, eating from a box of chocolates, and watching a comedy on TV. My mood dropped in an instant.

I should be sat with them, enjoying good food and drink. I should be sat on the sofa next to my brother, laughing and celebrating with him. I couldn't even do that right. I couldn't, for one day, put aside my own issues and do something for someone else. I couldn't put someone else above Ana, and I hate that. I was having my afternoon snack, a nature valley bar, and I remember sitting down, facing the TV, turning my face away from my family. I let the tears fall. My brother had wanted me to have some chocolates for my snack. He pleaded with me and asked if I could just have one. I couldn't do it. I couldn't allow myself to have that one piece of chocolate. Oh no! Instead, I had to cry and ruin everything. They all comforted and hugged me, telling me they understood, and I had nothing to be sorry for. That the most important thing was that we were all together as a family. Their words did help soothe me and calm me down, but they did not quieten the anorexic voice. I felt like I had let them all down. I should have just been able to have that tiny chocolate. I had eaten chocolate at April House, so why couldn't I do it for my own family? I think the difference is that at the day support programme, I didn't have a choice. The food was given to me and I ate it. Every week we would have something called 'surprise snack' and, as the name suggests, we would have an unknown snack on any day of the week. We didn't know when it would happen until we sat down at the kitchen table and saw what was on the plate in front of us.

Here, I HAD to have what was given to me. I only had two options to pick from the weekly menus and sometimes both the snack options were chocolate. Whereas at home, I don't have to do anything. To voluntarily choose to have chocolate instead of a 'healthy' cereal bar with known calories… well, that would have been an insult to Ana. But the truth is I have anorexia nervosa. I know how much I have suffered, how much I have put my body and my family through. I have been on the receiving end of Ana's harsh words for nearly a decade. As each year passed, my anorexia grew stronger. With each truth I withheld, Ana thrived. With each time I went for a run, she would gain more control. With each time I weighed myself, she would make me feel worthless. With each breath I took, Ana would shout at me and tell me off for being a waste of space. I owe her nothing. I may not have been able to join in with the celebrations last year or this year, but there is always next year.

I have a whole life ahead of me to make up for lost time. Next year, I hope to be able to eat the same foods as my family and enjoy a drink. I hope to give them the best present they could ask for – my recovery. My health. A life that is not dominated by my eating disorder. I wish to show them that Steph is back where she belongs. A few weeks after this wobble, I had another one. My brother invited his Chinese girlfriend to our home for the week. I had never met her before; I didn't know if she knew anything about mental health or eating disorders. My brother had told me that she was aware of my condition and had done research into it after he had discovered the truth himself. I was thankful that I had April House during the week, so I would be out most of the time and would still have all my meals and snacks at the right time. I was so worried about meeting her for the first time. I was ashamed of my eating disorder, and I didn't want to ruin her time in the UK.

The first time I saw her was on a Monday afternoon, when I returned home from April House. I met her only briefly as I think her and my brother were going out, but I remember feeling like I wanted a trap door to open and swallow me whole. I remember folding my cardigan over my stomach, trying to hide how big I was. Trying to protect myself. We said a brief 'hello,' but the fact it had gone half three meant I wasn't really open to conversation as I was panicking about the time. They soon left as my brother explained that I had to have a snack and I bid them goodbye. How was I going to manage a whole week of this? How was it going to work with my strict meal plan? What was I going to do?

To my relief, it wasn't as bad as I anticipated. They were out for most of the week, so I didn't have to worry about eating in front of her. I think I had managed to get through most of the week without any major hiccoughs. But on Thursday afternoon that all changed. I cried solidly for over four hours. Sat on my bed, hunched over, with a blanket wrapped around me, wallowing in my own self-pity. I had rushed my snack, thinking that they wanted me out of the way. Thinking that I was just being a nuisance and they all just wanted me to go to my room and stay out of sight and mind. I genuinely believed that. I genuinely believed that they thought I was being a pain in the arse and wanted me to leave so that they could get on with their own lives. That they were getting fed up with me. That I was trapping them, putting a halt to their own plans and hopes. I was a burden. It was because of ME that my brother and his girlfriend had to go out for most meals. It was because of ME that my parents had become stay at home carers. It was because of ME. I had ruined everything. I didn't want people to stop living just because I couldn't handle being me. I didn't want to upset people or make them feel like they had to be with me. That evening I had my mum, dad, and brother, all come into my room to help calm me down. To show their love and support. To tell me that I was worthy of their love. To hug and cling onto. I sobbed into my dad's chest, apologising for being a burden. Apologising for everything. I didn't want to let people down. I didn't want to force people to do things just for my sake. I couldn't stand being so vulnerable and weak.

***

There were many tears and tantrums and, the following day I went to my GP to get my anti-depressants increased. There was also talk about coming off my laxatives. Whilst I was under April House and back in the community, I was having laxatives prescribed from the doctor's surgery rather than buying them over the counter. My health professionals and parents were keen for me to come off, but I did not share their enthusiasm. The truth is I was scared witless of coming off them. I had been dependant on them for about a year and a half. The thought of not being able to go to the toilet was horrendous. Fear, anxiety, worry, grief... what if I had damaged my bowel? What if I wouldn't be able to go to the toilet by myself again? What if I needed to take laxatives for the rest of my life? What if I couldn't empty myself for days? I have mentioned grief a few times throughout this book. About how I am grieving my anorexic body, grieving my eating disorder. In a similar way, I am grieving laxatives. They were a safety net for me. They guaranteed loose, regular, bowel movements. I would be going around two or three times a day and I loved that feeling of emptiness they gave me. Feeling like I had nothing lurking inside of me. Feeling weightless. I had already given up Ana and running. I couldn't give up laxatives as well. There is only so much a person can take.

The tricky thing with laxative abuse is that you don't know what damage has been caused, if any, until you test the theory. Until you start reducing them. It is not a sensible idea to go cold turkey, so I spoke to my key worker at April House as well as the dietician, and we came up with plan. I was taking three laxatives a day at this point, so we decided that for one week I would alternate between taking three and two tablets a day. So, on Monday, I would have three, On Tuesday, I would take two… and so on. The week after that I would alternate between taking two tablets and one. Then I would alternate between one tablet and nothing. We had a three-week plan in place. What could possibly go wrong? I had finally been allowed to walk home from April House. We agreed that my parents would drive me in but then I could walk home. This was on the condition that my weight continued to go up and, if at any point, the trend started going down, I would have that freedom stripped away from me again. This was a chance to prove myself. And I am sad to say I blew it. As soon as I was able to, I went straight to Superdrug on my way home, and bought a pack of forty laxatives. I took them out of the packet, discarding the empty packet in the bin, and I shoved the tablets down my bra so my parents wouldn't discover them.

I would do this four times a week. Whenever I finished with day support, I would buy a pack of laxatives on my way home. I went to Poundland, Sainsburys, the One Stop, Superdrug, and Savers. Each day, I went to a different shop so as not to arouse suspicion. I would shove the tablets either down my bra, or in my pockets, or tuck it under my high waisted trousers. I had to get creative with my hiding places. I had been able to get down to alternating between one and two laxatives, but this put pay to that idea.

I would take eight a day, in addition to the tablets my dad was giving me in the evening. I noticed an instant change in my stools. It was a lot runnier; the smell was a lot more pungent, and I would go more frequently. Sometimes five times a day.

I remember I was walking home, and I soiled my underwear. Nowhere near as bad as it used to be, but still enough to shock me. I reverted to wearing period pads on my underwear, and I felt like a baby. I was a twenty-two-year-old woman who was losing control over her bowel… again. I had been making real progress, and once more I had failed. I couldn't tell anyone I had slipped up because then they would kick me off the programme. That was what I was afraid of. Losing this support network that I relied upon so heavily. It worried me how easily Ana took over. It worried me how easy it was to relapse. How easy it was for Ana to make her mark again and take advantage of you. I kept this up for several months, but I don't think I had my parents fooled.

My mum took to questioning me about my laxatives. She was convinced I was still taking them. I vehemently denied these accusations. I swore blind I wasn't taking any. The lies fell all too easily out of my mouth. Ana weaved her web of deceit once more. I had stashed all my laxatives in a draw on my dressing table, and every day I was buying more and more to add to my collection. It was growing out of hand, and my obsession with emptying my stomach was increasing again. This was bad news. On top of this, my recovery reached a point that I never imagined it would. That no one could have ever predicted. COVID-19.

***

No one could have envisaged a global pandemic. The coronavirus has really altered my support network. It has thrown everything into chaos, and as my treatment moved from physical contact to telephone, I have found myself at a bit of a crossroads. I hate not being able to meet my team in person. It unnerves me the fact that I can't see their facial expressions or gauge their thoughts. Picking up the telephone is an anxiety-provoking experience for me. And it hasn't gotten any easier. It was just before the official lockdown was announced in March that I received the news about April House. There were five patients at the time, including myself, and we were told that, due to the virus, they would be closing the programme and all 1:1 sessions were cancelled. That did not, however, mean that we had no support at all. They might have been closing their doors, but they were still offering their support.

They weren't leaving us out to rot. They weren't abandoning us. They weren't going to let our eating disorders take control again, and they certainly weren't leaving us to Ana's merciless violence. All our support turned remote. The materials that would have been used in the groups were emailed to us instead. We would continue to have weekly reviews via the telephone, and staff would phone us every weekday to check in with us. We would do the food diaries on a word document and email them to the dietician, who would then chat to us all individually on a Thursday, just the same as before. We would still be expected to weigh ourselves twice a week, and they would phone us to find out the results. It wasn't an ideal situation. It was far from perfect, but it was better than nothing. They didn't have to phone us every day. They didn't have to send us worksheets and resources. They didn't need to send us inspirational messages and quotes of the week. They *wanted* to do it. They were determined to help and do anything they possibly could in such uncertain times. They wanted to provide a bit of certainty when so much was unknown. Whilst I did appreciate their efforts, it didn't take away from the fact that I find phone calls really challenging. They were there to help us but, in a weird way, it only made me more stressed. I never know what to say over the phone and I am aware a lot of my emotions can be seen through my expressions, rather than what I say. I can say all the right things, I can say that I'm okay, but that doesn't mean it's the truth. Saying something does not make it a reality.

The coronavirus has not just disrupted my treatment from April House. It has also impacted my outlook on life. Let me explain what I mean by that.

April House was working with me towards building my life back up. About reconnecting with people and doing things that I, Steph, enjoy. They helped me ring up the Princes Trust to try and arrange a meeting to help me get out and meet new people. The lockdown means I am unable to do that. My life doesn't feel much different to what it was like this time last year, and that is hard. All throughout recovery, I have had people telling me how it's worth it, how much better my life will be without my eating disorder. But I found myself in a unique situation where I was unable to meet up with friends or family. Everything I was working towards had been moved even further away from my grasp. I was this close to reaching them, and now I felt further back than ever before. They were tantalizingly close, and I was struggling to see the benefits of recovery.

In one way, lockdown has almost been a blessing, because it has enabled me to really think about my eating disorder. It has allowed me to focus on the things I need to, without worrying about the pressures of getting a job and daily life. Working is not on the top of my list of priorities now. Staying well is. In all the jobs I have had, my eating disorder has gotten worse. Ana has become stronger, and I used work as an excuse to not eat. As an excuse to get more steps in and lose some more weight. The longer the hours the better, because it meant I didn't physically have time to eat, and that gave me a warped sense of satisfaction. That I had so much self-control and was able to do a ten-hour shift on one meal a day. Not many people would have the willpower to refuse all the food I was. Ana made me think, if I didn't have that biscuit or sweet, that I would be the best person in the room. Ana turned me into a person I really didn't want to be. I don't have a big ego, Ana does. I am not selfish, Ana is. I am NOT my anorexia! I am NOT that person.

***

Whilst grappling with Ana and trying to separate myself from her, I was hit by another blow. It was bound to come out sooner or later, but my parents had discovered my secret stash of laxatives. I had gone out for my daily walk and when I returned home, my parents called me into the lounge. My heart skipped a beat, and I wondered what I had done wrong. They sat me down and my mum asked me if I was taking more laxatives. I denied it. I swore I wasn't taking them, and I started shouting. I was angry they were questioning me, even though I know they had every right to be worried and they were only looking out for me. They wanted to help, but Ana wouldn't let them in. To admit I had a problem would be to ask for help, and Ana wouldn't allow me to do that. She asked me three or four times and, each time, I lied. Each time I was asked, I said I wasn't taking them, and I was getting fed up with being questioned all the time. My mum then left the room and came back with all my laxatives.

HOW BLOODY DARE YOU!?!?

That was Ana's immediate reaction.

YOU HAD ABSOLUTELY NO FLIPPING RIGHT!?!?

She was fuming.

HOW DARE YOU GO SNOOPING AROUND, INVADING MY PRIVACY. YOU'VE RUINED EVERYTHING NOW!

She was in full throttle, really gearing up to the peak of her anger.

YOU'RE GOING TO PAY FOR YOUR STUPIDITY STEPH!

I stormed upstairs, after having a go at her for going into my room. I felt so pissed off. I was angry with myself for hiding them in such an obvious place. If I'd only used my brain, I would have been able to get away with it. I was worried about how this would impact my place at April House, and whether my parents would be able to trust me ever again. That was a horrible day. My mum had made a mark on one of the packets so she could see exactly how many I had taken the previous day, and that just was just like rubbing salt into the wound. I had also hoped I could ween myself off them without my parents having to find out about my little blip.

***

I had FINALLY been assigned a CBT therapist after nearly a year of asking. She is so lovely and, whilst we have only been able to speak over the phone, I trust her. I believe in what she is saying, and I feel like she listens and tries to understand everything I say. She never judges me or makes inappropriate comments. I know it is early days, and I have only had a few sessions, but I already have a better relationship with her than I ever did with my previous therapist. I feel able to tell her how I really feel, and I don't have to hide my emotions or bottle things up. I can say what I think, how I feel, what my head is telling me, and she is always supportive and empathetic. She lets me talk and she listens. That is the greatest gift any therapist can give – just to be able to listen to you and respect you. She asks me to tell her if I don't agree with anything she says, and she encourages me to say what is on my mind and not hold back.

I was rather surprised with myself when, during my first or second, session with her I revealed to her my struggle with laxatives. I admitted that I was taking them again and, more than that, taking more than I was before. I don't know why I told her. Normally, I would be very hesitant to say anything that might lead to Ana losing some of her secrecy. But the words came tumbling out before I could stop them. I had never seen her face, only heard her voice over the phone, but I just knew I could trust her. We came up with a plan to come off them which basically mirrored the one I was supposed to do earlier. Gradually reducing them over a period of a few weeks. I really hoped I could keep this a secret from my parents, but obviously things didn't turn out the way Ana wanted.

My therapist, of course, had to pass on this information to the rest of the team. In my next review my parents brought it up, much to my discomfort and shame. I had been able to walk by myself once a day, so long as I was under an hour, but now they wanted someone to always come with me. I wasn't allowed out of someone's line of vision, and it was almost as bad as being on a 1:1. I felt trapped. I understand why they did it, and I know it was the right thing, but it was just so frustrating. I had taken several steps backwards. I had been doing okay, apart from this. I had reached a maintenance weight and I had been complying to my meal plan. I was no longer hiding food or trying to get out of things, I was having everything I was supposed to. But everyone has their limit. I felt like all my safety nets were being taken away from me all at once, I needed something familiar to lean on. I needed something that felt 'safe,' that made me feel in control just a little bit. Whilst everything was spiralling out of Ana's control, she grabbed hold onto whatever she could and, for me, that happened to be laxatives.

My biggest fear about telling anyone was that I would be kicked off the day support programme. I am beyond grateful that this was not the case. They said to me that they wouldn't kick me off just because of one little slip up. I had been working so hard, they weren't going to punish me for having a wobble. I couldn't believe my ears. They were saying that it was okay. That it was normal to have wobbles. But it doesn't take away from all the other progress I had made. I had been working with them, trying to put my best foot forward, and they could see how much effort I was putting into this. They didn't want to let this get in the way of all the work I had done. Of all the battles I had conquered. This was one trip. Admittedly, it was quite a big rock I had fallen over, but I wasn't staying down. I picked myself back up, brushed myself off, and carried on. I had a new plan of action. I had to keep going, or I would only end up at the bottom of the mountain again. I had already climbed halfway up; I wasn't about to stop and let all my efforts be in vain. I had been through so much, I had pushed aside massive boulders, and kicked away smaller stones… I wasn't going to put myself through all of that again. Once is too much; I fear I will not have the strength to climb that mountain a second time.

Recovery is a hard mountain to climb, there is no doubt about it. My eating disorder was about avoiding things I feared, but the only way I can conquer those fears, is by facing them head on. By climbing up that mountain and not giving up, even when times are tough. Giving up is the easy option. Staying with your eating disorder is the easy option. For me, it meant I avoided having to work, having to move out, start a family, have adult responsibilities... it meant I was protecting myself from failure. If I didn't try, then I wouldn't be letting anyone down. I couldn't fail at something I never did. You can avoid things indefinitely, but not forever. At some point, you will have to face what you have spent so long trying to avoid. You will have to face your demons. Do it now rather than later. There is no better time than the present. Tomorrow never comes, remember that. I could say 'recovery starts tomorrow,' but then I would keep pushing it back because tomorrow is never here. There will always be a tomorrow, but there will only be one here and now. Don't fight something you can't win. Don't keep fighting a battle that you are bound to lose. Make your own battles, pick the ones you can win. There will always be battles that are worth fighting for, and battles that are a waste of time. Choose wisely. Choose the ones that you stand a chance in and give it your all. There is no right way or wrong way, there is no perfect answer to anything. Just do your best, and that is more than enough.

Has my journey to recovery been perfect? Don't make me laugh? Of course not! It has been perfectly imperfect. Full of ups and downs, tears of both joy and sadness, despair and hope. Laughter and arguments... fights and apologies... it has been downright messy at times. But I am still here, still plodding on up that mountain of mine.

Exercise will always be a problem for me. Having maintained a healthy weight for a while now, I am running again, but it is done in a very controlled way. I run with my dad and, together, we are making sure that I do everything sensibly. Exercise will always be Ana's Achilles heel. I am already finding myself addicted to the sport again. If I could, I would run every day for hours on end, but is that what I really want? NO IT IS NOT! I cannot let running rule me, it must be other way round. I must stay in control and the first step is to acknowledge that I have a problem. Steph does love running, but I am not doing it for my own benefits. The desire to run is fuelled purely by Ana and I know that. I am trying to talk things through more with my family and therapist, to try and manage my addictions. There is a fear around gaining weight in lockdown, and the media latches onto that and gaining weight has almost become synonymous with being unhealthy. Gaining weight means gaining 'fat' and that is not true. I am gaining strength and the ability to fight back against Ana and my inner critic. What is so wrong with gaining weight? I'm not talking about ballooning in size, but so what if you gain a few pounds? So what? It doesn't matter, and the most important thing you can do to yourself is to be kind. Give yourself permission to not go for that walk, or to have a bit of a lie in. Give yourself permission to rest some days and eat foods you enjoy. I do not have to do ab exercises or yoga for hours every day. I do not need to run every day. I don't NEED to do anything, apart from telling myself that it is okay to gain weight. Losing weight is not always good, and gaining weight is not always bad. It depends on each circumstance, and everyone is unique. You do not need to be skinny to be successful. It is okay to eat and be happy and enjoy life. That I am not gaining fat, but a life. The whole fitness and diet culture can be so damaging to someone with an eating disorder, so please just be careful.

***

I WILL NOT DIET! I will not lose weight just to fit into other people's ideals. I will not die for the 'perfect body.' I will not exercise to the point of collapse and physical injury just to earn that extra potato. I am not putting myself through that again. I started off with good intentions, trying to lose just a little bit of weight and get healthy, but it spiralled out of control. I fixated on 'good' foods and 'bad' foods, on exercising and cutting out carbohydrates. I can't let myself exercise for just half an hour.

Why are you stopping?

Why aren't you doing more?

You're spending too much time sitting on your arse all day doing nothing!

If you give up now, you'll be nothing but a weak bastard!

EXERCISE MORE YOU BITCH!

That's what goes on inside my head. Those are the constant thoughts I have when I start exercising or reducing my food intake. That is how cruel and violent Ana is. How demeaning and critical she is. I am asking you to be kind to yourself and give your body what it needs. I am not suggesting that you go and have a takeaway three times a day for seven days a week. I am not suggesting you have a family sized bag of crisps or massive chocolate bar every single day. What I am saying, though, is you can still have those foods. You can still enjoy food and be healthy. You can still occasionally indulge and maintain your weight. You do NOT have to eat only bland foods, you do not have to eat only vegetables or salad, you do not have to live off fruit and diet drinks. Sometimes, you need to give your body what it wants, not necessarily what it needs. My body craves chocolate and pasta and cheese... all the foods I have starved myself of for such a long time. Part of the process of recovery is allowing yourself to eat those foods. To give yourself permission to eat what you WANT.

I am not going to say 'no' to any more foods. If I want something, I will be kind to myself and allow myself to live just a little bit. Life with an eating disorder is hell. When I properly start listening to my body and feeding my mind and soul, I know that the cravings I have will decrease. I crave the foods I don't allow myself to have. I crave the foods my eating disorder has forbidden me to even touch. You want what you cannot have, and this extends to your diet. Your body craves what it doesn't have. It wants what it is not given. It wants to live. I am eating six times a day to survive. I am eating six times a day to keep my hunger at bay, to keep Ana locked away. I am feeding the angel and not the demon. I am feeding myself.

There is far greater strength in saying 'no' then going along with what everyone else says. For my own health and my own safety, I cannot diet. I cannot exercise as much as I would like to. I am addicted to exercise, and as much as I hate saying that it is the simple fact of the matter. I hope one day, my relationship between food and exercise will be healthy. I believe that, one day, I will find the right balance. That things will sort themselves out in the end. My time at April House is ending, but as one chapter finishes another begins. I wish I could tie this book up nicely and have a great ending. But I can't end something I haven't finished. My journey to recovery has only just started, and I know I still have a way to go. I have not fully shaken off Ana. I have put her in a coffin, but I have not nailed down the lid. I might look well, but I am still anorexic. I might laugh and joke, but I still feel empty inside at times. I am recovering, but I am not recovered. I have reached a place I never thought was possible, I have found a light I never really believed existed. It might only be a small glow, but in time the light will spread, and it will take over the darkness, getting brighter and brighter, stronger and stronger. Choosing recovery is one hell of a decision, and it's a hard mountain to climb. The process is slow and gradual, and setbacks are going to happen. But that is okay.

It is okay to struggle; it is okay to fall. Just make sure you get back on your feet and keep holding on. Don't give up the war just because you lost a battle. Don't give your eating disorder the satisfaction of winning. Don't die for her. Don't die for Ana. Don't die for bulimia. Don't kill your family and friendships, don't kill your hopes and dreams, don't kill your future. Just don't! Stop and think, and remember, that it is okay. Whether you feel sad or happy, it is all okay. You don't have to feel a certain way but embrace how you do feel and know that tomorrow is a new day. That a bad day doesn't have to turn into a bad week, or a bad week doesn't have to turn into a bad month. You don't have to lose your life to this bastard of an illness. You have nothing to prove to anyone, only yourself. Realise how strong you are, how precious you are, and how loved you are. Realise you are WORTHY. You don't have to be emaciated to have an eating disorder. You don't need to have physical problems to have an eating disorder. You don't need to be hospitalised to have an eating disorder. It is about the inner torment you go through. The violent torrent of abuse. The constant stream of anger you feel towards yourself. The never-ending cycle of hatred and disgust you are cruelly trapped in. IT IS A MENTAL HEALTH CONDITION!

It is never too late to ask for help. Prevention is better than cure. Whether you have an eating disorder, know someone who has an eating disorder, or don't know anything about them, let this book be a lesson to you. Open up your eyes to the brutal reality that eating disorders are killers. That they are not born out of vanity or attention-seeking but are complicated and dangerous mental health illnesses. There are so many different layers to my anorexia. My body dysmorphia, addiction to laxatives and exercise, fear of failure, fear of taking up space... these are all the different parts to my eating disorder. You don't have to fully understand eating disorders (trust me, I don't understand them myself half the time,) but just understand that there is more to it than just not eating. There is more to it than just watching the number on the scales go down. If I had spoken up sooner, I may well have been saved from hospital-isation. I didn't need to come so close to death. I should have got help sooner. I should have had the courage to speak up, but I have the courage now. Better late than never, I guess. Let people guide you and help you, let those who care about you in. Let them save you. That is all they want. They want you to live and have a happy life, and that means ditching your eating disorder. My journey has not finished, so even though this book is ending, my life is just starting. I will rediscover who Steph is. I will find my freedom and zest for life. I will survive, I will thrive, and I will beat my eating disorder. That's a promise.

Ana, this is for you, so listen carefully.

I am DONE with you. You are a bully and a tyrant, and I don't need to punish myself every waking minute of every day. I am NOT taking up too much space. I do not have to die to prove my worth. I do not need to be dead and gone to please you. You have done nothing but cause me pain and misery. You have made me cry and scream and shout. You have stopped me from living and trapped me in my own hell. You turned my brain and body against me. You are NOT going to win. You are NOT going to define who Steph is. I am better than you, and my life will be a hell of a lot brighter without your filthy, little lies. Ana, you are a heartless bastard and I refuse to let you dominate my every waking moment. Even when I sleep, you are loitering, just waiting to pounce and maim me. You can't keep using me as your own personal battering ram. Not anymore. This ends today. But my life, Steph's life, starts today.

Look to your future, and not to your past. Let go of Ana and say 'hello' to the real you!